ZOLA

ZOLA

Philip Walker
Professor of French Literature
University of California, Santa Barbara

Routledge & Kegan Paul
London, Boston, Melbourne and Henley

First published in 1985
by Routledge & Kegan Paul plc
14 Leicester Square, London WC2H 7PH, England

9 Park Street, Boston, Mass. 02108, USA

464 St Kilda Road, Melbourne,
Victoria 3004, Australia and

Broadway House, Newtown Road,
Henley on Thames, Oxon RG9 1EN, England

Set in Baskerville, 10½ on 12 pt
by Fontwise
and printed in Great Britain
by Thetford Press Limited, Thetford, Norfolk

Library of Congress Cataloging in Publication Data

Walker, Philip D.

Zola.
Bibliography: p.
Includes index.
1. Zola, Emile, 1840–1902. 2. Novelists, French—19th
Century—Biography. I. Title.
PQ2528.W33   1985   843'.8[B]   84–27556

British Library CIP data also available

ISBN 0-7102-0518-X

To Corlette

Contents

Preface   ix

1   Childhood, Boyhood, and Youth   1
2   Young Manhood   46
3   The Continuing Struggle   92
4   First Great Triumphs   123
5   Full Summer   152
6   Life Persisting, Recommencing   189

    Selected Bibliography   246
    Index   251

Preface

Zola's place as one of the towering figures of modern civilization would today seem secure. A major shaper of the twentieth-century novel, most notably the twentieth-century American novel, he has never ceased to be enormously popular with the public at large. His best works have lost little or none of their power over the years. Moreover, since the current revival of critical interest in him began about 1950, his literary reputation has soared ever higher. Few commentators would now deny that *L'Assommoir, Germinal,* and *La Terre* and probably also *Nana* and *La Débâcle* are supremely great novels. Zola still remains, furthermore, along with Michelet and Hugo, one of the chief embodiments of republican France, and what Anatole France said of him is still undeniably true: 'he was a moment of the conscience of man.'

Like most other contemporary students of Zola, I have been impressed above all by the artistic, poetic, and prophetic aspects of Zola's fiction. No doubt because, in my youth, I also dreamt of becoming a creative writer, I have also been especially fascinated by Zola's artistic development, his mature aesthetic theories, and his long, hard, and ultimately successful struggle to achieve lasting literary fame. To provide a complete image of the man while emphasizing these aspects of his life and works is the purpose of this book.

Naturally, I have drawn not only on my own studies of Zola but also from those of a host of other critics, historians, and biographers too numerous to list here in their entirety. I should, however, like to acknowledge my considerable indebtedness in particular to F. W. J. Hemmings, David Baguley, E. M. Grant, Henri Mitterand, René Ternois, Joanna Richardson, and Halina Suwala and to all those scholars, especially B. H. Bakker

ix

and Colette Becker, who have made the unfortunately still incomplete edition of Zola's correspondence published by the University of Montréal Press the mine of precious information that it already is.

I am grateful to Penguin Books Ltd for permission to quote two passages from L. W. Tancock's translation of Zola's *L'Assommoir* (Penguin Classics, 1970, Copyright © L. W. Tancock 1970, pp. 226 and 423).

I am also greatly indebted to Louis Blancolli for the verses that I have cited in Part V, chapter 5, from his translation of Dante's *Inferno* (*The Divine Comedy, I, Hell*, Washington Square Press, New York, 1966, pp. 18-19).

[1]

Childhood, Boyhood, and Youth

I

Émile Zola was born on April 2, 1840, in a very ordinary Parisian house at no. 10 *bis*, Rue Saint-Joseph, a short, narrow street only a few steps from the Bourse. The event took place at eleven o'clock at night on a camp-bedstead near the bedroom window of the Zolas' apartment on the fourth floor.

His mother, Émilie Aurélie Zola, was the daughter of Louis Auguste Aubert, a glazier and occasional house-painter. Her mother, Henriette Aubert, had been a seamstress before her marriage. The Auberts were from Dourdan, a small town between Paris and Chartres. In the early 1830s they had joined the hundreds of workers then migrating from surrounding country districts to Paris. Since their arrival there, they had done fairly well by the standards of their class, but they were far from being prosperous.

Zola's father, Francesco Zola (originally Zolla) was an Italian from a family of soldiers who had served in the army of the ancient Republic of Venice for generations. His paternal grandfather, Antonio Zolla, had been an infantry captain, his father, Carlo, a captain in the engineers. Francesco himself had started out by following in their footsteps. At the age of fifteen, he had been admitted to the military school in Pavia and, two years later, on his graduation, had been commissioned second-lieutenant in the Franco-Italian army of Prince Eugène Napoléon. After the fall of the First Empire, he had continued his military career in an Italian regiment in the service of Austria. His real interests, however, were mathematics and engineering. In 1817 he had obtained permission to complete his studies in mathematics at the University of Padua and, the

1

following year, had received his doctoral degree. His dissertation, on the art of making geodesic surveys, had soon become a standard civil engineering textbook in Milan. In 1820 he had left the army and joined his brother Marco's construction firm. Too ambitious to spend his whole life in an oppressed, neglected corner of the Austrian Empire, he had shortly afterwards gone to Austria and, in 1823, had helped plan the first public railway in Europe, connecting the Danube and the lower stretch of the Vltava River. While still engaged in this project, he had conceived the idea of a second railway extending the first one south from Linz to Gmunden on the Traunsee. This railway had ultimately been built, but he had had no hand in its completion, for, after the French Revolution of 1830, he had gone to France, his adopted country from then on.

In 1831, he had submitted to the French Minister of War a plan for the fortifications of Paris, which, while officially recognized as meritorious, had been rejected for political reasons. That same year he had volunteered for service in the French Foreign Legion, recently founded to help out in the conquest of Algeria, and had been admitted as a lieutenant. His stay in the Legion had, however, been a brief and disastrous one, because of his fondness for a certain Madame Fischer, the all-too-attractive wife of a retired sergeant. Persuaded by her to give her 1,500 francs, he had taken the money from the clothing store, fully intending to replace it before anyone found out. When informed of all the facts, the authorities had dismissed the charges against him, but they had accepted his resignation.

After landing in Marseilles in January, 1833, he had found employment once again as a civil engineer. By 1835, he had established his own firm, employing three draughtsmen and two apprentices, on the Canebière, the city's main artery. When his proposal to supply the principal streets of Marseilles with gaslight had come to naught, he had thrown himself heart and soul into promoting his plan for enlarging the city's main port. It involved among other things the use of certain ingenious mechanical devices which he had invented. In 1836, he had gone to Paris to obtain approval and support for it and secured an audience with Louis Philippe, who had shown considerable interest. It was during one of his protracted stays in the capital that Francesco had encountered Émilie for the first time, one

Sunday as she was coming out of mass at Saint-Eustache. He had fallen in love with her at first sight. She was only twenty, twenty-four years younger than he, full of life, well-shaped, slightly on the plumpish side, and had lustrous brown hair. Her father had not been able to give her much of a dowry – only a few transferable stocks, but that had meant little to Francesco; he had been more than happy to marry her for herself alone. The ceremony had taken place at the *mairie* of the first arrondissement on March 16, 1839.

Since his arrival in Paris three years before, he had made no money whatsoever. In fact, he had spent all his savings and piled up debts of over 20,000 francs. They went on mounting every day. The couple's newly rented fifth-floor apartment on the Rue Saint-Joseph, where, a year after their marriage, Émile was born, alone cost 1,200 francs a month, four times the wages of an ordinary clerk or craftsman. Nevertheless, the prevalent mood in the Zola household was one of hope, rather than one of despair. A gifted, sober, hard-working, expansive, cheerful man with enormous self-confidence and a gift for making powerful friends, Francesco never doubted that he would achieve success sooner or later, if not with one project, at least with another. It was true that the Marseilles harbor plan, which would have brought in from 80,000 to 100,000 francs, had fallen through at the last moment, just when he had thought that the government was on the point of buying it. A second scheme for the fortifications of Paris, submitted in October, 1840, six months after Émile was born, was disdainfully rejected, even though the great statesman Thiers had backed it. But meanwhile he had undertaken another less grandiose, yet still ambitious project, with a good chance of coming to fruition. In 1837, the municipal council of Aix-en-Provence, nineteen miles to the north of Marseilles, had budgeted 1,000,000 francs for the construction of a canal capable of providing that perennially dusty, thirsty city with at least one-and-a-half cubic metres of water a second. A year and a half later, Francesco's plan, calling for the construction of three dams in the Infernet Gorge and a canal seven kilometers long, had been accepted, and the contract to do all this was his.

Despite Thiers' support, getting the project actually under way was slow going. The rich local landowners whose property

3

would be crossed by the canal – particularly the Marquis de Galliffet – resisted it at every turn. Moving with Émilie and Émile to Aix in 1843, Francesco kept on, however, doggedly fighting, much as he had for his previous schemes. Royal approval was obtained the following year and a joint-stock company, the Société du Canal Zola, at last floated in 1846. Finally, after eight years of constant struggle, active operations could begin. At the inauguration ceremony, the engineer, short, but heavy-set, with his large head and face, his big nose deeply cleft at the tip, his thick brown mustache, and proud military posture, cut an imposing and heart-warming figure. As the first pickaxe struck the earth, he gripped his seven-year-old son's hand in his own. Émile would never forget that moment.

But then, only three months later, before he could reap the fruit of all his effort, this man, who had almost never been ill, suddenly caught a cold while supervising his workmen in the mountains. It was one of those days when the mistral was blowing. Instead of taking care of himself, he insisted on going to Marseilles on some urgent business. While there, he developed pleurisy. Since it was impossible to move him, his wife was hurriedly summoned to his room in the Hotel Moulet, Rue de l'Arbre. A week later, March 28, 1847, he died there as she held him in her arms. His body was transported back to Aix in a hearse draped in black. A delegation of clergy met it outside the city's gate. Émile, looking very small and pale, headed the long funeral procession winding through the streets crowded with people come to pay their last respects. The sub-prefect, the mayor, and the chief engineer of the arrondissement marched among the pallbearers. So also did Alexandre Labot, *avocat au Conseil du Roi*, one of Francesco's closest Parisian friends. A local newspaper, *La Provence*, raised a fund to pay for a tombstone to mark Francesco's grave until the completion of the canal, when, it was expected, a more splendid monument would be built.

Émile, his widowed mother, and her aged parents, the Auberts, who now moved in with them, could not help but feel proud; but, except for Émile, they were also profoundly anxious. Francesco had left behind him little more than his shares in the Canal Company and debts of over 90,000 francs. Émile's sole income was a company pension of only 150 francs a month. Within five years, some of her worst fears were justified. In

January, 1852, the company went bankrupt due to the shady manoeuvres of the principal stockholder, a certain Jules Migeon, intent on taking it over at a reduced price. The stipend was cut off. At the same time, needless to say, the shares that she had inherited, most of which had been given to creditors as collateral, became worthless. In December, 1847, a physician who had taken care of her husband in Marseilles had threated to bring her to court if she did not pay him the 864 francs that she still owed him. Now she had even more serious legal problems to contend with, chief among which were her battles with Migeon, battles that seemed destined to drag on for ever.

She had no business sense. Disregarding Maître Labot's advice to go out and use her political connections to obtain a stamp or tobacco concession – or, if that failed, to look for work in some big Marseilles department store – she foolishly placed all her hopes in the canal, even after it failed and passed into Migeon's hands. Her mother, a cheerful, energetic, pious woman, provided moral support and helped keep the family together, but neither she nor her semi-invalid husband, Aubert, simple working-class people that they were, could give their daughter any very sound advice, nor could they proffer her much financial support. Indeed, she had them on her hands, as well as Émile. The servants, of course, had had to go almost at once after Francesco's death. Soon after that, she had been obliged to sell articles of furniture. In the summer of 1851, it had at last become necessary to give up her big two-storied house, formerly occupied by Thiers and his parents, on the Impasse Sylvacane. They moved to a more modest house that they had rented on the Pont-de-Béraud, outside the city. The spacious, airy, well-furnished rooms and the large garden where Émile had spent most of his time happily playing since the age of three became just another memory from a happier past.

II

Émilie and her parents did everything they could to shelter Émile from the effects of these misfortunes – this only child who was all that she had left from her marriage, on whom all the family's hopes rested, and whom they all dearly loved. He was a delicate,

5

sensitive boy with her and Francesco's dark hair and eyes, Francesco's broad face, prominent brow, and the same large, curiously shaped nose. The brow was permanently marked by long horizontal lines. The nose could be very expressive. The left eye opened wider than the right eye, due to a permanent contraction of the orbicular muscle. He frequently had a somber look about him. From an early age on, he had been more thoughtful, serious, quiet, and reserved than most other children. At two, he had suffered from an attack of brain fever. The leeches had refused to take hold, and he had nearly died. Between the ages of six and seven, he had come down with a whole series of new illnesses requiring numerous plasters on both arms. His poor health had left him thin, pale, lymphatic, almost feminine in appearance. He was also very high-strung. Among other things, he was excessively afraid of thunder. Whenever there was a thunderstorm, they had to carry him wrapped in sheets and blankets down into the basement or, after he became too old for that, do their best to calm him while he covered his eyes with a handkerchief.

He had had a hard time learning how to talk, until the age of five pronouncing *s* as though it were *t*. His speech still bore traces of this defect. Fortunately, he was blessed with a fine intelligence, extraordinarily sharp senses, and an amazing memory. Hours after seeing something, he could recall it in complete detail and with such vividness that, for example, the memory of the sun would nearly dazzle him or the memory of some strong odor almost suffocate him. He could at times be quite imperious, pampered as he was by his adoring family; but he was generally gentle and sweet tempered. He had an enormous need to love and be loved. Among other things, he was intensely fond of animals. He would refuse to eat his meals if he could not share them with his white cat.

His mother kept putting off sending him to school, but finally, when he was seven and a half, she had enrolled him as a day-pupil in the Pension Notre-Dame, a primary boarding school catering to middle-class people of modest means. It was run at that time by a good, kindly, somewhat permissive man named Father Isoard. Since Émile balked at learning his alphabet, Isoard was obliged to take him into his office and give him individual reading lessons – using for the purpose an illustrated

6

edition of La Fontaine's *Fables*. The five years that the boy spent under Isoard's benign, undemanding rod were happy ones. Although Émilie sometimes took him with her when she went to see her lawyers, he had no inkling as yet of the desperate straits his family was in. He went to class only when he wanted to. As he always had, he played in his garden or, after their move to the Pont-de-Béraud, romped freely through the surrounding fields, visiting a nearby gypsy camp or whiling away the time on the banks of the Torse or in a sunny abandoned cemetery he had discovered, full of tall grass and gnarled pear trees. He had unconsciously acquired by now an intense love of nature – a love that as yet, however, had nothing literary about it. He much preferred spinning his top or playing marbles or saddle-my-nag to poetry. Often two of his schoolmates. Philippe Solari and Marius Roux, as fond of playing hooky as he was, would accompany him. All this time, he was growing stronger and more vigorous.

He was also approaching puberty. At the age of five, he had been sexually abused by one of the servants, a twelve-year-old Arab boy named Mustapha. When this had been discovered, there had been a terrible to do. Poor Mustapha had at once been arrested and packed off to jail. But that had been only an isolated incident, something to be quickly forgotten, breaking for just a brief, painful moment the long sexual tranquillity of childhood. Now, however, Zola's sex instinct was becoming more powerful. He began to have erotic fantasies. He developed sudden, brief infatuations. By twelve, he already knew the pangs of passionate love – no less overwhelming for being limited to the confines of his own head. Despite this precocity, girls still played only a small part in his life. Except with his family and closest companions, he tended to be reserved. Some might have taken him as shy.

During the same period, Zola also began to acquire some of his first religious ideas. From a mural over the school altar, he formed his first notion of God – a colossal, venerable old man with a long white beard that inspired him with feelings of mingled admiration and terror. When threatened with God's ire for stealing fruit or telling some unpardonable lie, he would imagine this same venerable, yet frightening patriarch striding down from the wall, switch in hand, and administering the

7

memorable corporal punishment he so richly deserved. He learned about the other members of the Holy Family from other pictures in the school chapel or from the sacred images in his prayer book. Then at last the time came to learn the catechism. On June 6, 1852, he took his first Communion, at Saint-Sauveur.

III

That same year, his carefree days at the Pension Notre-Dame came to an end. His mother, citing her dead husband's past services to the city, had persuaded the City Council to grant their son a scholarship so that he could enroll in the town's official preparatory school, the Collège Bourbon (now the Lycée d'Aix). A former convent, situated on the edge of town, it faced a small peaceful square, in the midst of which stood the Fountain of the Four Dolphins, rococo monsters with fiercely twisting stone tails and perpetually open mouths spewing out jets of water. As one entered the school past the concierge's lodge, one came upon a big courtyard shaded by four aged plane-trees full of chirping sparrows and containing another fountain with a large mossy basin where the boys were permitted to swim once a week. On the other side of the fountain, there was a second, smaller courtyard containing trapezes, swings, and parallel bars. The study-halls, on the ground floor, were dismal and airless, with leprous, dank plaster walls, but the classrooms, on the floor above, with their rough-hewn tables and benches, could be cheerful enough. Through the windows, one could look down on shady neighboring gardens. There was also the refectory with its foul kitchen odors, the dormitory rooms holding up to forty cots, the infirmary presided over by kindly nuns in black gowns and white hoods, and the chapel with its big outside door, painted black at that time, and always kept tightly shut.

The school's academic standards, like those of most French provincial schools, left much to be desired. The curriculum, in full conformance with the national educational plan imposed by Fortoul, the current, highly conservative Minister of Education, was deadening. Anything that smacked of innovation had been excluded. The students were expected to master the rules of Latin, Greek, and French grammar, do exercises in style, and

8

learn many passages and summaries by rote. No instruction in contemporary literature or history was allowed. A teacher who dared mention Victor Hugo or talk about the Revolution of 1848, the Second Republic, or the coup d'état ushering in the Second Empire, risked immediate dismissal. The teachers, mostly tired-looking, gray-faced men who had given up hope of a great career, were rigidly supervised and poorly paid. All but a few taught perfunctorily, glad when the class was over, uninterested in all but the best students. Most of them had completely lost contact with the nation's cultural life, centered in far-away Paris. All in all, the Collège Bourbon was what one might have expected to find in the Aix of Zola's time, no longer, as it had been in the middle ages, the capital of Provence and a major center of art and learning, but only a remote, dead little provincial town with grass growing between the cobblestones in its streets.

The pupils, mostly sons of well-to-do barristers, solicitors, notaries, merchants, and farmers from Aix and the surrounding countryside, had little incentive to put themselves out. Almost all would go on to assured futures in their family businesses or professions. For Zola, it was different. His mother and grandmother had by now begun to take him more and more into their confidence, apprising him of the family worries, seeking his advice. He knew how much depended on him. His fighting instincts were aroused. Poorly prepared, anything but a brilliant scholar, he started out at the bottom of his class, but he studied hard, methodically, doing only what was required, nothing more, anxious to finish as soon as possible. Before going to sleep, he reviewed what he had learned. The next day, thanks to his sponge-like memory, he could recall nearly everything. Soon, he was forging ahead. Almost every year, he won numerous prizes, doing particularly well in Latin, history, geography, French narration, arithmetic, geometry, physics, chemistry, and natural history, but also excelling in religion and Greek and doing honorable work in calculus and French grammar. At seventeen, he walked away with nearly all the top prizes in the courses that he was then taking – mostly scientific ones; for by then he had opted to major in the sciences, instead of letters. Not only was this a means of getting out of any further study of, if not Latin, at least Greek (he detested the manner in which both subjects were then taught); it would enable him to pursue his burgeoning interest in the natural sciences.

The school's four hundred pupils resembled schoolboys everywhere. They did not mind the lack of heat in winter, the hard mattresses, the decaying walls, the cramped quarters; but they complained loudly about the cooking and the heavy assignments. An usher foolish enough to treat his charges gently, far from winning their gratitude and respect, would only end up more despised than the rest of his wretched breed. Many of the teachers smarted from cruel nicknames like 'Rhadamanthus,' who had never been known to smile, 'Filth,' who, by constantly rubbing the back of his head against the wall, had left dirty spots behind each of his desks, and 'Thou-hast-deceived-me-Adèle!' a physics professor, well known to have been cuckolded by his wife. Three-quarters of the boys studied only when they wanted to or never worked at all. A good deal went on that they would remember later, if not with shame, with amusement. But to be respected by the others, the most important thing was to be good with one's fists. Like many other boys' schools, the Collège Bourbon was a jungle.

Zola's reserve, his unaggressive, almost girlish manner and appearance, his habitually somber expression, his status as a poor scholarship student, his obvious craving to be loved, his greater age, the Parisian accent he had learned from his mother, the trace that remained of his infantile speech defect – all of this made him the perfect butt. Day after day, his new classmates mercilessly teased him. For a mere nothing, they would fall upon him and try to cut him to pieces. It did not help, either, later on, to have one of his teachers conceive a dislike for him and discriminate against him in the classroom. (His fault had been to admit that no useful purpose could be served by learning Greek!) Especially during his first years at the school, there were many mornings when he hated having to face another day. But there were also many happy moments: the moments of escape, the first pipes smoked in secret, the furtively read novels, the card games in the dormitory at night after the proctor had fallen asleep, the dips in the fountain in the courtyard or in the river, the coming of spring with its fragrant odors wafted in from the nearby open countryside, the apricots and redcurrants stolen from neighboring gardens, the increasing liberty.

Almost from the outset, moreover, he had not been friendless.

During recreation one day, while he was still in the seventh class, it had seemed as though the whole courtyard had lit into him for some breach of the rules. A strong, black-haired, dark-skinned older boy, Paul Cézanne, a rich banker's son, had the courage to come up afterwards to comfort him. Cézanne had paid dearly for it. The next day, Zola had brought him a basket full of apples to express his gratitude, and from then on they had been like brothers. It was not long before Zola had also formed a close relationship with Cézanne's chum Jean Baptistin Baille, whose father was a humble local innkeeper. Their classmates called them the three inseparables. There was also another boy, a lawyer's son named Louis Marguery, with whom Zola became quite intimate, largely because of their shared passion for music.

Together, he and his friends would roam about Aix, the old town and the new town, the crumbling, ivy-covered ramparts, the crowded cafés, the splashing fountains, the plane-trees full of chirping sparrows, the aristocratic quarter with its closed shutters and silent streets. Side by side, they would participate in savage rock-throwing battles between the schoolboys and the town boys. During the Crimean war, when passing troops on their way to shed their blood overseas would march up the Cours Mirabeau, they would rush to see them, drums beating, trumpets blaring, the *cuirassiers'* helmets blazing like so many separate suns and race along beside them out through the gate, the suburbs, and along the road to Marseilles as far down as the river crossing. He took painting lessons at the Aix art academy and collaborated with Cézanne on the decoration of a large folding screen. Once he helped move a community of cloistered nuns. He carried the Crucifix or saints' images in some of those long Corpus Christi processions that were the major annual events in the town's life. In another procession, he played the clarinet as a member of the school band, along with Cézanne and Marguery, both puffing on their cornets.

What he liked most of all were his excursions with Cézanne and Baille in the open countryside, with its rows of silvery little olive trees, almond orchards vibrant with the shrill chatter of cicadas, dark grapevines silhouetted against the red earth, white roads where the dust cracked underfoot like fresh snow and, beyond, the high semi-wilderness, the terraced slopes, the goat paths along the edges of steep ravines, the plains, mountains,

11

giant rocks piled one upon the other like Pelion on Ossa, the periwinkle and wild roses, the sage, the thickets of oaks, holly, and pines. On holidays or during summer vacations, the first to wake up would toss pebbles against the closed shutters of the others' bedrooms, and they would race off, drunk with freedom, space, sunlight. Sometimes, especially in winter, they would hike to Le Tholonet, six miles to the west, or some other remote peasant village, and treat themselves to an omelet. In summer, they would spend many happy hours swimming stark naked in the deep parts of the Arc, wrestling or sun-bathing on the banks, or lying on their stomachs in the shallow water, enjoying the feel of the current flowing over their skins. In the fall, they would hunt for rabbits, partridges, ortolans, thrushes, or finches. One of their favourite places to visit was the canal Zola's father had planned, not far from Tholonet. They also liked to hike through the near-by Infernet Gorge, between Titanic walls of rock baked and gilded by the sun. They climbed Mont Sainte-Victoire. Once, they tried to camp out overnight in a cave, reclining on beds of lavender and thyme, but a strong wind came up, filling the cave with its howling, while a swarm of huge bats circled and darted above them in the moonlight. By two in the morning, they had had enough, and returned home. But before doing so, they set the lavender and thyme on fire, to enjoy the resultant romantic spectacle.

One stifling July afternoon, Zola discovered on the banks of the Durance an abandoned, crumbling eighteenth-century château with a ruined garden. Entering through a gap in the wall, he found himself in a kind of Eden. Here and there, he could vaguely make out the remains of a cobbled path, a fountain, a lawn, a flight of stone steps, an eroded Cupid, but wild nature had invaded the whole area, reclaiming it as her own, planting bushes in the fountains, trees in the middle of the paths, covering everything with moss, grass, climbing vines, transforming the whole garden into an impenetrable virgin forest.

His love of nature was growing stronger. In frequent close contact with it, he developed a tranquil faith in the power of life. He required – at least at certain moments – no other religion.

Despite the traditionally prominent place that the clergy occupied in the communal life of Aix, where the Corpus Christi

12

procession was the biggest civic event of the year, the town's inhabitants were generally no more devout than most other Frenchman. In the Collège Bourbon, as in most other schools not run by religious orders, priests played the same role as in the army; they were merely tolerated. After confirmation, most of the boys took Communion no more than two or three times a year and soon gave it up altogether. The older ones declared themselves atheists. Religious services were reduced to the strict minimum and celebrated as fast as possible. When one was marched to confession, the thing to do was to yawn broadly, without covering one's mouth, and to do one's best to be excused. Some boys flatly refused, deaf to the director's exhortations. In catechism or history of religion, three-quarters of the class paid no attention whatsoever to what was being said and never bothered to do the assignments. Even the better pupils, like Zola, tried to look bored. The priest knew perfectly well that almost no one was listening, but pretended not to notice.

Zola was now a solidly built, muscular, sun-tanned adolescent. He had reached puberty not long after turning thirteen. His body had become hairy all over, particularly on the chest. The sexual urges that he had already began to feel when he was ten had grown more imperious, but he still had not known a woman. His nervousness, lingering speech defect, and the very strength of his desires made him excessively timid. He spent hours lost in reveries in which Solari's little sister, Louise, or whatever other girl he happened to be in love with, merged with the insubstantial creatures of his imagination – Gratienne, L'Aérienne, Ninon. Infinitely more satisfying than reality was the endless idyll of his dreams. There, he had no problem of communication. His mistress and he spoke directly from the heart in a language worthy of the greatest lyric poets. She combined the beauty of a girl with the robust intelligence of a man. She was at once his bride, sister, and brother. She and he never parted, perpetually wandering through the countryside hand in hand or making love in hidden places.

With the advent of adolescence, not only his thoughts about girls but also his conception of nature had become more overtly sexual. He loved Provence, his adopted country, as though she were a woman. The harsh, desolate, sun-scorched beauty of the land between the rich meadows of the Durance and the orange

13

groves of the coast assumed in his imagination a deliciously erotic character. It seemed to him that a strange hurricane of passion had swept through the whole region, followed by an immense exhaustion in which everything, still ardent, had fallen into a slumber filled with dreams of love. His classical education colored his perceptions with recollections of bucolic poems. He was in Greece. Provence was a nymph reclining half-asleep in the noonday sun while satyrs, hidden in the thick foliage, lustily caressed her with their gleaming eyes. At other times, the blood-red soil became in his imagination the flesh of a female in rut, or he could feel the earth trembling underfoot like a wet nurse's breast in response to the famished kisses of her nurslings. Frequently, nature and the half-real, half-ideal girl of his dreams became one. The sound of the rivers recalled her voice; the stars gazed down with her gaze; the entire countryside smiled with her smile; the undulations of the landscape seemed patterned on the supple, rounded lines of her body.

IV

As he grew older, he was also becoming more and more interested in drama, fiction, and poetry. Aix had a small theatre, open three times a week. Tickets for seats in the pit cost only a few sous. He was always among the first in line, sometimes returning over and over again to watch the same play performed. He saw *La Tour de Nesle* no less than eighteen times, *La Dame blanche*, thirty-five. He gobbled down one novel after the other, never satisfied – especially novels of adventure. During the cholera epidemic of 1854, when he and his family had had to take refuge in a small, isolated country house for three months, he devoured a whole library. His grandmother, brave soul that she was, repeatedly went to town to fetch him books, returning with packages of fifteen to twenty volumes at a time. *Le Petit Poucet* and *Swiss Family Robinson* made the same indelible impression upon him as they do on most French youths. By fourteen, he was reading everything he could get his hand on by the Dumas, father and son, Eugène Sue, Paul Féval, Élie Berthet, and Emmanuel Gonzalès, and other popular writers.

14

When he was sixteen, he discovered *Don Quixote* and George Sand's *Indiana*.

That same year, Zola was also falling more and more in love with poetry. He had, of course, studied the great classical poets, but, like his schoolmates, he had been up till then woefully ignorant of the poetry of his own time. Then, one day, an exceptionally lively, courageous teacher, a young man from Paris whom they all adored, astonished Zola and the rest of the class by starting to talk to them about – not Virgil or Horace – but Victor Hugo, Musset, and Lamartine. If he had discoursed on the poets of the moon, they would not have been any more dumfounded. At just about this time, Zola also became familiar with Mistral, Roumanille, Aubanel and some of the other local Provençal poets. He had escaped from school to attend a poetry festival, held in the town hall, where many of them had been present. He had shared in the general excitement as their poems were recited and the prizes distributed. But nothing matched the enthusiasm that he and not only he, but Cézanne and Baille as well, had for Hugo, now that they had been introduced to him.

For a year, Hugo was their absolute idol. They would take some of his books along in their pockets or game-bags when they went hunting. After a few perfunctory shots, most of which missed their targets, they would flop down on their backs, and discuss him or read aloud selections from *Les Orientales* or *Les Feuilles d'automne*. Sometimes they would act out one of his dramas. They could recite hundreds of his verses by heart. His gigantic personality and rhetoric overwhelmed them. They became habituated to seeing the world through his visionary eyes, finding contrasts everywhere, transforming everything into symbol, fusing dream and reality, subject and object, making reality loom like clouds or swarm like bees. Along with Lamartine, Hugo initiated them into the religion of the romantics with its cults of love and nature. As they returned home at dusk, they would march in time to the cadence of his verse, sonorous as trumpet blasts.

Then, one morning, one of them brought along a volume of Musset, and before long, he had become their new favourite. More and more, Hugo left them cold. Like thousands of other French adolescents of their generation, they identified with Musset, the *enfant terrible* of the romantic movement. They thought of him as an older brother. They were thrilled by his splendid, brattish impudence, his self-mockery, his disdain for rhetoric, his light, satirical romanticism, so different from the convinced, solemn romanticism of Hugo or Lamartine. They were seduced, too, by his deep humanity. His scornful, yet adoring attitude towards women inflamed them. Was he not really Romeo under his Don Juan's mask? But the better they knew Musset, the more they were attracted above all by his doubt, his despair, his bitterness. Through him, they imbibed in long drafts the delicious poison of romantic melancholy. When they were reading him, the best moments were those when he would bring tears to their eyes. They read and reread *Rolla* and *Les Nuits* over and over again.

During this same period, they began to engage in creative literary activity of their own. Cézanne penned hundreds of verses in French or Latin. Baille dreamt of synthesizing epic poetry and integral calculus. Zola wrote a long novel about an episode of the Crusades. He also composed some narratives and dialogues in verse. In one of these pieces, an imperfect yet comical imitation of Musset's *Dupont et Durand,* a devil popped out of a street lamp and dragged a school assistant down a sewer. Meanwhile, another, more ambitious project began to take shape in Zola's mind. He was intrigued by the idea of writing an epic poem recounting the history of the world as it was being revealed by natural history – a subject to which he had been introduced in the third form and in which he had won the first prize. His discovery of the vastness of time and space filled him with awe and terror. The endless series of gigantic floods, eruptions, earthquakes, and conflagrations, the continents swallowed by the abyss, the strange worlds preceding the world of man, created only 6,000 years before, the perspective of the new worlds that would follow man's destruction in his turn, the superior creatures that would inhabit these new worlds – what could provide a more sublime, challenging, or original subject? A great deal of research would, of course, be required. For the moment, he was content with just meditating on it, letting it solidify and grow in his imagination.

He had, moreover, much more urgent matters to think about. On October 16, 1857, his grandmother Aubert died. Again he had to cope with death – all the more traumatic now that he was older and more reflective. Then misfortune struck another blow. Year after year, his family's financial situation had grown increasingly difficult. After moving a total of five times in ten years, always on the lookout for cheaper quarters, they had ended up in two wretched rooms on the Rue Mazarine, a decrepit alley inhabited only by poor working-class people, next to the city wall. In 1855, Aubert had sublet a bread oven and gone back to work – this time as a baker; but even this had not been enough to stop their decline into ever greater poverty. They had now sold most of their furniture. Their debts went on piling up at a frightening pace. Émilie's lawsuits were getting nowhere for lack of money. Her only recourse was to go up to Paris to try, as she had once before, to enlist the support of her husband's powerful friends in her efforts to continue her struggle to salvage something from his estate. Accordingly, towards the end of the year, she returned to the capital to see what she could do. In February, she wrote Zola, who had stayed behind with Aubert: 'It is no longer possible for us to go on living in Aix. Sell the four remaining pieces of furniture. That will give you enough money to buy a third-class ticket for yourself and your grandfather. Hurry up. I am waiting for you.'

Zola, Cézanne, and Baille went on a long farewell hike to Tholonet and his father's dam. 'We'll be back together again, in Paris,' he assured them. His heart breaking, he gave each one a parting hug.

V

His mother had found them a place to stay in the Latin Quarter – a modest three-room apartment at no. 63, Rue Monsieur le Prince, one of those houses inhabited mostly by a shifting population of employees, small artisans, and a few students. She had also managed, with M. Labot's help, to obtain a scholarship for him at the Lycée Saint-Louis. Even his books were to be paid for. On March 1, he started out as a day pupil in the science section, taking up his education where he had left off.

He was desperately unhappy. He longed to be back in Aix and hated his new school as much as anything else in this strange, disquieting city. At eighteen, he was now going through much the same kind of nightmare that he had when, at twelve, he had entered the Collège Bourbon. As before, he was a new boy, friendless, an outsider. He was made to feel ashamed of his poverty, his peculiar accent, his odd lisp, his inadequate scholastic preparation. But whereas his classmates in Aix had made fun of his 'Parisian' accent and called him 'Frenchy,' his new classmates taunted his meridional accent. He was now 'le Marseillais.' As he tried to draw one of his poor provincial circles on the blackboard, he could hear them snickering behind his back. They were all – or so it seemed to him – fantastically rich, elegant, and brilliant. All that really interested them was their appearance, their perfumed gloves, their elegant canes. Yet when they recited they sounded like professors. They spoke rapidly, eloquently, effortlessly, and with infinite irony. They could discuss anything, read the newspapers and journals, and adored the latest fashionable actresses.

After having been an outstanding pupil in Aix, Zola now ranked to his great chagrin only twentieth in a class of sixty. To be sure, he was not doing badly at all in French narration. The professor, a young Normalian named Pierre Émile Levasseur, was, in fact, so impressed by one of his exercises, 'The blind Milton dictating to his older daughter, while his second daughter plays the harp,' that he read it aloud in class. Even so, at least one other pupil was doing better than he did in the same subject, and even the mediocre ones were very good by Aix standards. As for his other courses, he had quickly despaired of distinguishing himself in them and had largely given up trying. What was the use of competing with such obviously superior scholars? His unhappiness, his homesickness, his independent literary interests, and his growing urge to write would have made it hard to concentrate on his non-literary studies even if he had wanted to. He hated chemistry. Instead of paying attention to a lecture, he read one of his favourite books behind the back of the youth ahead of him. (He was particularly absorbed at this time in Michelet, Barbier, Gautier, Dumas fils, Hégésippe Moreau, Lamartine, and, again, Hugo, as well as Musset.) In study hall he composed long letters to his friends in Aix, especially Cézanne and Baille, or he worked on his literary projects. He wrote a poem addressed to Cézanne, another to both Cézanne and Baille.

18

In June, he finished a poetic comedy in three acts, *Enfoncé le pion!* – about two schoolboys who successfully vie with a ridiculous usher for his girl friend's affections. Their school principal, named Pinguin, was likewise given a farcical role.

That summer, his mother somehow made it possible for him to spend his vacation back in Aix. Cézanne wanted them to write a five-act drama together to be entitled *Henri VIII de l'Angleterre*, but somehow it never got started. It was too tempting just to do what they had always done. They and Baille went swimming in the Arc again, climbed Sainte-Victoire and Le Pilon-du-Roi again, trudged up the Infernet Gorge again, inspected the dam and Roquefavour bridge again. They went hunting again. Needless to say, they also read and discussed their favorite authors just as they always had before.

Zola was hardly back in Paris before he fell gravely ill with what was later diagnosed as typhoid fever. It kept him at home for the first two months of the 1858-9 school year. He nearly died. His feet felt as though they were on fire. He kept vomiting. He was delirious. Like an apprentice shaman he entered the realm of death. He lost awareness of his emaciated flesh. He savored the sensation of being nothing but liberated, disembodied thought floating freely through the void above his expiring mortal self. The notion that he was dead, that he could now go on dreaming beautiful dreams for ever, that he would never have to suffer again filled him at times with an immense bliss. But at other times, his will to live again returned. In his hallucinations he was a seed struggling to thrust its way up through hard, rocky soil. He became more aware than he had ever been before of the never-ending, savage struggle between the forces of death and life. During convalescence his mouth was ulcerated and his teeth became loose. Unable to speak, he was obliged to write what he had to say on a slate. At about the same time, his myopia grew much worse. He realized this one day when he was unable to make out what was printed on the posters pasted on the wall facing his window.

After he returned to school, it was much the same story as the year before. Although his rhetoric professor, M. Etienne, criticized his compositions for being too romantic, he too was impressed by his literary talent and read his work aloud in class. Yet his overall performance was again mediocre. Algebra made

his head ache. He loathed geometry so much that the mere sight
of a triangle made him tremble. He went on doggedly reading his
favorite authors and writing. With his closest friend at the Lycée,
a pharmacist's son name Georges Pajot, he composed a poem
lauding Napoleon III's Italian expedition. They dedicated it to
the Empress Eugénie. He even got *La Provence* back in Aix to
publish it along with a poem he had written on the Zola Canal.
At about this time he started to draw up plans for a three-act
tragedy about Hannibal in Capua and a drama, *Rollon l'archer*.
He also wrote another comedy in verse, this time a short one
illustrating a popular proverb: *Il faut hurler avec les loups*. None of
his works from this period was a masterpiece. The best thing that
could be said about any of them is that he had finished it.

Paris still depressed him. Going out that Mardi Gras, he could
not help comparing the people whirling in the overheated air of a
public masked ball to dead souls furiously thrashing about in the
waters of Lethe, the mythical river of forgetfulness.

Like many late adolescents, he was troubled by the question of
what he should do with himself. He was sick of school. He hated
being a burden on his mother, whose financial situation was
growing more and more desperate. Unable to afford the
apartment on the Rue Monsieur-le-Prince any longer, they had
moved to a still more modest one on the Rue Saint-Jacques.
Should he not break off his studies and try to find a job right
away in some business firm or government bureau much as he
hated the idea? For a moment he thought so, but allowed himself
to be dissuaded. 'Life is a battle,' an inner voice adjured him.
'You must accept this battle and go on fighting no matter how
tired you are or how great your problems are.' One possibility
was to plan to seek admission to the prestigious École Centrale,
to become an engineer like his father. Another was to prepare for
a law career. What he wanted was to be a man of letters. As a
barrister he might be able to do this. Yes, he would become a
barrister! 'You can rest assured,' he wrote Baille in January,
1859, 'that the ear of the writer would stick out from under the
lawyer's robe.' He resolved to master the necessary Greek and
Latin on his own as much as possible. 'I've always said there's
only one way to succeed, and that's by hard work,' he concluded
in the same letter. But unfortunately he lacked his former inner
strength. He had sunk into a dangerous lethargy. He spent hours

daydreaming. 'It is our fate to be born out of nothing in order to return to nothing,' he wrote Marguery in June. 'All that matters is to spend our stopover between these two voids as agreeably as possible.'

Towards the end of the same month, he applied for the baccalaureate exam, the one great hurdle that anyone intending to go on to an institution of higher learning had to pass. He did astonishingly well in the writtens. On August 4, he also breezed through the scientific part of the orals – so well that a classmate, assuming that he had as good as passed the whole exam, ran to announce the good news to his mother. He was confident that he would do equally well in the last part, devoted to modern languages and literature. However, when the literature examiner asked him what the date of Charlemagne's death was, his answer was five hundred years off the mark. They violently disagreed as to the interpretation of one of La Fontaine's fables. He knew no German. He had failed. The science examiners did their best to make the literature examiner change his mind but he obstinately shook his head.

In mid-August, still smarting from his failure, Zola returned again to Aix, where the joy of being reunited once more with Cézanne and Baille (both of whom, however, had passed their 'bachots') somewhat consoled him. He spent part of the summer writing a long poem, 'Rodolpho,' about a youth who discovers his mistress, Rosita, in the arms of his best friend, Marco. After placing the flowers he had picked for her on her brow, he kills her. This project, too, momentarily distracted Zola from his own troubles. He stayed on in Aix until the end of November, when he took the exam again, in Marseilles. But this time he did not even make it through the writtens. It was a terrible blow. The door to a career in engineering or law was now tightly shut. He had failed not only himself but also those who had counted on him to make something of himself and rebuild the family fortune. A third try was out of the question. Even if he had been willing to let his mother go on supporting him, she would not have been able to do so. Poor woman, she had reached the end of her rope. Her protracted battle to recoup something from her husband's estate had ended in defeat. She had been reduced to begging the Aix municipal council for an annual stipend in recognition of her husband's services to the city. As for Zola himself, he would have to earn his living as best he could. But what kind of a job could someone like himself, with no trade or profession, possibly find? He wrote Baille that he felt as though he were walking on quicksand and was about to be swallowed up.

VI

M. Labot, once again coming to the rescue, used his connections to obtain for him a situation as copy clerk in the Excise Office, on the Paris docks. He had hoped to start in January, but as it turned out the job was not actually available until April. In the meantime, his mother and grandfather and he had been evicted from their apartment on the Rue Saint-Jacques for failure to pay the rent and had had to move into new lodgings in no. 35, Rue Saint-Victor, on the slope of the 'Montagne' Sainte-Geneviève.

Although grateful to Labot, he hated the job from the outset. It paid only sixty francs a month, not even enough to live on. There was not the slightest chance of promotion. The work was dehumanizing. Day after day from nine to four, he perfunctorily recorded customs declarations in ledgers, transcribed official correspondence, read his newspaper, yawned, paced back and forth. There was hardly any space to move between the tall piles of yellowing forms and documents. The constant noise of scratching pens irritated his overwrought nerves. So did the chatter of the other clerks, most of whom struck him as stupid, and many of whose words and phrases he had a hard time understanding. None had had anything like his education. The sunlight filtering in through the windowpanes seemed, he wrote Cézanne, to be taunting him. Outside, the eternal festival of nature, in which he had once participated, went on as joyously as ever. But he was now nothing but a drudge, a slave. In losing his freedom, he had also become, he reflected, something less than a whole man, just another minuscule specialized part in the monstrous machine of civilization. He dreamt of running away and living all alone in a cave on some high far-off mountain. He wrote Cézanne that he felt trapped in a hellish maze. 'I can't stand being only a passive instrument. I loathe this brutish toil that society imposes on us,' he wrote Baille. 'I would rather lead the life of an American savage and be self-sufficient than go on with this civilized existence where each of us has to depend every day on others just as wretched as we are.' His health declined along with his morale. He suffered from frequent nervous pains in his intestines. Finally, in June, he could stand the job no longer and quit. 'Was this right or wrong? The question is relative,' he wrote Cézanne. 'It is a matter of temperament.'

About nineteen months went by during which he was unemployed except for a brief period when he earned some cash going over and polishing the style of a technical author's manuscripts. He repeatedly tried to find, with or without M. Labot's help, something more permanent. He was willing to do anything. He had once toyed with the idea of being a typographer. Now he considered, among other things, working for a railroad, possibly as a superintendent. But none of the officials, some courteous, some self-important and abrupt, into whose offices he managed to penetrate for interviews had the slightest desire to hire him. He was timid, thin, hungry looking, and shabbily dressed. There was something almost feminine about his sad, wistful little face despite the fringe of beard running around his lower jaw from ear to ear. His high, chiming, slightly lisping voice did nothing to counteract this impression. A far more serious handicap was that his interrupted bourgeois education had taught him nothing of practical worth. If he had not had his mother to think of, he would have enlisted in the Army. To keep body and soul together he had to borrow small amounts of money from Baille and other friends. He pawned everything of value, including his clothes. He could afford no more than one meal a day. Sometimes it consisted of bread and coffee and a pennyworth of Italian cheese, or perhaps a few fried potatoes or some apples, or roast chestnuts bought at a street corner. Sometimes he had to content himself with bread alone dipped in oil. At still other times, in desperation, he would catch a sparrow on the roof outside his window and roast it on the end of a curtain-rod. This poor diet made his nervous disorders worse. Along with the digestive troubles, he felt unbearable pressure on his chest and coughed up blood. He woke up at night feeling feverish. Hardly a day went by when he was not in pain. To comfort himself, even if it meant going hungry, he would occasionally buy a bouquet of sweet peas when they were available and place them on his bedside table. Their light fragrance, similar to that of orange blossoms, would make him dream about his childhood.

In February, 1861, his family and he had to change residences again. This time, it was no longer possible to be together – even in the same building. His mother and grandfather, who was now bedridden and moribund, moved to a boarding house at no. 21, Rue Neuve-Saint-Étienne-du-Mont, he to a belvedere, a kind of glassed-in cage, poised on the roof of no. 24 on the same street. In April, evicted for failure to pay the rent (always the same story), he was obliged to make yet another move, to 11, Rue Soufflot, a sordid lodginghouse inhabited mostly by poor students, common prostitutes and their pimps and frequently raided by the police.

Yet jobless, poor, and ailing as he was, he had many happy moments. He had loved his lofty rooftop belvedere on the Rue Neuve-Saint-Étienne-du-Mont, cold and windy as it was during the cold winter days. Not only did it have a magnificent panoramic view of Paris. He had learned that Bernardin de Saint-Pierre had written most of his works there. While Pajot pissed into the chimneys of the tenants below, he had dreamt of conquering in his turn this vast, cruel, but also beautiful and glorious city spreading out beneath their feet in every direction as far as the horizon.

Since his arrival in Paris, he had, moreover, little by little acquired a circle of companions: Pajot, a fellow Aixois named Aurélien Houchard, several obscure young artists also from Aix, and, among others, a mediocre, aging, but amusing poet named Pagès du Tarn, a member of the Académie des Jeux Floraux of Toulouse. Some of them would regularly go out together on Saturdays, strolling about the town, going to street fairs or popular bars or dance halls. Or they would assemble at each other's places, drink cheap wine, smoke their pipes, and lose themselves in animated conversations. Sometimes on these occasions Zola, Pagès, or some other poet would read his verses aloud. Those gifted with voices would sing. When sufficiently drunk, the whole group, sometimes amounting to a dozen people, might break into Bacchic dancing. At one party, Zola posed for one of the artists, a likeable fellow of peasant stock named Jean Baptiste Chaillan, as Amphion, scantily draped, grasping a lyre, and gazing skyward. While doing so, he dictated verses to Pajot, who, for lack of paper, wrote them on the wall.

In April, 1861, Cézanne arrived. 'I've seen Paul!!!' Zola wrote Baille. 'Do you know what that means to me? Have you caught all the melody in these four words?' The two friends leapt into each other's arms, had lunch together, and, smoking one pipeful of tobacco after another, went on a whirlwind tour of the Luxembourg and other public gardens. But not everything was the same. 'It's not like Aix, when we were eighteen and unworried about the future,' Zola complained to Baille a few weeks later. There were times when Cézanne was so absorbed in his work at the Atelier Suisse that it was difficult for Zola to see him as much as he would have liked. Cézanne was often moody, plagued by self-doubt, easily discouraged. Zola, whose situation was in reality much more desperate than his, spent hours trying to stiffen his resolve to go on with his plans to be a painter. Although he was convinced that Cézanne had the genius of a great artist, he sometimes wondered now if he had the genius to become one. But they were still as close as ever. For weeks they would spend at least six hours together every day. He would sit as still as he could while Cézanne drew him – 'like an Egyptian sphinx' – in semi-profile, his head bowed, his hair and beard shaggy, his eyes shadowy and soulful. Or they would saunter through the Luxembourg Gardens, puffing away on their pipes, or drink beer at left-bank bars. Often he would meet Cézanne at the atelier. In May, they visited that year's Salon.

VII

During this whole period, from the autumn of 1859 through January 1862, he was also deeply engaged in activities central to his formation as an artist. His thoughts and emotions were in a constant state of turmoil. Like many other late adolescents, he spent many moments wrestling with the great eternal questions about the nature of reality. He was also more seriously concerned than ever with those problems that are peculiar to aspiring young writers. You could have seen him browsing for hours in the bookstalls along the Seine – the poor man's library, as he called them. He continued to follow *Le Siècle* and other left-wing publications. For months at a time he treated himself every evening to a few verses by Hugo, Lamartine, or Musset, especially Musset. He read Dante, Ronsard, Shakespeare, Chénier, Casimir Delavigne, George Sand, Victor de Laprade, Sainte-Beuve, and Montaigne. Above all, he took advantage of his enforced leisure to devote himself to his own writing.

December, 1859, and the first nine months of 1860 were an immensely active, fruitful, and, on the whole, happy period in so far as his artistic development was concerned. The greatest disaster that could befall him was not to have enough money to buy a candle to provide the light he needed to write at night. He corresponded with Cézanne and Baille more frequently and at greater length. Some of his letters were veritable epistles containing, in addition to long accounts of his activities and intellectual progress, colorful descriptions of Paris, character analyses of various friends and acquaintances, or detailed literary essays. Towards the end of 1859 he wrote and managed to get published in *La Provence* 'La Fée amoureuse,' a fairy tale about two lovers turned into flowers. He composed at the same time 'Les Grisettes de Provence,' a realistic short story based on his and his friends' true experiences with some Aixois working-class girls. In March, 1860, he finished another comedy in verse, *Perrette*, inspired by a fable of La Fontaine. In June, he penned the last verse of 'Paolo,' another long poem, about a youth's pure love for a maiden whom he adores from afar as if she were the Virgin Mary. He also, during this period, wrote a number of songs, one of which, set to music by Marguery, would appear in a Parisian paper, *Le Journal du dimanche*, in October, 1861.

His old idea of composing a vast, all-embracing epic account of the history of the earth continued to haunt him. Its larger outlines were still slowly taking shape. Its title, he wrote Baille on June 15, 1860, would be *La Chaîne des êtres*. The poem would be divided into three cantos: 'Le Passé,' 'Le Présent,' and 'Le Futur.' The successive creation of all the beings that had preceded man – 'all the upheavals that have occurred unexpectedly on the globe, all that geology teaches us about destroyed countrysides and the animals now swallowed up in their debris' would provide the material for the first canto. The whole history of humanity from its primitive beginnings up to modern civilized times, resuming everything that physiology had discovered about man's physical nature and philosophy about man's spiritual nature, would make up the second canto. The third canto, he told Baille, would be 'a magnificent divagation': 'Seeing that God's creation has done nothing but improve with the passage of time, one could imagine that this creature is not the Creator's last word and that after the extinction of the human race other more and more perfect beings will come to inhabit the earth. Description of these beings, their mores, etc., etc.' It was, one had to admit, a magnificent idea! 'I don't know whether you can perceive the horizons of this poem, but for me they appear so vast, so luminous, that I have postponed up to now the formidable task of rhyming my poor verses on this grandiose theme.'

He was toying with other projects, less grandiose, but still ambitious. On December 29, 1859, he informed Baille that he was going to undertake a volume of short stories on the theme of love. The next day, he apprised Cézanne that, despite his lack of any practical experience with the subject, he planned to write a 300-page book, 'a kind of poem,' tracing the path of love from its birth all the way to its consummation in marriage. In the letter in which he summarized for Baille what he intended to do in *La Chaîne des êtres,* he confided that he was also determined to make a study of poetic love in all its different forms throughout the ages:

> Nothing would be more piquant than a comparison of Horace, Petrarch, Molière (in a few scenes), Lamartine. I will only mention these four; naturally each century would be represented. The way men make love to women has always been more or less the same. I mean that when men are with the women they love anywhere on earth they say pretty much the same things. How then do you explain that in every century poets have had a different way of addressing their beloveds, in verse, needless to say, for I imagine that they do not amuse themselves citing all that nonsense when they are at their beloveds' feet?

He had by now pretty well decided to become an author. His reasons for doing so were legion. Not only was writing the only profession now open to him after his failure to pass the 'bachot'; it was the only one that he had ever really wanted. He passionately loved poetry, fiction, and drama, and he loved doing all those things that he associated with writing – building beautiful structures out of words, verbally expressing his thoughts and feelings, describing things, telling stories, letting his imagination go. He aspired after the immortal fame that society has always reserved for the greatest writers. But even if there had been no possibility of recognition, he would still have wanted to be an author not only because of the sheer pleasure that writing gave him but also because it was a way of preserving his freedom and wholeness. Through words he could escape from harsh reality into the realm of dreams, as in 'La Fée amoureuse.'

But in his less escapist, more positive moods, he also wanted the power that words can give. With this writing, he could fulfill his need – poor, obscure, timid young man that he was – to assert himself, make a dent on the world, live out loud. He could prove how strong and virile he really was under his weak-looking, almost girlish exterior. He could satisfy his enormous need to love, to give freely of himself, but, as he confessed to Baille on July 4, 1860, he could also take vengeance on all those imbeciles who had treated him and his loved ones with contempt, hatred, and cruelty – Migeon and his likes, the brutal, snobbish schoolmates who had teased him at school, the literary examiners who had failed him in his 'bachot,' and all the others. 'I could have tried to exculpate myself, but instead I thought of another plan: I would crush them with my superiority, I would make them green with envy.'

But among Zola's many motives for becoming a writer, there was another, even more compelling one. Since the decline of traditional religion in the eighteenth century, poets had been called upon to play an increasingly sacerdotal, even vatic role. Were not Hugo, Lamartine, and Michelet, three of his favorite authors, supreme examples of the poet magus, the poet prophet? Hungry, unemployed, academically a failure, completely un-known except to a few readers of *La Provence*, Zola dreamt of becoming a great magus, a great prophet, in his turn. 'In my opinion,' he wrote Baille on July 25, 1860, 'the poet's role is to be a regenerator, that of a man devoted to human progress. What he advances are admittedly dreams, but dreams that ought to be turned into reality. If God will only grant me the inspiration that I need, I stand ready.' Two weeks later, he asked rhetorically in another letter to Baille, 'Is not being an artist the same thing as being a prophet? Are they not both God's anointed ones?'

There was so much to do if he was to achieve all his literary ambitions! Did he have the genius to accomplish all this? It seemed an impossible task, but he was determined to try, putting everything he had into it. 'If I definitely take up a literary career,' he wrote Baille towards the autumn of 1860, 'my watchword will be: *All or nothing!*' If he failed, he told himself, he would at least be a noble failure.

When Cézanne complained about the difficulties that he was having mastering his art, he had to admit that he was having trouble with his too. Yet in fact he was gradually making considerable progress. By dint of writing every day, he was developing greater and greater facility. He was developing a conscious aesthetics. He was slowly establishing the perimeters within which he would have to work. He was forming an idea of the role he would have to play, the destiny that he would have to accept in his struggle for enduring literary fame. (He foresaw among other things that he would always be hated as well as loved, hissed as well as applauded.) He was settling on certain themes. He was developing his powers of observation, increasing his knowledge of human nature in general and of the psychology and mores of his contemporaries in particular. He was acquiring that self-knowledge which is essential to the mastery of art, testing his own limits, probing his strengths and weaknesses, discovering his tastes, exploring his own personal temperament.

As a schoolboy, he had never given much thought to aesthetic theory, uncritically accepting the principles that his teachers taught him or that he had picked up haphazardly in his independent readings. His method, which he had not reflected much upon either, consisted of developing an initial idea and a vague conception of what he wanted to do with it and then starting out to write – or, preferably, just lying on his back and letting the poem, play, or novel unfold itself in his imagination, perhaps never to be written down. In any case, the final product tended to differ considerably from what he had originally had in mind. As he approached the conclusion, he would merely go over what he had done so far in order to be able to tie the end to the beginning.

'I know very well that I am still floundering about, that I am not mature yet,' he confessed to Cézanne on August 1, 1860. He was confused about a lot of things. He was torn, for example, between his love of dreaming and his interest in reality. He could not reconcile his conviction that literature should be concerned with eternal things and the idea that it should concentrate on the realities of its own time, serve the cause of progress, fight materialism, reveal God to man, uphold and defend the weak, demonstrate the existence of individual immortal souls. His attitude toward science was also ambivalent. It seemed to him that there was more truth – that is, eternal human truth, the only kind of truth that ultimately mattered to the artist – in one page of Homer or the Bible than in all the proud discoveries of modern science. Yet his most ambitious project, *La Chaîne des êtres*, was largely to be based on geology, history, and physiology.

Little by little, however, he was deliberately forming a body of other artistic principles, some of which he would soon reject but all of which struck him for the moment as solid. He adopted as one of his basic aesthetic doctrines the then widespread doctrine that a great work of art was a great poetic idea communicated to the public in a well-made form that it could understand. He warned Cézanne about the dangers of commercial art. An artist should never, he said, be guided by a desire for financial reward while creating a work, but after the work's completion it was only fair that its creator should receive part of the profits. On May 2, 1860, he wrote Baille that, like George Sand, he preferred fiction that depicted the world as it ought to be to realistic fiction as a means of improving his fellow men. He believed that beautiful ideal visions ennobled a poet and that it was impossible to seek out and expose corruption without having some of the muck rub off on oneself. Strongly coming out against realism in painting as well as literature, he advised Cézanne on March 25, 1860, to imitate the spiritual painters Jean Goujon and Ary Scheffer: 'Scheffer was passionately in love with the ideal, all his types pure, airy, almost diaphanous. He was a poet in the full sense of the term, almost never depicting reality, attempting the most sublime, the most delirious subjects.'

As for the realists, he professed that he had never been able to understand those fine gentlemen. The most realistic subject in the world, a farm courtyard with its dunghill, splashing ducks, fig-tree, and so forth could, he argued, be made poetic with the help of a ray of light and one of Greuze's farm girls. In the last analysis, spiritualism and realism, he concluded, were only words. Everything had its poetry, dunghills as well as roses.

While working out his general artistic principles, he also began to establish the very particular artistic traits that he wanted to cultivate. Like most other beginning writers, he had started out by imitating the authors whom he most admired – the classical models held up to him in school and the great romantics, especially Musset, the most widely copied poet of his day. He still did this, but more systematically; and, without abandoning his former models, he acquired new ones. Furthermore, he questioned everything. No matter what author, great or small, he happened to be reading, he always, as he told Baille in April, 1861, related his methods and artistic ideals to his own, constantly comparing himself with him and trying to decide whether he was on the right path. He tried to define what he liked and what he did not like, to put his finger on what he should emulate and on what he might do differently.

Reading Shakespeare, he discovered several qualities that he would like to possess himself. He loved the way Shakespeare dramatized the truth that while some people lie suffering by the wayside others pass by singing. He admired Shakespeare's mingling of the real and the ideal just as they were in life itself. He was impressed above all by Shakespeare's genius for finding in each of his dramas the material for a general portrayal of life. 'Each play is like a separate chapter in a work about humanity . . . Othello is not a jealous man, he is jealousy, Romeo, love, Macbeth, ambition and vice, Hamlet, doubt and weakness, Lear, despair. No paltry or strange exceptions, just a grandiose generality.' He liked André Chénier's attempt to express modern ideas in forms inspired by the Greeks and Romans, but concluded that the genius who would arise someday and attempt, on the contrary, to express new thoughts in new forms would, if successful, be acclaimed by the public and win immortal fame. He sympathized with his pathetic old friend Pagès du Tarn's attempt to write a bourgeois *Phaedra* in modern dress. But he thought it was perfectly ridiculous of Pagès to employ for this purpose confidants, emphatic tirades, and other worn out tragic accessories and to make his modern middle-class characters speak like the heroes and heroines of Corneille and Racine.

Rereading Hugo, comparing himself with him, he became aware of some of his own particular artistic traits – for example, the love he shared with Hugo for strong contrasts or his Hugo-like fondness for luminous conclusions resuming the full thought behind a piece of writing in a few words.

In the summer of 1860, after rereading a poem Cézanne had sent him about the choice of Hercules between vice and virtue, he had sadly to admit that even though he wanted to be a poet more than anything else he was not perhaps so temperamentally suited to being one as Cézanne. 'Yes, old friend, you are more of a poet than I am,' he wrote him solemnly on August 1. 'My verse is perhaps purer than yours, but yours is plainly more poetic, more true. With you, it is the heart that speaks, with me, the brain. You really mean what you say. For me, it's only a game, a brilliant lie.'

By the 1860s, the notion that a man has to be of his own time had become a critical commonplace. Zola enthusiastically embraced it, including it among his most fundamental assumptions. 'All my excuse,' he wrote Baille on June 2, 1860, 'is in the time in which I live.' Influenced by Hugo, Michelet, and his favorite newspaper, *Le Siècle,* he optimistically pictured in the same letter his century as an age of transition carrying humanity forward from the odious prerevolutionary past to the longed-for future. Like them he also saw it as marked by impatient, fiery, all-consuming activity on every cultural level – science, technology, politics, religion. The railroads were expanding everywhere. Electricity was being applied to the telegraph, balloons soaring into the air, steamships conquering the seas. The peoples of the world were rising up in revolt. The great empires were coalescing into one. Traditional religion was in shambles. The new world about to be born would require a fresh, vital new faith. From these ideas, colored by liberal republicanism, he deduced, also in the same letter, those qualities which distinguished nineteenth-century poets, including himself, from those of other centuries. That is to say, he established the archetype to which, if he was to be truly of his own time, as indeed he must if he wished to be great, he would have to conform:

Even if we wanted to deny the date of our birth, we

could not do so; a poet can borrow the form of a Rabelais, Corneille, or Voltaire, but his ideas will always be modern. It will always be these yearnings for God, these cries of a soul longing for the sacred beliefs of evangelical times, the sacred love of woman; it will be these blasphemies of a heart ulcerated by doubt and, denying all that is pure and sacred, searching with anguish for some truth that will prove it wrong. It will always be this poet seizing a pen in his cradle, making literature not with a treatise on rhetoric, but with the wounds of his own heart, turning his back on pedagogues, who are not of his time, and recounting his favorite visions, interrogating the future, digressing and losing himself in the clouds, piling one utopia upon another, always devoured by his feverish activity.

All the while, he was asserting more and more his predilection for vast, all-embracing subjects. He was also turning increasingly outwards. He began to seek in the great historical events of his time the powerful original themes that he needed in order to realize his vaulting literary ambitions. 'One thing is certain,' he wrote Baille towards the fall of 1860,

> Every society has its own particular poetry, and, since our society is not that of 1830 and does not as yet have its own poetry, the man who finds it will be justly famous. The hopes for the future, the wind of liberty arising everywhere, the purification of religion – these are all certainly powerful sources of inspiration. The whole problem is to find a new form, to sing worthily of the peoples of the future, to show in a fittingly grandiose manner humanity ascending the steps of the temple.

His realistic bent was also asserting itself despite his initial preference for idealism. He inserted realistic passages into his letters, poems, and short stories – a description of a Paris street in the rain, a colorful, La Bruyère-like contrast between a proper gentleman and a poor workman. The sight of the workman with his hungry face, work-soiled blouse, ragged tie, illiteracy, ignorance, and quiet acceptance of his fate moved him to indignation and made him call out for vengeance. In late August, 1860, reading Hugo's *Le Dernier jour d'un condamné* – a moving pamphlet against capital punishment – he finally conceded that the poet had a right to expose the ills of society in order to cure them.

When Zola had come up to Paris from Aix he had been woefully ignorant of the movement of ideas of his own day. Now, like his former classmates at the Lycée Saint-Louis, he avidly followed it and was caught up in it. If he still read Hugo it was because Hugo had never been more adulated than he was during those years. In exile, due to his heroic opposition to the Second Empire, the poet had assumed in the eyes of thousands of French youths an ineffable grandeur. They pictured him as a colossus in chains still singing in the midst of the tempest, a Prometheus, a superhuman figure dominating France, brooding over it from afar with his eagle eye. If Zola read Shakespeare, it was because a new, highly publicized edition of his complete works in French translation had just come out. Nor was there anything extraordinary at that time about Zola's passion for Michelet, who had by then become along with Hugo and Musset one of the chief shapers of his thought and art. During the first dozen dark, repressive years or so of the Second Empire, Michelet's humanitarianism, his republican enthusiasms, his grandly optimistic faith in the future had won him a host of new admirers.

VIII

Throughout this whole initial stage of his career, Zola was also struggling to forge for himself a new faith. The natural tendency of late adolescents to question their inherited values and beliefs and where necessary adopt new ones was reinforced in his case by his ambition to play a prophetic role and by the extreme metaphysical and religious crisis through which France, along with numerous other Western countries, was then going.

Like many other thoughtful French youths of his age, he had lost his original faith soon after reaching the age of reason. The same pattern endlessly repeated itself: the first twinge of doubt, then the painful inner conflict, and then the final break. While still at the Lycée Saint-Louis, he had already concluded that Catholicism was irrational. The chaplain had tried to dissuade him, but to no avail. Like Michelet or the journalist Louis

Jourdan, whose articles he could read in *Le Siècle*, and many other republicans, he had also become violently anticlerical. It was impossible to forgive the Roman Catholic Church and the clergy for having supported the coup d'état of December 2, 1851. 'Prayer is the only intermediary that I accept between the Lord and myself,' he wrote Baille on August 10, 1860. 'In this age of philosophical inquiry, what has killed the faith are the priests and commentators.' Meanwhile, what remained of his specifically Christian beliefs was, in large part, fading away – not without an occasional brief flare-up, like a dying flame. Like most of his more thoughtful, open-minded, intellectually curious contemporaries, he was torn between violently conflicting philosophical and religious ideas and attitudes.

He was often plagued by the romantic melancholy that he had first imbibed in his readings of Musset. Sometimes he would sink into a state of utter doubt and despair. The world would seem absurd and meaningless. Not only were there moments when, as we have seen, he regarded life as nothing more than a brief stop between two dark voids; he deplored his inability to perceive the spirit hidden in the flesh, the face behind the mask. Like Michelangelo's bound slaves, he suffered from the soul's imprisonment in the body. He was tormented by the inability of his soul to communicate with other souls, the eternal solitude to which it would seem to have been condemned.

At certain moments, he tended to substitute for his old Catholicism a vague, nebulous, constantly changing Romantic Christianity, or, more precisely, syncretism dominated by Christian elements. Still devoted to the Holy Virgin, he dedicated to her 'Paolo,' but, as he confessed in that same poem, he sadly suspected that she was only a myth. 'Each religious sect has its profession of faith,' he wrote Baille, also on August 10, 1860. 'Here is mine: "I believe in one God, omnipotent, good, and just. I believe that God created me, that he directs me here below, and that he awaits me on high. My soul is immortal and, in granting me free will, the Master has reserved for himself the right of reward and punishment. I should do good, shun evil, and above all trust in the justice and goodness of my judge." ' In the same letter, however, he rejected the doctrine of the Holy Trinity as illogical. Yet even though he denied the divinity of Christ, he still, he went on to say, loved him, prayed to him, and regarded

35

him as his master. 'If to be a Christian means to be a disciple of Christ, I openly take this name. His precepts are mine, his God mine.'

But nothing was more fragile than this new, makeshift, still predominantly Christian religion. Even as Zola clung to whatever remnants he could save of his former faith, he went on accumulating ideas mostly drawn from the chaotic secular thought of his day. In doing so, he was governed not so much by logic as he was by intuition and feeling. He scorned systematic philosophy and theology and boasted of his own lack of order and methodicalness.

He retained that pagan reverence, going back to his excursions in the Aix countryside, for the power of life. Like Voltaire – or Michelet for that matter – he regarded just plain hard work as in itself a powerful, if prosaic, source of happiness and intimated that if he could rewrite the Beatitudes, he would include one beginning: 'Blessed are they who work.' He had been struck by Michelet's conviction, expressed in *La Femme*, that in times of religious eclipse such as theirs woman alone might serve as a transitional religion. He also tried like Michelet and others to make a religion out of Eros. His chief motive in writing 'Rodolpho' and 'Paolo' was, indeed, nothing less than to regenerate society by bringing men back to the path of true love. In 'Rodolpho,' he condemned the soulless, exploitative sexuality that he blamed for much that was wrong with the society of his day. In 'Paolo,' based on his own experience with a girl in Aix, his objective, as he wrote Cézanne on June 25, 1860, had been to make platonic love 'more attractive than carnal love' and 'to show that in this century of doubt a pure love can serve as a religion, impart to lovers belief in God and the immortal soul.'

Through his readings of George Sand, Michelet, Hugo, and others, he was drinking in romantic humanitarianism with its religious exaltation of mankind, its utopianism, its republican and socialistic tendencies, its cult of France as a Messianic nation, its glorification of the French Revolution and the nineteenth century pregnant with a new and better world. He was particularly entranced by Sand's vision of society transformed into one big, cooperative, prosperous family.

But at the same time, he was also influenced by certain philosophical and religious ideas then current in the sciences, particularly natural history – ideas rooted quite as much in traditional philosophical cosmology and natural theology as in modern scientific discoveries and theories. In his more scientific moods, he conceived of God as the 'creative principle,' or 'first force,' and wanted to discover the workings of the divine mind and achieve union with it through scientific study of the laws governing creation. Like many other more scientifically minded Westerners, he no longer considered man as the center and chief beneficiary of creation, tending instead to regard man as only a small, ephemeral part of an ever-changing, progressing universe.

IX

As has been noted, he finished 'Paolo' in May, 1860. In composing it, he had tried to express the gospel of platonic love that he was preaching in it with all the eloquence at his command. It was not long, however, before his ideal of love changed again. In June he fell in love with a young florist. She was blonde, with small hands and feet. She lived in the house next door, and he would religiously watch her pass by under his window twice a day, every morning at six-thirty, and every evening at eight. She would look up at him, respond sometimes to his smile, and that was as far as their relationship had gone. But by now he had reverted to his earlier notion, inspired by Michelet, that the best kind of love available to mere mortals involves the complete commitment of the body as well as the soul. In 'Un coup de vent,' which he completed on September 3, he imagined that Stephen, a timid adolescent like himself, and Nini, a young florist like the one he loved, actually carried their passion to the happy conclusion that he had, for lack of courage, vainly desired for himself.

Like most of his other writings so far, it was all very sentimental and romantic. 'Yes, yes!' Nini cries in the ending, as her lips and Stephen's finally touch, 'brother, become my lover, or, rather, retain both these names ... let us have this terrestrial love, these effusions of the body as well as the soul. Let us love with all our faculties and worship God in his secret designs.' The narrator comments that the angels in heaven must surely have smiled down approvingly on these young lovers' 'sacred and pure embrace where earth fraternized in a way with Heaven.'

On September 8, his heart madly pounding, he slipped a copy of 'Paolo,' together with a laudatory letter, into an envelope and sent it off to Victor Hugo. He might as well have mailed it to the man in the moon.

The most crucial and painful stage in his artistic and intellectual development during these initial years of his career began at just about this moment. He had many reasons to feel depressed. His plans to revisit Aix in the autumn of 1860 had collapsed. (His mother and he had not been able this time to raise the money.) His persistent failure to find a job depressed him, and so did his almost constant ill health. He was mentally and physically exhausted. Then, as the weeks went by, it became increasingly hard just to keep warm. Few Parisians could remember a harsher winter. Meanwhile, it was becoming harder and harder to hold on to his few meager possessions, including indispensable articles of clothing, and scrape together the money to buy his next meal. He especially hated his one, increasingly threadbare and shiny old greenish overcoat, but desperately needed it, and there were occasions when even it had to go to the pawnshop. For two or three days at a time, he would have nothing to wear except his bedclothes.

Not long before he moved to his belvedere on the Rue Neuve-Saint-Étienne-du-Mont, he had, moreover, become involved with a poor prostitute named Berthe. It was one of the most traumatic experiences that he had ever had. The sight of her, huddled up in her dirty, ragged dress and strangely inert, more like an object than a human being, filled him with a curious mixture of lust and pity. Influenced by his romantic ideas about the redemptive power of love, he dreamt of saving her with his love, of being for her what Hugo's Didier had been for Marion de Lorme. A few days after Christmas, 1859, he had picked up an injured warbler fallen in the snow outside his door and carried it close to the fire. For an instant, it had opened its eyes, and he had felt it palpitating in his hands. Then it had died. In a way, the same incident now repeated itself, but more painfully. This was partly because so much more was at stake, including not only one of his most cherished and poetic beliefs but his very self-respect. Yet it was also because, no matter how tenderly and

38

generously he treated Berthe, no matter how eloquently he pleaded with her to change her mode of life, no matter how passionately he made love to her, Berthe never did respond in the way he had hoped that she would – even for a moment.

No doubt women like her, he reflected, had been born with good instincts, but through force of habit they had acquired a second nature. She was sick of kisses, self-centered, grasping, easily annoyed, unkind, essentially hostile to men in general, incapable of being faithful to any particular man. The more he tried to help her, the more she resented it. She accused him of acting like a tyrant and evoked other lovers who had been more handsome and generous than he was. As for himself, he soon became disgusted with her vulgarity, her obscene stories, her foul language. When he made love to her, he now did so less tenderly. He wondered if she had a soul at all. What had started out as a noble experiment ended up as sheer debauchery. He loathed himself as much as her. Finally, they broke up. As for his romantic belief that he could save her, he was completely disillusioned. 'I have just graduated from a rough school,' he wrote Cézanne on February 5, 'the school of real love.' 'Love a lorette and she will hate you,' he wrote Baille a few days later. 'Despise her and she will love you.'

Much as he loved his belvedere, he had to admit that it was at first sometimes almost unbearably cold, exposed and vulnerable to every glacial wind. There was no fireplace. The big windows were white with frost. Sometimes the only way not to freeze to death was to stay in bed. Even when he was writing, he would remain there, under the covers and anything else he could put over him, holding his candle with one hand while he scribbled away with the other.

What was even more depressing, he was having a harder and harder time with his writing. For weeks on end, he would have no new ideas. Nor could he summon the energy to go on trying to express his old ones. His transitions were causing him trouble. He had difficulty saying exactly what he meant. 'The Muse has left me for a while,' he complained to Baille on March 17, 1861.

To make matters worse, he was going through another metaphysical and religious crisis. As the cruel winter wore on, his chief pleasures were to smoke his pipe in front of his mother's fireplace, daydream with his eyes fixed on the flames, and, occasionally, read a few pages of Montaigne. At first he found this author a great source of comfort. He loved what he termed his sweet and tolerant philosophy, common sense, unfailing good humor, lack of pedantry, elevated thoughts, and colorful, concrete, trenchant style. 'He's the one for me,' he wrote Baille later on that year, in June. 'In a word, I am his disciple, his fervent admirer; and the least I can do is give all my love and devotion to this man who has given me his fortitude, his cheerfulness.' But, as he would confess later, he was horribly mistaken. Little by little, as he read Montaigne, he had absorbed without realizing it Montaigne's radical skepticism. He had lost his ability to believe in anything but lacked Montaigne's gift for living comfortably with doubt. He felt betrayed by his new master and henceforth regarded him with horror. Thanks to Montaigne, he had lost his last certitudes. He deplored man's ignorance. He despaired of finding the answers to the great metaphysical questions that were increasingly tormenting him. What was man's principle and end? What was life all about? Why had the world been created? What was God like? Why did there have to be so much suffering? How could he, Émile Zola, communicate with other souls, break out of the prison of his isolation, discover the soul behind the face, penetrate to the reality underneath the appearances of things. Neither in the stars nor in other men nor in himself could he find the answers. He was more than ever devoured by metaphysical anguish – that same anguish which was one of the main traits of the thought of his intellectually and spiritually confused and troubled age.

'I am young,' he had written Baille on October 2, 1860. 'The future belongs to me, and all I need to conquer it is the courage to do so.' But for the moment that precious sine qua non was hard to come by. Sometimes when he thought about his career and the need to pursue it courageously, he would wonder what courage is good for, when luck is everything. He was afraid that he was growing lazy – not 'lazy' like a poet lost in creative reveries, but lazy in the ordinary, truly disreputable sense. Often the slightest exertion troubled him. Nothing on earth could have made him budge from his chair in front of his mother's fire. At times he sank into a deep apathy. At other times, he was furious, cursed his career, found all his earlier writings disgusting, tore up all his new verses. One feverish night, while only half-awake, he had imagined writing a long poem that would make the multitude howl or applaud at his feet, but the subject was so vague that he had not even been able to define it in the letter he wrote Baille the next day. In his moments of greatest exhaustion and discouragement, he suspected that the most he could hope for in life was to have some day, no doubt in the distant future, a dog that might love him a little and a mistress who would probably love him not at all.

But he was not one to give up completely. The soldier in him always sooner or later fought back. Even after the Muse had left him, one of the worst apparent misfortunes that can befall a young writer, he was not utterly discouraged. 'Thank God!' he wrote Baille on March 17. 'This is only – and I feel this strongly – a period of transition. Sometimes I even think I should be happy about it. Art still exalts me, I understand, I sense beauty, and if I tear up my verses, it is because they don't content me, because I realize that I must, that I can, do better. My task now is to find this better form. With courage, you always succeed, especially when you know exactly what you are looking for.'

The truth was that he had grown tired of romanticism. He had absorbed all he could from Musset and his other romantic models. For a long time, he had realized that his own generation needed something new. But it was difficult for him to see exactly what that was.

Yet simply to realize that there was this longing for something new was already a step forward. Little by little, moreover, he was actually making some progress in his quest for an alternative to romanticism whether he was always aware of it or not. For a while he suspected that he might have found it in Laprade's icily spiritual, highly elevated poetry, devoid of anything carnal, aiming at the superb tranquillity of plants – a reaction to romantic passion. But he quickly realized that this was not what he was looking for, that he wanted something more human, something that appealed to the brute as well as the angel in man. He realized, reading Laprade, how much he himself craved in literature living human beings just like himself whose joys and sorrows interested and moved him. He envisaged a kind of poetry that would eliminate the passionate effusions, violent stage effects, glaring colors, and physiologically odd heroes of the romantics but retain their vitality, their concreteness, their protrayal of human life in all its fullness.

In July, 1861, he had a great idea, an idea of genius: to write a long treatise, to be entitled *Le Poète,* whose purpose would be to discover what one had to do to become a great poet by finding out what all the great poets throughout the ages have had in common. In particular, it would study the conditions that produce a great poet, the major motives and themes shared by the great poets, the effects produced by them on their contemporaries, their major qualities (originality, harmony, grace, sublimity, etc.), their use of form. When he had rolled all the great poets into one composite great poet, as it were, he would have established the model that he himself must follow. He already suspected what some of the most general conclusions would be: that there are two kinds of poets, those who concentrate on their own epoch and those who study what is eternal in man; that those who follow the second course are more likely to win lasting fame; that one should portray one's own time, but in doing so focus on what is eternal in it.

Among other things, his meditations on this project augmented his urge to create an original kind of epic, his epic, the epic that his age needed. He did not know exactly what it would be like, but he could already dimly perceive its form stirring in the shadows. He wanted to change his style, make it more sober, nervous, and graceful. He was more and more convinced that the wisest course for himself and other would-be great poets of his generation was to exploit the fascinating new material that their century offered. By this he now meant not only the growth of freedom and world unity, the changes going on in religion, and all the other major aspects of the unfolding drama of progress, but also the astonishing discoveries of contemporary astronomy, natural history, physics and chemistry. 'This is what the century offers you,' he wrote Baille on July 18. 'Take as much of it as you can. Become great with this subject matter.' He had come to admit that the exact sciences now provided the standards by which all other knowledge should be measured. He recognized that mathematics and science also had their poetry.

His ideas were evolving and expanding in other respects. The preceding December, a group of opposition intellectuals including Émile Deschanel, an eminent literary scholar and republican intellectual just returned from exile in Belgium, had inaugurated a public lecture series in a hall at no. 7, Rue de la Paix. Presumably, the lectures were to treat of literature and other 'harmless' subjects. The purpose was, as Deschanel put it, 'to do with the spoken word what newspapers do with the pen,' that is, to become 'one of the instruments of progress, one of the forms of liberty.' Yet it was easy for a speaker to slip into his talk, even when he was discoursing on something nonpolitical, allusions to the current political situation. The series had created a sensation. The hall was packed three times a week, month after month. Latin Quarter publications reproduced many of the lectures in their entirety. They were also discussed in the cafés. Zola was as much influenced by them as anyone else. They helped determine his selection of books to read, the subjects he meditated on, the topics he treated in his letters – topics that, as the months went by, became ever more deeply rooted in his thought: the causes of social progress, the applications of physiology to literary criticism, the doctrine that a work of art should be the expression of a temperament reacting to a milieu, the ways in which a writer's style reflects his century, country, climate, temperament, sex, and profession.

For about five months, beginning in October, 1860, his literary activity had slowed down almost to a halt, but by February, 1861, his creative powers had begun to stir again – at least on a prosaic level. It had occurred to him that an interesting novel might be based on his disillusioning affair with Berthe. It would make more or less the same point as a novel by Auguste Vermorel, entitled *Desperanza*, that had appeared in the bookshops just that January: that the courtesan as depicted in contemporary literature was a myth and the widespread romantic notion that prostitutes could be saved by love a dangerous illusion. Rapidly, this new project took shape in Zola's mind, chapter by chapter.

Soon, despite more lethargic spells, he was writing verse again. Towards the end of May, he finished another long poem, 'L'Aérienne,' exalting much the same view of love that he had preached in 'Un Coup de vent.' Comparing it with 'Rodolpho' and 'Paolo,' he realized that the three poems went together. 'Rodolpho' was the hell of love, 'L'Aérienne' the purgatory of love, and 'Paolo' the paradise of love. Delighted by this

43

discovery, he entitled his new trilogy *La Comédie amoureuse*.

After completing 'L'Aérienne,' he returned once again to *La Chaîne des êtres*, now rebaptized *La Genèse*. Still undaunted by the immensity of the subject, he started doing all those things which had to be done before he could plan it in detail. He reread Lucretius, amassed notes on Cuvier, Zimmermann, Flourens, and others. But the more deeply he delved into his authorities, the more disheartened he became by the great disagreement between them and by the precariousness of their hypotheses. He was unable to get beyond the first eight verses:

The Birth of the World

Creative Principle, unique First Force,
Who with the breath of life made matter animate.
Thou who livest, knowing neither birth nor death,
Give me the golden wing of the inspired prophet.
I shall sing of thy work and on it traced
In time and space I shall read thy thought.
I shall rise towards thee, borne upwards on thy breath
To offer thee this mortal song of immortality.

In the grips of the black, absolute skepticism provoked by his readings in Montaigne, he wrote a poem of about 150 verses expressing the terrible metaphysical anguish and the pessimistic view of the human condition that had resulted from them. He called it 'Doute,' and headed it with an epigraph culled from Montaigne: 'Oh to believe, how thou dost prevent us!' But in another poem, almost identical with 'Doute' except for the ending, the dark night of the soul evoked in 'Doute' is followed by a leap of faith. In his despair, the seeker after truth whose words are recorded in the poem suddenly hears what he takes to be the voice of God addressing itself not to his reason but to his heart:

Love, love! that is the secret word!
Each wave is followed by another; the swallow's nest
Sees with each new spring hatch within its down
New eggs, frail hopes of a new mother.

A rose fades, a bud opens;
The wind loses its perfumes, then dies in space;
A new song always follows the song that must end . . . .

44

Writing Baille in the summer of 1861, Zola admitted that he had not as yet done anything of value. He was, he said, the first to smile at his works. But he added optimistically, 'I am doing better day by day, and every day the horizon seems brighter.' On January 20, 1862, he wrote Cézanne, 'I am very ill, but not yet dead. My spirit is alive and doing wonderfully. I even suspect that all this suffering is helping me grow. I see better, hear better. I am developing new senses.'

[2]

Young Manhood

I

On New Year's day, 1862, Zola went around to various houses in Paris delivering New Year cards for another old friend of his father's, a professor of medicine named Boudet. Boudet had been shocked to see Francesco's son reduced to such a sorry state. Zola's threadbare, tattered overcoat had now turned an almost yellowish hue, and he looked more famished than ever. Some of the houses he stopped at belonged to former classmates at the Lycée Saint-Louis. He hesitated to knock, but he needed the money, and the twenty-franc gold piece that Boudet gave him after he had made his rounds did wonders for his morale. He had all the more reason to be happy, because, thanks to Boudet's recommendation, he had been promised a job! He was to be a clerk at Hachette's publishing house. His long search for employment had at last ended.

He liked the idea of working for a publisher and a major publisher at that. It was the stroke of luck he had been hoping for. All he needed now was the wit and courage to take advantage of it in order to advance his literary career.

He started in on February 1. The salary was 100 francs a month. At first he did nothing but wrap books, but all the while, he studied the business and the people he had to deal with and planned his strategy.

He was now part of one of those aggressive, perpetually expanding enterprises characteristic of the last half of the nineteenth century. The founder and head, Louis Hachette, a solidly formed, benign looking, clear-eyed old gentleman with mutton-chops, was the very type of the brilliant, educated, liberal nineteenth-century entrepreneur. Perceiving the potential market created by the rapid spread of public education initiated by Guizot, as Minister for Public Instruction, in 1833, he had become the major publisher of textbooks and teaching manuals in France. He had been the first to place bookshops in railroad stations, cramming the shelves with popular novels, children's books, inexpensive editions of the classics, and scientific vulgarizations published by his firm or its subsidiaries. He was also the editor and publisher of Littré, Michelet, Sainte-Beuve, Deschanel, Taine, and some of the other most brilliant and influential authors of the time. Although the firm's policy was reasonably eclectic (its stable also included Gobineau and the spiritualist philosopher Caro), the atmosphere was, like the founder himself, a close friend of Littré's, primarily positivistic and liberal.

During the first two of the four years, from 1862 to 1866, that Zola was employed at Hachette's, its crowded headquarters on the Boulevard Saint-Germain, where he worked, were constantly undergoing expansion. Day after day, the air was filled with the din of pickaxes, shovels, saws, hammers, pouring concrete, whistles, workmen's shouts. The whole city reverberated with the same, by now familiar noises as it went on violently changing and growing to meet the needs of the Empire and the new century already emerging out of the dust and debris of the old. Hundreds of ancient houses were being pulled down to make way for Baron Haussmann's broad new boulevards and the huge new, floridly embellished stone, concrete, iron, and glass palaces of modern commerce. At some construction sites, electric arc lights, a recent invention, would burn on all night as work feverishly continued. This provided, as it were, a fitting accompaniment to Zola's own struggle to change, grow, keep up with the times, assert himself, prosper, become the great writer he wanted to be.

The new shipping clerk lost no time in his efforts to attract the attention and secure the confidence of his employer. At closing time one Saturday evening, only a short while after he had begun working for the firm, he gathered the courage to slip into M. Hachette's empty office and deposit on his desk a copy of *La Comédie amoureuse*. Monday morning, he anxiously studied the old gentleman's face to see if he could find on it any indication of what his reaction had been, but there was none. That noon, however, Hachette summoned him and invited him to sit down. Hachette had no intention of publishing the manuscript, but he encouraged the young poet to go on writing and from then on treated him with more consideration. He doubled his salary. He tried to find him extra work. He invited him to submit a short story for a children's magazine the firm published – a generous gesture even though he was obliged to reject the actual piece Zola gave him, 'Soeur des pauvres,' finding it 'too revolutionary.' When, that May, Zola submitted to him a written proposal for a new magazine to consist entirely of selected first efforts by talented beginners, he turned this down too because it was not in Hachette's line, but he was impressed by the proposal itself. Zola had had the astuteness to present his suggestion as a financially profitable venture for the firm. Following a sure instinct, he promptly transferred Zola to the publicity department and made him its director.

Zola now had his own office, a small upstairs room at the end of a long corridor reached by a spiral staircase and lined on both sides by piles of unbound sheets.

II

He was acutely aware that his life had entered a new stage. His childhood in particular seemed terribly remote. When, seven months after he had started working for Hachette's, his old friend Marguery, just arrived from Aix, paid him a visit, he was overcome by nostalgia. Marguery had not changed at all. Never having left Aix, he had been preserved by it, as if in a glass jar. 'Suddenly all my youth was standing there in front of me, come alive again,' Zola wrote Cézanne. 'That time is so far off, so many sensations have erased those of my early years that I remained in a near tremulous state for a good quarter of an hour afterwards.'

But he was not dissatisfied with his present life. To be sure, even with 200 francs a month it was still hard to make ends meet. He had debts to pay off, his mother to support. (His grandfather Aubert had died in 1861.) His mother and he, back together again, still found it impossible sometimes to pay the rent on time. In the spring of 1864 they were evicted from their current address, no. 7, Rue des Feuillantines. Another place they lived in, on the Rue de la Pépinière (now called the Rue Daguerre) overlooking the Montparnasse cemetery, was a noisy working-class tenement house jammed with over two hundred people. But the nightmarish poverty of his Bohemian years was over.

Once more it was good to be alive! More than ever, he could enjoy being with his friends, and their number was growing constantly. Towards the end of 1861, Baille had arrived to begin his studies at the École Polytechnique. In November, 1862, Cézanne returned. The three inseparables' old dream of sticking together no matter what, one for all and all for one, in their struggle to conquer Paris now became a reality. Marius Roux and Philippe Solari, Zola's oldest friends, had come up to Paris too. So had another companion from Aix, Numa Coste. Pajot often joined them. Through Cézanne, other young artists were introduced into their circle, among them Frédéric Bazille, Théodore Fantin-Latour, Camille Pissarro, Armand Guillaumin, Francisco Oller, and Antoine Guillemet.

They all passionately loved art and literature and shared the same artistic and literary tastes. Almost without exception, they were in revolt against tradition and looking for new subjects and forms of expression. With Cézanne in particular, Zola never tired of discussing the problems that they had in common, reviewing the past, interrogating the present, trying to work out a complete, infallible artistic creed. Sometimes they went on animatedly conversing until dawn.

There were once again the long Sunday walks in the countryside around Paris, most often with Cézanne. Cézanne would bring his painting things along. Zola would slip a book into a pocket. Frequently they would get off the train at Fontenay-aux-Roses, and hike to the Forest of Verrières, where they would spend the rest of the day. One of their favorite spots in the forest was a small, remote greenish pond called La Mare à Chalot in the Forest of Verrières. It was full of rushes and reflected in its clear, motionless surface the overhanging foliage of the surrounding trees. It made Zola think of the goddess Diana bathing, dipping her snowy feet in hidden sylvan springs. A mysterious charm seemed to rain down from the trees, while a secret voluptuousness, the silent love-making of the forest, rose

49

from the still water, over which would pass an occasional broad, silvery shimmer. Cézanne would paint, Zola read or doze.

III

In putting Zola in charge of publicity, Hachette had made a shrewd business decision. The firm's sales soared. But knowingly or unknowingly, Hachette had also done Zola himself, the man of letters, a stupendous favour. He now stood at the crossroads where writers, publishers, and critics meet. He was in the best possible position to study the workings of the book market from the inside. He was learning the then still rudimentary, yet rapidly growing, art of publicizing books. He was making valuable contacts. He met not only most of Hachette's own current authors, among them Littré, Michelet, Sainte-Beuve, and Taine themselves, but also scores of publishers, authors, and critics outside the firm. Many became personal friends, but all could be counted on to do him favors when he needed them to further his own literary career – not, of course, out of pure generosity or admiration, but because he had become, due to his position, a man who could bestow favors as well as receive them.

At Hachette's, he took account of the capital importance of journalism and advertising in the contemporary world. One day he decided to engage in journalism himself, not only because it would increase his income but also because of the powerful leverage it would give him. He also made up his mind to make full use of everything he had learned as publicity director to promote his own writings and reputation.

He no longer harbored any illusions as to what the world of letters was like. Writing in September, 1865, to Antony Valabrègue, a younger aspiring writer back in Aix, he offered to help him if he would come up to Paris.

> I'll be able to pass on to you what I've learned from my own experience, and we'll seize the bull by the horns. If you only knew, my poor friend, how little talent counts for in achieving success, you would put aside your pen and paper and set

about studying literary life, the thousand and one dirty tricks
that open doors, the art of using other people's credit, the
ruthlessness that you must have to step over the bodies of your
dear colleagues.

Very quickly after starting in at Hachette's, he had regained
his old faith in the value of work. On weekdays, he almost never
stopped working, except to eat and sleep. In the evening, after
he had finished supper around eight thirty, he shut himself up in
his room and read or wrote until midnight. If even fools can
succeed through hard work, he reasoned (and it seemed to him
that in his new job he had met plenty of good examples), he,
Émile Zola, certainly should be able to. At least, it was worth
giving another try. After he had done so for a while, his morale
improved. He thrived on all this exertion. He enjoyed trying to
do the impossible. He discovered strengths and capabilities that
he had not known he had, and his self-confidence went on rising.
So did his sense of his own superiority. One of his visitors at
Hachette's in 1864, the journalist and novelist Jules Vallès, was
struck when he met him by his 'disdainful, almost supercilious
mouth.' After they had been chatting for a while about their
mutual struggle to get ahead, Zola astonished Vallès with the
point-blank question: 'Do you feel you are a power?' Vallès was
at a loss to reply. But Zola, paying no attention, went on to say
as though simply stating a fact, 'Speaking for myself, I feel that I
am one.' When he finished, his mouth, Vallès noted, assumed
the same strangely contemptuous curl.

During the four years Zola was employed by Hachette's, he also
participated more than ever in the tumultuous, swiftly changing
cultural life of the capital. Not only might one have seen him, as
in his student or Bohemian days, applauding or booing in the
paradise of the Odéon, Le Gymnase, or Le Théâtre Français, or
standing in clusters of young men animatedly discussing some
painting or sketch at the Académie Suisse, Gleyre's studio, the
Louvre, a Salon, or listening with rapt attention to Deschanel,
Jean-Jacques Weiss, or some other idolized public lecturer in the
crowded hall on the Rue de la Paix. He and his friends swelled
the crowds snickering, guffawing, scowling, and gesticulating in
front of Manet's revolutionary *Déjeuner sur l'herbe* at the Salon des
Refusés in 1863. He shared Cézanne's, Guillemet's, Pissarro's,

and other artist friends' enthusiasm for Manet and their outrage at the official and public response to this masterpiece. But above all, he acquainted himself with everything going on in the world of letters. For his own private as well as business reasons, he read as he never had before – fiction, drama, poetry, criticism, philosophy, history, scientific vulgarizations. He had, of course, to read or at least leaf through everything put out by Hachette's in order to prepare his publicity material, but he also devoured many books published by other firms. Everything he read was either hot off the press or of current interest.

He abandoned *La Genèse*. The theme was too vast, the hypotheses he had to deal with too contradictory. He still dreamt of being a new Lucretius, of setting forth in beautiful verse the entire philosophy of science of his age. But one had to be practical, acknowledge what one could and could not do, and choose forms and subjects that were right for one. In the fall of 1862, on September 18, he began a long poem on Joan of Arc – a currently fashionable topic – in the style of Molière. Nothing came of it. Then he gave up writing verse altogether. His faith in his poetic gifts was shaky. He did not like the kind of poetry his generation was producing. He loved nature too much to sympathize with Baudelaire's cult of the artificial. Art for art's sake was not for him. He also saw that he could make his reputation faster with the rude tool of prose than with verse. He had observed that the novel was the genre in favor. He told himself that some day when he was famous he would come back to the Muse, if she would have him. Meanwhile, he was turning out one short story after another. By the end of 1862, he started working seriously on *La Confession de Claude*, the novel that he had wanted to write about his disillusioning affair with Berthe. He was also, while employed at Hachette's, trying his hand more and more at literary criticism.

At first he still turned to the classics in his efforts to go beyond romanticism. In September, 1862, he acknowledged as his new master Molière, the topic of a recent, very popular series of lectures by Jean-Jacques Weiss at no. 7, Rue de la Paix. Then he attempted to emulate Voltaire, whose star, in the early 1860s, after declining in the preceding decade, was once again rising, due to the reaction provoked by recent victories of retrograde elements within the Church. What he wanted to do was not abandon romanticism, but combine what he liked in it with what he admired in the classics. He retained the romantics' belief that art should be absolutely unhampered by external rules, their cult of originality, their conviction that an artist's prime duty is to manifest his personality, and their delight in portraying life in all its concreteness and immediacy. On the other hand, he wanted to recapture the great classics' reasonableness and self-discipline, their love of simplicity, their focus on what was most common in human experience, and their emphasis on universality, typical characters, and general human truths.

IV

He was trying very hard now to get himself published. On June 5, 1863, he wrote Jules Claretie, editor of *L'Univers illustré,* to which he had submitted two short stories, 'Please note that for me as a writer it is almost a matter of life or death, and that I await your decision with all the impatience of a twenty-year-old poet.' Despite the fervor of his appeals, no one seemed interested at first. That February, he had made the mistake of sending the prestigious *Revue des deux mondes* his rhymed 'proverb,' *Perrette.* After letting it gather dust for six months, the review sent it back with a curt, disdainful note of rejection. But by then he had already realized that he had been too presumptuous. He was not ready for the big reviews. It was not a good idea, furthermore, to expose himself prematurely to the editors that really mattered. Thereafter leaving the great literary periodicals alone, he tried out his powers and honed his style and ideas by publishing a few short stories and book reviews here and there in journals with lesser reputations and smaller circulations, mostly in Belgium or the French provinces.

Towards the end of March, 1864, he observed that he had enough short stories to make up a small book. On the advice of Deschanel, whose public lectures he had been attending and favorably reviewing, he sent one of them to Pierre Hetzel, the publisher, a friend of Deschanel's. When Hetzel took his time answering, Deschanel wrote him a prodding letter. The publisher read the story, liked it, and agreed, together with his associate, Albert Lacroix, a small, willowy, red-bearded Belgian with a passion for literature, to publish the entire collection. 'I've just had my first victory,' Zola exultantly wrote Valabrègue in July. 'The battle was a short one, and I'm surprised that I'm not more bruised by it. I'm on the threshold! The plain is vast, and I can still break my neck. But who cares! Since it is just a matter of marching on, that's just what I'll do!'

The volume, *Contes à Ninon*, came out in the bookshops in November. Except for 'La Fée amoureuse,' composed in 1859, he had written all the stories in it after his attempt to combine the best of romanticism and classicism was already well under way. Most of the classical authors he admired are strongly reflected along with his favorite romantics. The variety of all these incongruous influences results in a curiously discordant mêlée of genres, styles, motifs, and themes. Perrault rubs shoulders with Molière, Voltaire with Hugo and Musset. Not only in 'La Fée amoureuse,' but in most of the other stories – 'Simplice,' for example, or 'Soeur-des-pauvres' – the romantic dreamer is still in evidence. Simplice escapes from the ugly world into an enchanted forest where he falls in love with a nymph whose kiss is fatal to them both and they die happily in each other's arms. A kind fairy gives the charitable Soeur-des-pauvres a coin which endlessly reproduces itself to help the poor. But some of the other stories are anti-romantic. In 'Celle qui m'aime,' the narrator discovers to his great dismay that the immortal enveloped in a cloud of white muslin whom he glimpses through a side-show peephole is only, when he sees her afterwards in the street, 'a poor daughter of the earth, dressed in a faded cotton print.'

The longest and most ambitious story in the collection, 'Adventures du grand Sidoine et du petit Médéric,' is based on Voltaire's *Micromégas* and *Candide*. It is about a giant and a dwarf who set out to discover the mythical Kingdom of the Blessed. The story not only satirizes the politics of Napoleon III; it makes bitter fun of the excesses of romantic utopianism, personified in Primavera, the fey girl queen of this happy realm. Primavera founds a school to teach animals to live together in peace and harmony like her subjects. Naturally, the lions end up devouring the lambs they were supposed to lie down with, for, as the narrator dourly observes, 'Lions will be lions!' The story also gibes at theology in general. The moral recalls Voltaire, or, more precisely, the morals, for the narrator invites his readers to take their pick among 'fifteen or twenty' possible morals, one for everybody – but only two of which he has time to spell out. One may, if one wishes, agree with the narrator's own serious, desperately pessimistic conclusion that man's ignorance about the great mysteries of life is absolute, that even modern science will never solve them, that the one truth necessary to cure his sick soul will always elude him, that the best thing would be for every man to commit suicide, each in his own corner. But if one lacks the stomach for this, one may choose to ignore it and opt for the more obliging, optimistic conclusion, again recalling Voltaire, that the wisest course for those tormented by metaphysical questions is to lose themselves in some form of hard, healthy, constructive work and that happiness is to be found in love.

The style of *Contes à Ninon* is for the most part emotional, mincing, affected, and precious. There are numerous imprecisions and gratuitous assumptions. Yet there are also memorable pages – the description of the aimlessness and futility of the street-fair crowd in 'Celle qui m'aime,' or the evocation in 'Le Sang' of a drowsing soldier's hallucination that a river of blood is flowing from the wounds of his dead comrades. The book shows talent yet contains no hint of anything more than that.

Zola himself had a low opinion of it – even before its publication. But he did feel that these stories were as good as much of the other stuff that was getting published, and he needed a book to advance his career. He would have time later to show what he had it in him to do. Weeks before the publication date, he planned in minute detail his campaign to launch the book. He used his position at Hachette's to get the book noticed in over a hundred newspapers. Benefiting from what he had learned as publicity director, he sent friendly editors blurbs he had composed himself and offered to 'have a friend' write reviews which lazy critics could publish over their own names. He begged Valabrègue and Marius Roux to write critical reviews for their newspapers. 'You can then send me copies of the papers in which your essay appears,' he wrote Valabrègue on November 4. 'That way I'll know your opinion without your having to take the trouble to write it to me directly.' The immediate critical reception was favorable. Reviewers, half sincerely, half out of self-interest, found in the author a disciple of Musset, Heine, and

Murger, and agreed that the book was charming. Then no one mentioned it again. But Zola had what he wanted. His name had appeared in all the papers. From now on other writers would address him as 'my dear colleague,' His reputation, small as it was, predisposed newspaper editors in his favor and helped him place articles. He was thrilled with the thought that he was no longer just another face in the crowd. His campaign to conquer the public had begun. He had savored his first victory. But he wondered anxiously if he had the strength to keep up his reputation.

V

It was just at this moment, when he was savoring the modest success of his first book, that he fell in love again. The object of his passion was a tall, handsome, dark-haired, black-eyed young woman a year older than he. Her full name was Gabrielle Eléonore Alexandrine Meley. He called her Gabrielle, Sandrine, or – along with most of her other friends – just Coco. Like him she had led a hard life. She was an illegitimate child. Her mother, Caroline Louise Wadoux, a florist, and her father, Edmond Jacques Meley, a hosier, both still in their teens when she was born, had quickly tired of each other. Each had ended up marrying someone else. Alexandrine's mother had died when Alexandrine was ten. Her stepmother had treated her badly. Her stepfather, a riding master, and his sister had done what they could, but more and more she had had to fend for herself, just as Zola had. When he met her, she was earning her living as a seamstress. He assiduously courted her. In the spring of 1865, they wandered hand in hand in Fontenay-aux-Roses. They picked strawberries and made love in the Forest of Verrières.

At just about the same time, he started holding regular receptions for Cézanne, Baille, Solari, Pissarro, and other very close friends every Thursday evening after supper. He looked forward to these occasions as impatiently as he did his rendezvous with Alexandrine.

In 1864 and 1865 what was most essential in his mature artistic doctrine finally took shape. He renounced none of the elements that he had earlier decided to retain from the classics and the romantics. But the particular form that these partly romantic, partly classical elements now assumed in his thought was determined by more modern influences. He was more certain than ever that the main thrust of his age was in the direction of science, and he agreed more enthusiastically than ever with those who had called for a marriage between art and science. To be original, to be of its own time, art had to participate, he felt, in the great modern quest for scientific knowledge. In particular, he was convinced that it had to take part in the attempt of naturalistic philosophers like Deschanel and Taine to discover the explanation for psychological phenomena in the physical and material world.

He had read Deschanel's *Physiologie des écrivains et des artistes ou Essai de critique naturelle* when Hachette's had brought it out in 1864. He had also read Taine's history of English literature, published by Hachette's at about the same time. The theories of these two thinkers, quite similar in some ways, on the relationship between a work of art and the artist's race, temperament, and environment both appealed to him, but he preferred Taine's, more materialistic and deterministic. Taine's definition of an artist as a unique product of a specific race, moment, and milieu satisfied him, and he adopted it. Thanks to Taine, he became an enthusiastic admirer of Flaubert, Stendhal, and Balzac, then considered by most fashionable critics 'bad' authors. During the same period, he discovered Champfleury, Duranty, the Goncourt brothers, Dickens, Thackeray, Poe, and Hawthorne. He became aware of Darwin, whose *Origin of Species* had appeared in French translation in 1862. His new heroes, especially Balzac, Stendhal, Flaubert, and the Goncourts, exemplified all those qualities he now admired in the classics and the romantics while adding new ones that he also wanted to emulate.

Searching for cogent formulas and striking images to sum up his ideas, he was influenced by the tendency of many of his contemporaries, including such great artists as Gautier, Flaubert, and Baudelaire, to conceive of a work of art as nature viewed through some kind of optical medium, stained glass, a lens, a filter – all metaphors, of course, for the artist's eye, style, imagination, personality, or temperament. As he read Deschanel's *Physiologie des écrivains et des artistes,* he could not help but be impressed by the remark: 'A too fine style is like a piece of stained glass that alters the true appearance of things. This glass is, no doubt, beautifully colored, but in imparting its color to objects, it distorts their real appearance, their physiognomy, the truth, and forces me to think about itself too.' He did not agree. In August, 1864, he set forth in a letter to Valabrègue his own 'Theory of Filters.' Classical art, he said, is a fine, very pure slice of talc that dampens colors and brings out lines, romantic art a somewhat clouded, disturbed, but brilliantly rainbow-hued mirror or prism. As for realism, it is just a simple clear pane of glass which leaves out nothing, distorts nothing. Speaking for himself, he went on to say, he liked the realistic filter best. It satisfied his reason better than the others. He perceived in it immense beauties of solidity and truth. Yet he could not accept the realistic filter entirely. What he really wanted, he said, was a filter that would lie just enough to make him feel the presence of a man in an image of creation. But in the last analysis, he did not care whether an artist portrayed an object as blue, green, or yellow, square, or round. What kind of artistic distortion one prefers is purely a matter of taste, he wrote. The artist places himself face to face with nature, sees it in his own manner, lets it penetrate him, sends back the luminous rays after having, like a prism, refracted and colored them according to his own nature. The really important thing is to be a genius, to possess a powerful temperament. All the different filters that geniuses have created are equally acceptable.

Resuming his ideas the following year in an essay on Proudhon and Courbet, he at last found what was for him the perfect definition of a work of art: 'A work of art is a corner of creation seen through a temperament.'

At the root of his emerging mature aesthetics was the quasi-religious love and respect for life that he shared with Cézanne and his other closest friends. A picture, poem, or novel without a powerful, individual life of its own, he concluded, is nothing but a stupid lie. That was why there could be for him no such thing as an absolute ideal, or fixed standard, of beauty contrary to what so many idealists maintained. Beauty could reside only in life, in the free workings of a personality. A beautiful work, he insisted, is a living original work, a transubstantiation of its creator, his very flesh and blood. 'If you ask what I have come to do in this world, me, the artist,' he said, 'I will answer, "I have come to live out loud." '

VI

During this whole period he went on struggling to find or work out the new faith that he needed both as an artist and as a man. But this was even harder to do than forge an aesthetics. He had come over the years to accept many of the supreme values of his time. Nature, life, love, fecundity, work, truth, progress, force, the nineteenth century – these were the things that he held sacred. But in themselves they did not constitute a religion or even a vision of reality. They could at most provide a nucleus, a center. The thousand and one dreams, intuitions, myths, hypotheses, many exceedingly tentative, some barely conscious, that were associated with them in his mind formed no system. As before, his ideas were in a state of turmoil, like angry wind-swept clouds.

How could he ever create a new world out of this chaos? After he had read Montaigne most of what remained of his Christian faith had evaporated, including even his belief in individual souls. Occasionally he still lost himself in romantic reveries of a vaguely religious character, but in his serious thinking romantic idealism was giving way to the increasingly widespread cult of science. Like Taine and Renan he wanted to believe that science would reveal the religion of the future. 'We are becoming scientists,' he ecstatically announced in *Le Salut public* of Lyons on October 5, 1865. 'All the different social and religious problems are going to be solved one of these days. We are going to see God, we are going to see the truth.' Although he had given up *La Genèse*, the sublime vision of natural history behind it, largely based on Kant and Cuvier, had continued to evolve in his mind, becoming increasingly pantheistic. The Great Whole, Life, the World Soul, continuously creating itself, approaching ever closer to perfection. Man just a tiny link in the great chain of being, but destined as part of the Great Whole, to observe creation in its final state on the Last Day. The more perfect beings of the future were already adumbrated in man's dreams. In the October 14, 1865 issue of *Le Salut public*, he inserted into a long book review a few paragraphs proposing this vision as a new philosophical and religious faith. But his manner was a curious mixture of evangelical fervor and philosophical caution. His 'new faith,' he claimed, was better than Christianity and all other traditional religions, but he modestly acknowledged that it was still only a hypothesis.

He could not really believe in anything. He identified himself with Pascal the anguished skeptic but lacked Pascal's capacity for faith. At the thought of his own incredulity, he would sometimes break out in a cold sweat. He was as mistrustful of philosophical systems as he had ever been. In his approach to the great questions of existence, despite his occasional attempts to emulate Voltaire, he was now influenced above all by Taine or more purely positivistic thinkers, such as Littré. There were many moments when he believed only what he could see before his eyes. The immense skepticism provoked by his readings of Montaigne had heightened his need for infallibility. Like thousands of his equally troubled contemporaries, he found it not in religious dogma or the ex cathedra pronouncements of the Pope, but in unvarnished empirical fact. It was this, as much as anything else, that lay behind his growing preference for realism over romanticism. Criticizing the then fashionable artist Gustave Doré, he remarked, mindful of his own painful experience: 'One suspects that he has never known that life of suffering and doubt which makes one deeply love naked, living reality.'

VII

Throughout the whole of 1865 he devoted every spare moment to advancing his literary career. He began to acquire a reputation as a journalist and fiction writer. That spring, he submitted to the editor of a new Parisian daily, *L'Avenir national,* an audacious plan for a major series of articles reporting the drama of progress as it went on unfolding on every level of society. The objective, he explained, would be not only to satisfy their contemporaries' curiosity as to where they were and where they were going but also to record for the men, the society, of the future, 'how they were born, in what gigantic suffering and travail.' The proposal was rejected. He managed, however, to place other things elsewhere. Up to then, he had published only sixteen pieces, most in Belgium and the provinces. This year, he published forty-eight. Among them were book reviews, Parisian chronicles, short stories, and even a poem. The newspapers and magazines they appeared in were nearly all Parisian, and several, including *Le Petit journal*, *Le Salut public*, and *Le Figaro*, had large circulations.

Lured as always by the stage, he also composed two plays, *La Laide*, an insipid, excessively sentimental piece which the Odéon wisely rejected, and a dark melodrama, *Madeleine*, which, the following year, was turned down by two theatres. Lemoine-Montigny, director of Le Gymnase, found it too crude and melodramatic for his public. Harmant, director of Le Vaudeville, on the contrary, found it too sweet and mild for his.

But Zola's biggest project for 1865 was his maiden novel, *La Confession de Claude*. He had completed most of it by the end of 1863, then put it away in a drawer. Now, excited by the modest success of *Contes à Ninon*, he took it out and feverishly penned the final chapters. He wanted at all costs to have it appear before the start of the winter book season. This time, Lacroix, Hetzel's old partner, who had just formed a new firm with a Flemish colleague, accepted it. It went on sale at the end of November, less than twelve months after his first book.

Like most first novels, *La Confession de Claude* is highly autobiographical. Claude's ambition to save a prostitute with love had been Zola's own. So also had been Claude's grim poverty. Like Zola, Claude is torn between reality and a 'doleful gift for dreaming, the faculty to create out of whole cloth characters that seem almost real.' Like Zola, he has something of the priest about him and, as Zola puts it in the preface, 'is looking with immense despair for some sustaining truth.' Claude's account of his love-making with Laurence reflects Zola's own tormented nights with Berthe: 'I hugged her tight, felt her body abandon itself disdainfully to my embrace. But nothing on earth could make her open up her soul to me. Her heart and her thought shunned me. I was holding nothing but a lifeless rag, a body so weary, so worn out, so inert that it was incapable of answering my embrace with anything at all.'

But Claude is more than a mere reflection of Zola as he really

61

was. Like most of the central figures of Zola's earlier short stories, he is Zola's dream-self, a fictional alter ego through whom Zola can live out his fantasies. Although Claude's attempt to redeem Laurence ends in failure, like Zola's to save Berthe, Claude's quest for truth, in contrast to Zola's, has a happy ending. At the story's close, Claude, staring out of the window of his sordid room at the clear nocturnal sky, sees 'all the way to God.' In turning himself into a fictional character, Zola also acquired a mythological dimension. He entered the sphere of archetypes. He invested his experience with the meaning he wanted it to have, but could not be sure that it did have, in real life. There is a parallel between Claude, whose name means 'lame,' and Jacob, lamed by the angel in their famous struggle. As Claude himself understands his experience with Laurence, it is, like Jacob's, an ordeal of the sort that God visits upon his elect. 'Perhaps he wants, by making me responsible in this way for another soul,' Claude surmises at the beginning of the story, 'to test the limits of my spiritual strength.' As with Jacob, Claude's defeat is actually a blessing in disguise. Both Jacob's spiritual struggle and Claude's end just before dawn. Both emerge from their suffering stronger and better than they were before.

The style is barer, more sober and realistic than that of *Contes à Ninon,* but still too rhetorical and lachrymose for modern taste. Both the style and the theme recall Musset's *Confession d'un enfant du siècle.* The story is overdramatized. The language spoken by the characters is too poetic. But there are pages more memorable than anything Zola had previously written. Among the best are those in which Claude, suspecting that Laurence is being unfaithful to him with his friend, Jacques, stares at Jacques' lighted window and finally perceives the shadows of Laurence and Jacques in an embrace. The whole scene, in which reality turns into hallucination and nightmare without ever ceasing to be intensely real, possesses genuine power.

Again, as with his previous book, Zola stopped at nothing in his efforts to promote himself. He regarded the public as his prey and was now stalking and attacking it like a famished young lion. His main object was to shock, to create a scandal if possible. He preferred that to the mild praise which had greeted his short stories. He had learned at Hachette's how effective a properly phrased attack could be. If he could not yet provoke wild applause, he could at least make himself hissed. That way, the public would never forget him. 'The author reveals in it a strange talent combining exquisite delicacy with mad audacity,' he wrote in the blurb he composed himself and sent out to friendly editors. 'One will applaud, hiss perhaps, it being impossible to remain unmoved by this drama full of anguish and terror. There is in this work an indescribable talent, a passion and force that announce a writer of rare energy.'

Most critics, while expressing some reservations as to the subject, warmly praised the book. Others, however, reacted with just the sort of indignation Zola had been hoping for: 'shameful and degrading love,' 'filth,' 'hideous realism.' Barbey d'Aurevilly, whom Zola had dubbed an 'hysterical Catholic' in *Le Salut public* seven months earlier, warmly excoriated it, much as Zola had hoped others would. Writing for *Le Nain jaune*, Barbey declared that Claude was a toad and that Zola had simply spun out over 320 pages what Cambronne, who commanded the Old Guard at Waterloo, had expressed in a single word. A review editor who also happened to be a professor wrote Zola, *'La Confession de Claude* will have been your pistol shot. You wanted us to stick our heads out of the window and look at you. Well, we have seen you. Now it's up to you to exchange your pistol for a harp and charm us.'

Zola himself had almost as low an opinion of his novel as he did of *Les Contes à Ninon.* 'It has a lot of weak spots,' he wrote Valabrègue on January 8, 1866. 'It isn't a virile work. It's the cry of a whining, rebellious child.' He had to agree with Pajot's private comment that it was too exclusively psychological, that it told in detail what Claude thought, but did not tell the reader how Claude ate. But he was pleased again by the critical reaction in the press, even though he would have preferred something more thunderous, like the angry uproar that broke up the premiere of the Goncourts' *Henriette Maréchale* on December 5. Sitting in a box seat, courtesy of the Goncourts, whose novel *Germinie Lacerteux* he had enthusiastically praised in *Le Salut public* eleven months earlier, he had enjoyed the spectacle – the endless boos and hissing, the actors, their voices worn out by having to shout so loud, reduced to miming the third act. It had made the Goncourts famous. But at least, as he told Valabrègue, he himself was now known. 'People fear me and insult me,' he boasted. 'I am now classified among those writers whom the public reads with horror.' Yet this success only whetted his appetite for more. His goal of becoming an immortal was still far, far off.

VIII

After the publication of *La Confession de Claude* his position at Hachette's became awkward. The firm's partners (Louis Hachette was now dead) were disturbed by the notoriety that had resulted from the novel. They did not deal in that sort of fiction and did not want their employees associated with it. To make matters worse, an agent from the Public Prosecutor's office showed up at the firm to ask questions about the author. One of the partners gently hinted to Zola that he was a fool to go on working for only 200 francs a month at Hachette's when he could do much better devoting himself completely to literature and journalism.

He agreed. To be sure, it would be a long time before he could expect to gain much from his books. The whole edition of *Contes à Ninon,* all 1,500 copies, now sold out, had brought him a total of only 375 francs. The most the novel, printed up in the same size edition, could yield him was 450 francs. Yet just by contributing to periodicals in his spare time he was already earning as much as his salary. Trying to live solely by his pen was a risky thing to do. The newspaper world was a jungle. But he had faith in himself. He was eager to work on furthering his own literary career full time. He resigned as of January 31, 1866. This gave him two months to prepare for the battle ahead.

In the course of his duties at Hachette's, he had entered into relations with Gustave Bourdin, son-in-law of Hyppolyte de Villemessant, one of the first great modern French press lords. Villemessant, a huge, dynamic man with a bull neck, bulging eyes, and a tiny black moustache, the illegitimate son of a plebeian Napoleonic general and a noblewoman, was a mixture of P. T.Barnum and Balzac's Mercadet. Along with such rivals as Emile de Girardin and the bankers Mirès and Millaud, he had created the mass-circulation periodical in France. His aim was to make money by entertaining the public, and *Le Figaro,* his first successful venture, had made him a millionaire. His newspapers shunned politics and consisted of short articles on nonpolitical subjects of current interest, bits of gossip, interviews, disaster news, fashion reports, cultural items, and serialized fiction – all laced with plenty of ads. Tirelessly interrogating everybody, including his barber, Villemessant knew at any moment what the public wanted to read at that moment. He also possessed an inerrant nose for talent and used up young writers in droves. As soon as they were no longer useful to him, he fired them. He called it 'throwing them a cane,' because he would offer everyone he dismissed a new cane – for taking a walk.

He had just founded another newspaper, *L'Événement.* One of its objectives was to announce news before it happened. Late in January, after sounding Bourdin out, Zola applied for a job on the staff. He proposed to write a regular series consisting of news about books that had not yet been published, before any other critic had mentioned them. He would use his Hachette connections to obtain inside information and proof excerpts. In response to the possible objection that all this free publicity might cut down on advertising revenues, Zola noted that in his experience the more a newspaper talked about a book the more likely its publisher was to place ads in that newspaper. Villemessant liked the idea and hired Zola.

The series, 'Livres d'aujourd'hui et de demain,' started on February 1 and continued at the rate of one, two, or three a week. On January 31, Villemessant had introduced him to the newspaper's readers: 'If my new tenor succeeds, so much the better. If he fails, no fuss at all! He himself assures me that in that event he will annul his engagement.' At the end of February, Zola, not knowing yet what his pay would be, presented himself at the cashier's table. To his great surprise, he was handed 500 francs. He had never received so much money in one lump sum in his life.

That same month, a long study that he had done on Hippolyte Taine's aesthetics came out in *La Revue contemporaine.* In March, he started contributing literary articles again to *Le Salut public.* He had also agreed to write a big three-volumed work for Hachette's – *Les Héroïsmes.* The first volume would treat the heroes of humanity, the second, the heroes of the fatherland, the third, the heroes of the family. Each chapter would amount to a short historical novella with true decors. It would cover the whole of history.

Also that January Alexandrine and he set up housekeeping in an apartment on the Rue de l'Ecole-de-Médecine, near the central wine market. In May they moved to her apartment, complete with a small dining room, guest room, and terrace, on the seventh floor of no. 10, rue de Vaugirard, next to the Odéon.

He kept on receiving his closest friends every Thursday. Cézanne, turned down by the judges of the 1865 Salon, was still struggling to gain recognition with portraits influenced by Courbet and grandiose, vehement, tumultuous paintings reminiscent of Delacroix, Rubens, and Tintoretto. Baille was writing a book on the marvels of electricity, to be published by Hachette's. It was the first of its kind in French. Solari, who used to play hooky with Roux and Zola when they were enrolled in the Pension Notre-Dame, now a promising sculptor, did a bust of Zola for the approaching 1866 Salon. Since they were both too poor to afford to have it cast professionally, they and Cézanne mixed the plaster, made the mouldings, and cast the bust themselves. According to an admiring critic, 'It communicated through its excessive projections, the violence of its lines, and the romanticism of its inspiration a strange impression: that of something tumultuous and clashing, grandiose and savage.'

One day in February, Duranty, a man Zola respected for the battles he had fought on behalf of realism a decade earlier, took him to the Café Guerbois, on the Avenue de Clichy in the Batignolles district of Paris. It was patronized by artists, critics, and others interested in art such as the famous photographer Nadar. Usually on Fridays, a group headed by Duranty met there around two tables reserved for them on the left of the street entrance to work out a common artistic creed. They were already being referred to as the 'Ecole de Batignolles.' Guillemet, Bazille, and Fantin-Latour could always be counted on to come. Cézanne, Pissarro, and Monet showed up occasionally. Whistler sat in now and then for a few moments, and sometimes, though quite rarely, Degas would join them. Soon Zola was a regular member. Like Cézanne, Baille, and himself, they formed a genuine brotherhood dedicated to the artistic principles they held in common and to fighting side by side in their struggle for success.

They were all rebels, dead set against the state-supported artistic tradition, looking for a new way to paint, rejecting all the old, stale tricks, too-facile techniques, and slick deceptions of Academic art, calling instead for faithful analysis and precise interpretation of nature. Despite the frayed and patched clothes that some of them wore, they acted as though the world was already theirs. Each of them felt that he had only to strike the pavement with his heel to bring forth a masterpiece that would dazzle the age. Zola loved joining in their discussions around the tables or outside in the streets, shouting himself hoarse like them. He identified himself with the revolution they wanted to bring about. Being a member of 'the gang,' as they called themselves, provided him with a new, badly needed source of moral support.

One of the most burning topics was the approaching Salon, to start, as usual, on May 1. He persuaded Villemessant to let him write that year's report for *L'Événement*. The jury was less indulgent than the 1865 jury, which had admitted Manet's *Le Christ insulté par les soldats* and *Olympia*. The works he submitted this time, *Le Fifre* and *L'Acteur tragique,* were refused. The young revolutionary painters, including Zola's friends, organized a protest march up the boulevards. Then, on April 16, one of the artists whose offerings had been rejected, a certain Holtzapfel, committed suicide.

The first installment of Zola's report, published on April 19, 1866, was a resounding indictment: 'Truly, I would not want to be one of those who condemned this man. If I were a painter and had had the honor of excluding one of my colleagues from the Salon, I would have nightmares tonight.' In the following installments, he tore the jury and the traditionalist critics apart. He insulted each of the jury members individually, except Corot and Daubigny, who had tried in vain to have Cézanne's *Portrait de Valabrègue* accepted. Some of the rejected painters and their supporters agitated for a new Salon des Refusés. The government turned them down. The battle grew more bitter and violent. Protests against Zola's articles became shriller. But Zola, undaunted, kept on. This was his first great battle, just what he had always been waiting for. For the first time, he was one of the leaders on the field. His warrior's blood was boiling. He was championing 'the great masters of tomorrow,' as he put it. He was helping clear their way. He was in Heaven.

With redoubled fury, he attacked one by one Gérôme, Meissonier, Vernet, and all the other most fashionable Academic painters of the day. He criticized Courbet for recently having conceded too much to public taste. He praised the Salon paintings he admired – Monet, 'a man in this crowd of eunuchs,' Pissarro, 'a great blunderer . . . . an artist I love.' Above all, he extolled Manet: 'I am so certain that M. Manet will be one of the masters of tomorrow that I would gladly if I were rich invest some money in his paintings. In fifty years they will sell for fifteen or twenty times what they are getting today, while certain canvases fetching 40,000 francs today will not get you 40 francs.' Manet's paintings, he maintained, punched a hole in the Salon wall, letting the light in, revealing the artificality and lifelessness of the surrounding works, the candied-sugar trees, the pastry-crust houses, the gingerbread men, and the vanilla-custard women.

Manet, a great painter! This was too much for most of the public. Zola was now receiving up to thirty letters a day, mostly angry ones, some unprintable. He almost got into a duel. Madmen were tearing up *L'Événement* in the streets outside the kiosks. Many readers cancelled their subscriptions. Ville-messant had been delighted at first by all the uproar. The paper was selling like hot cakes. Zola's 'Salon' had become the cultural event of the season. But now the publisher felt that he might have let things go too far. He hired another art critic to express the traditional point of view and permitted Zola to write just two more articles. Zola obligingly wound up with just one final broadside.

That June he published his first volume of essays on art and literature: *Mes Haines*. It consisted mostly of the pieces that had come out in *Le Salut public* the year before. 'Hatred is sacred,' he wrote in the preface.

> It is the indignation of strong, potent hearts, the militant
> disdain of those who cannot abide mediocrity and stupidity.
> To hate is to love, to feel one's soul becoming warm and
> generous, to live grandly, despising everything shameful and
> stupid. Hatred comforts, chastises, ennobles. I have felt
> younger and more courageous after each of my revolts against

the platitudes of my age. I hate impotent nullities. They get in my way.

Busy as Zola was this year, he and Alexandrine managed to escape several times between May and September to an ideal rural retreat that they had found in a remote part of the Seine valley beyond Mantes. At its heart was the small riverside village of Bennecourt and right beside it the tiny hamlet of Gloton, where they stayed at an inn (now a bakery) next to a blacksmith's shop. Cézanne was there too. Baille, Chaillan, Valabrègue, and other old friends from Aix occasionally joined them. Their favorite activity was to borrow the innkeeper's big, leaky old rowboat and explore the river, with its flowery poplar-lined banks, shady coves, narrow tributaries, and little, deserted, rush-encircled islands.

But even during these short vacations Zola doggedly kept on working. Alexandrine put on weight. He grew thinner. He spent every afternoon bent over a table, reading or writing. The clang of the forge bothered him at first. Then he grew to like it. It had an infectious force and virility. Almost every day he had to do another literary chronicle or essay for *L'Événement or Le Salut public*. This meant going through dozens of books – 'all our contemporary imbeciles,' as he put it. When he needed to relax, he worked on one of his own books. He was in the midst of a long essay on Manet, whom he had now met. It was to be published in January in the *Revue du xixe siècle*. He began a big critical treatise, *L'Oeuvre d'art devant la critique,* another ambitious project that he would never finish, like *La Genèse, Le Poète,* or, for that matter, *Les Héroïsmes.* He was also frantically churning out another novel, this time a pure pot-boiler, *Le Voeu d'une morte,* about a generous young man who gives the girl he loves up to his best friend, who loves her and whom she loves.

It illustrated none of his new aesthetic principles. He was doing it solely to make money. Villemessant had liked the plot outline. Serialized in *L'Événement* that fall, it aroused little interest, and, at Villemessant's request, he abbreviated it, to make way for another serial. There was nothing wrong with the basic story line, and he had conformed pretty well to the conventions of the popular novel with its Manichean characters, exaggerated pathos, sugary idealistic sentiments, and strange coincidences. But he had devoted too much space to dissections of his hero's psychology. Nevertheless, he managed to persuade a publisher to bring it out in book form that September. It still did not matter to him what he published, as long as he got published.

About the same time, however, he wrote for *L'Illustration* one of his most powerful short stories, 'Les Quatre Journées de Jean Gourdon'. Set in his beloved Provence, it takes up the theme, reminiscent of Ovid and Pythagoras, of the four seasons of man. Jean, the story's narrator and central character, passes through each of them. In the last, winter, the flooding Durance destroys the rich farm that he has acquired after years of hard work. All his family drowns in the raging waters except Marie, his little daughter.

At the heart of the story is the religious respect for life, nature, and work that marked Zola's own thought. The world, Jean's uncle Lazare, a curiously unorthodox priest, tells him, is a giant workshop tirelessly manufacturing life. This, he says, is the lesson of spring, the season of resurrection. He also asserts that man is made in the image of Earth, the Great Mother. As the young Jean lies on his stomach on the ground, pressing himself hard against it, its vernal forces penetrate him and he becomes one with the nearby willows. At the root of the story is the myth of eternal return. 'Like our common mother, we are eternal,' Uncle Lazare says as he lies dying just before Marie is born. 'Every year fresh green leaves come to replace the withered ones. I am reborn in you, and you will be reborn in your child.' In the conclusion, after the flood, Jean, remembering this, reflects, 'I have had my four seasons, and here is my darling Marie starting the eternal joys and sorrows all over again.'

The romantic adolescent in Zola was still far from dead in the young man of twenty-six. In his nonfictional writings, however, Zola identified himself with positivism and science even more strongly this year than the year before. 'We are becoming more and more scientific,' he stated in *L'Événement* of May 11, 1866. 'Whether we like it or not, the trend is towards the exact study of facts and things . . . . The movement of our times is certainly realistic, or, rather, positivistic.' On July 25, in the same newspaper, he declared himself to be 'the humble disciple of M. Taine.' On November 20, again in the same paper, he championed Spinoza, Taine's favorite philosopher, perceiving in him the principal ancestor of all the major contemporary French positivists, among whom he included Michelet as well as Renan, Taine, and Littré. (It must be admitted that his use of the word 'positivist' was, like that of most other mid-nineteenth-century Frenchmen, rather broad and vague.)

He did his utmost in his journalistic articles to advance his perpetual compaign to capture the public and impose his own personality and ideas, using shock and every other available attention-getting device. He hammered tirelessly on the same points – the relationship between art and temperament, art and truth, art and life, art and its time, the imperative for the contemporary artist to be realistic, scientific, and positivistic, and the worthlessness of art that did not live up to his criteria.

He was at the same time rapidly filling in the outlines of his aesthetic doctrine. Invited to write a paper for a session of the Congrès Scientifique de France to be held in Aix that December, he delightedly accepted. The result, entitled 'Deux Définitions du roman,' was at once a brief history of the novel and a literary manifesto. Embracing the thesis of Villemain, one of the founders of comparative literature, that the modern novel had evolved out of the classical epic via the Greek novel, he compared the Greek novel with its modern descendant. The former, he wrote, was 'an agreeable lie, a tissue of marvellous adventures, the tale of a love at first obstructed, then re-compensed.' Its purpose was solely to amuse. The latter, on the other hand, was best exemplified, he said, by Balzac, the modern Homer.

> If I had asked Balzac to define the novel for me, he would surely have answered: 'The novel is a treatise of moral anatomy, a compilation of human facts, an experimental philosophy of the passions. Its object is, with the help of some verisimilar action, to portray mankind and nature as they really are.'

Sometimes when he was tired he felt like withdrawing not only from Paris but from the whole of history. He took refuge in nature, where, as Hegel says, nothing new ever happens. In his fantasies, the myth of eternal return replaced the modern concept of history as a straight or spiraling line. He wrote in one of his articles that he envied the kings of the forest. They were the true priests, with their superhuman strength, their proximity to the sky, their divine serenity and immobility, their proud aloofness from the senseless and ephemeral agitations of mankind. But most of the time he loved history and was glad to be a part of it. He would not have exchanged his century of violent change and upheaval for any other. He did not care a fig for the so-called great ages of art. Now each artist, as he had come to see full well, was a rebel out for himself, competing to become the new lawgiver that mankind was waiting for, the creator of the archetypes of the future. The prize would go to the fellow with the most powerful fists. The old world had reverted to chaos. The air was full of plaster dust and the noise of demolition. The world of the future had not yet emerged. For all those who, like himself, looked forward to its advent and participated in this epic process, there were reserved the sharp joys and bittersweet anguish attendant on the birth of this new world. He could not imagine any better time for someone like himself to be alive.

After all these years of struggle, Zola's faith in himself was beginning to be confirmed. He really was, already, at twenty-six, a force to be reckoned with. 'You are on the right path,' the critic Alexandre de Lavergne wrote him on June 10, and Manet, a few days later, wrote, 'Decidedly, you have the reputation of being a powerful man.'

IX

Up to the middle of November, 1866 was indeed a splendid year. Then the bottom fell out. On November 15, the government suppressed *L'Événement* for a minor violation of the press law. *Le Salut public* terminated Zola's employment as of January 1, 1867. These two papers had been his main sources of income. He looked frantically for new sources. 'I am running every which way under the whip of necessity,' he wrote a fellow journalist on January 30. But for a long time his efforts met with little success. Throughout the rest of 1867 and much of 1868, he was able to make only 300 or 400 francs a month, less than half of what he had earned in 1866. This new bout with poverty was all the harder to bear because he had become accustomed in 1866 to a higher standard of living. He had to turn to his more well-off friends once again for financial assistance. Alexandrine made book bands for Hachette's and pestered the cashiers of little magazines for money owed them – magazines that were themselves hard put to survive. He was frequently depressed and fearful about the future. He suffered from spasmodic pains in his abdomen and intestines. The smell of ink nauseated him.

Thoughout the greater part of 1867 he spent most of his afternoons and many of his mornings slaving away on another potboiler, *Les Mystères de Marseille,* a rambling made-to-order novel serialized in *Le Messager de Provence* at two sous a line. He based it, in accordance with the specifications imposed by the editor, Léopold Arnaud, on various local news stories that had gripped the Provençal public over the preceding fifty years – most notably a sensational elopement that had taken place in 1823. This real-life scandal, fictionalized through certain modifications and additions including an illegitimate child thrown in for extra pathos, provided the central plot. His old school-friend Marius Roux, who had helped arrange the deal, did the research and mailed him the necessary legal reports and press cuttings. He put little of himself into it and got so bored with it that just writing the title, inspired by Eugène Sue's famous best-seller *Les Mystères de Paris,* made him feel sick.

Anxious to milk the serial for all it was worth, he and Roux concocted a theatrical version. Arnaud persuaded the director of Le Gymnase, a Marseilles theatre, to accept it. Towards the end of September, Zola went down to Marseilles and Aix to supervise the final rehearsals and attend the premiere on October 5. He was not impressed. The play was much too long. The serious playwright in him almost approved of the hisses with which some of the first-nighters greeted it, but he was surprised, nevertheless, that it survived for only three performances.

Meanwhile, he kept on trying, as he had ever since *L'Événement* folded, to find a position on the staff of another newspaper. In January, 1868, his efforts seemed for a moment to have paid off. He was hired as a literary and dramatic critic by *Le Globe,* a brand-new liberal daily. Unfortunately, it was banned from the streets only a few days after the first edition and lasted only a month.

Shortly afterwards, his luck improved somewhat. Between April 20 and September 1, 1868, *L'Événement illustré* published fifty-nine articles by him. Towards the middle of May, that same year, he managed, with the help of a good friend and fellow journalist, Théodore Duret, to obtain a coveted position on the staff of *La Tribune*, one of the biggest of the 140 Parisian papers founded after the new liberalized press law of May 11, 1868 had gone into effect. He remained with *La Tribune* until January 9, 1870, the date it went out of business. During the first nine months of 1869, he also contributed regularly to *Le Gaulois*. Other papers occasionally bought pieces from him. Even so, his financial situation throughout the last half of 1868 and the whole of 1869, if not so desperate as in 1867 and the first half of 1868, was uncomfortably tight.

Yet things could have been a lot worse during these last three years of his twenties. On the whole, it was a period he would look back on with nostalgia as well as pain. The sudden, disastrous drop in his income after the relative prosperity of 1866 had been a cruel blow. But even in the dark days immediately following the suppression of *L'Événement*, he had never lost his self-confidence or love of life. He had constantly exhorted himself and his friends to be courageous, to go on fighting. Was not life, as he had always said, a battle? He had remarked, in a letter to Valabrègue, that being penniless and reduced to pounding the streets looking for a new job had, if nothing else, at least the virtue of forcing him to come to closer grips with the world. It was much better to be doing that than sitting, like Valabrègue, in a comfortable chair in Aix and writing dreamy verse.

Moreover, even in those dark moments Alexandrine was there, enduring his tribulations with him. So was his mother, holding her head high, proud that, hard pressed as he was, her son had never sunk so low as to have to soil his hands with rough physical labor. In April, 1867, Alexandrine and he moved across the Seine to the Batignolles quarter so that he could be nearer his artist friends. They had found a place they could afford on the corner of the Rue Moncey (now Dautancourt) and the Avenue Clichy. In the early spring of 1868, they moved to a little detached house with a small yard at no. 23, Rue Truffaut. The rent was only 550 francs a year. His mother, now living with them again after vacating her apartment on the Boulevard Montparnasse, liked being back on the right bank, in a more middle-class neighborhood. The following year, they took up residence in another tiny detached dwelling with a private yard, no. 14, Rue de la Condamine. He loved working (it was his only form of physical exercise) in the garden, with its roses, peonies, dahlias, lettuce, cabbages, vines, and trees. He and Alexandrine built a hen-roost and a kennel for Bertrand, their labrador. They let Rhunka, their little female Macaco monkey, run free indoors and outdoors, wherever she liked. He went on receiving Cézanne, Baille, and his other most intimate friends at home every Thursday night. Alexandrine and his mother would clear the dining room table, and they would all sit around it, drinking tea and chatting as usual. Some evenings he would call on Michelet or show up at Manet's. On Fridays he went religiously to the Café Guerbois. In the spring and summer, when they could get away, he and his artist friends returned to the dappled shade, watery reflections, and joyous boating parties of Bennecourt.

Although most of his closest companions were still artists, he also expanded during these years his circle of literary friends and acquaintances. He sometimes attended, along with Manet and Roux, the Tuesday-night literary and artistic receptions of the wealthy business man, author, and publisher Arsène Houssaye. (An amusing feature of these very worldly occasions was that the society women present all wore masks.) In November, 1868, Paul Meurice, one of Hugo's most devoted friends and disciples, impressed by some pieces Zola had written about him and his exiled idol, as well as the long essay on Manet, invited him to attend his famous Monday soirées. There, in Meurice's little ground-floor Montmartre apartment dominated by David d'Anger's bust of the master, Zola encountered, along with Manet, Charles Hugo, Hugo's son-in-law Auguste Vacquerie, François Coppée, Paul Verlaine, Théodore de Banville and other members of Hugo's Parisian circle. Always a bit timid and awkward in strange company, he could not help feeling a little out of place among so many impenitent romantics. Moreover, the whole place had the air of a chapel. Yet he kept coming back.

On December 14, 1868, Jules and Edmond de Goncourt invited him to lunch with them in their little house in Auteuil. Although they had already begun corresponding with him while he was still employed at Hachette's, they had never seen him before, nor he them. He tried to be as charming and deferential as possible to these two observant, somewhat precious, middle-aged aristocrats. He respected and wanted to emulate them almost as much as he did his supreme hero, Balzac. They were delighted to have met at last this remarkable young man who had been the first to understand and champion their fiction and whom they had already come to regard as their admirer and disciple. In their journal that evening they recorded in detail their first impressions: 'a worn-out Normalian, at once strong and weak,' 'waxy, bloodless complexion,' 'the delicate moulding of fine porcelaine,' 'the furious planes of the nose.' They were struck above all by the ambiguous, indecipherable aspects of his personality as they saw it, a remarkable amalgam of male and female qualities. 'A creature impossible to pin down, profound, mixed, after all; sorrowful, anxious, troubled, full of doubts.'

On September 15, 1869, Valabrègue showed up at Zola's door with a newcomer from Aix, Paul Alexis, another young writer who admired him and with some of whose writings he was already familiar. In fact, eight months earlier, he had helped launch him by the stratagem of publishing one of his poems, 'Le Lit,' as an unedited piece by Baudelaire, who had recently died. After critics had praised the poem, he had disclosed the name of the true author. The two men had no sooner met than they knew they would be inseparable for the rest of their lives. Alexis had found an older brother, Zola another disciple. One of his ambitions had long been to form a tight-knit brotherhood of writers sharing the same ideals and fighting side by side for fame and glory – like his artist friends or himself, Cézanne, and Baille. There were plenty of literary precedents – the romantic clubs of the 1820s, for example, or the circle of Hugo-worshippers into which he had been introduced by Paul Meurice. It was still too early to realize this objective completely, but he was confident that sooner or later he would do so, and he was already laying the foundations.

Meanwhile, he continued his campaign to promote his artist friends. He went on publicly praising Courbet, Monet, Pissarro, and, of course, Manet, whose portrait of him was shown at the 1867 Salon. He did his best to introduce to the public Bazille, Renoir, Jongkind, Corot, Degas, and the other painters he admired. He consecrated an entire laudatory essay to his old friend, the sculptor Solari and wrote the first public defense of Cézanne. Like them and most of his other avant-garde friends, he had also by now become an ardent partisan of Wagner and enjoyed taking part in the battles that Wagner's music still provoked whenever it was performed, jumping to his feet, furiously applauding, and loudly shouting for an encore.

In the summer and fall of 1868, he waged a campaign, in the form of a polemic with *Le Mémorial d'Aix* and an eloquent written appeal to the mayor and municipal council of Aix, to force the city to honor his father's memory. If he had remained silent for so many years, he wrote the paper's owner, Remondet-Aubin, it was because he had waited until he was strong. His efforts on his father's behalf were successful. On November 6, the council voted unanimously to change the name of the Boulevard du Chemin-Neuf to the Boulevard François Zola.

After he joined *La Tribune,* he was also able to participate more actively in the stormy political and ideological conflicts of his day. He did so with the same furious relish and energy that he had shown in his other articles written on behalf of this or that noble cause. This newspaper was a major organ of the liberal republican, anticlerical opposition, to which, like other members of his generation, he belonged heart and soul. The days when he could dedicate an ode to the Empress Eugénie were long gone. He hated the tyranny and corruption of the Second Empire, its hypocritical, crass, pleasure-bent society, its indifference to the atrocious suffering of the poor. In one after another of his *Tribune* articles – little 'chats' on whatever subjects appealed to him – he gave vent to this hatred. He lashed out at his rich contemporaries, warning them, like some Old Testament prophet, that their unbridled immorality would bring about the collapse of their society. He attacked Baron Haussmann, whose extensive alterations of Paris had so heavily benefited the rich while imposing new hardships on the poor. He castigated the licentiousness of ladies of high rank for whom adultery was a sin only when it was committed by members of the lower classes. He hit out hard against everything that he loathed in the theatrical world of the Second Empire – the bawdy operettas of Offenbach, the demimonde, the bordello atmosphere of certain theatres, the 'great' actresses like Blanche d'Antigny or Hortense Schneider,

77

whose reputations and wealth depended less on whatever talent they might have than on the way they swayed their hips. He also freely expressed his own anticlericalism, caricaturing Veuillot, the chief French Catholic apologist of the day, or ridiculing two Jesuit teachers, arrested for child abuse for having had their assistants disguise themselves as devils before whipping errant pupils.

His ideas about art went on evolving within the general framework that he had established in his mid-twenties. His conception of what he wanted to do as a writer grew richer, more complex, and more precise. Some of his earliest beliefs assumed a new vitality. His interminable conversations with Cézanne and other avant-garde painters had profoundly affected his thought. He expressed more strongly than ever his conviction that he and his fellow artists should portray contemporary life. More than ever, he was struck by the poetic possibilities inherent in the unfolding history of his own age. 'Come straight into our modern times,' he adjured the poet Frédéric Mistral in an open letter published in *La Tribune,* 'and after you have spent just one day in the midst of our giant labor, our feverish pursuit of justice and liberty, you will smile with pity at the thought of the languorous complaints of your troubadours, you will no longer sing of anything but our struggles and triumphs.' His old Hugolian ideal of the poet-prophet, the poet-magus, also reasserted itself. 'Poet, be true to your mission,' he wrote in the same open letter. 'You are one of those inspired spirits who should divine and preach the future.'

His conception of the philosophical basis of realism broadened. The canvases of Jongkind, Corot, Pissarro, and other landscape painters opened his eyes to the extent to which realism, or naturalism, as his artist friends also called it, could express not only his and his contemporaries' need for scientific certainty, but also their romantic pantheism. For if everything in nature, no matter how lowly or banal, even a mere blade of grass, was alive and divine, one could love it just as it was. There was no need to ennoble it.

He was tempted to expand the scope of his fiction to include not only man, but the whole of nature, as he had once planned to do in *La Genèse.* After reading an account in Michelet of how roses love and oaks are born and grow, he exclaimed, 'The epic of tomorrow is there, in the discovery of the profound, sweet mysteries of the sky and the earth, in the natural and sublime history of beings and things.'

His vision of reality remained unstable, fragmented, and full of contradictions, but the idealistic, optimistic elements of his thought were becoming stronger than they had been in his early and middle twenties. He was still plagued by doubt. The pessimist in him was far from dead. A part of him was still firmly attached to Taine and positivism in the somewhat vague sense that he and many of his contemporaries gave to that term. He rejected idealism and spiritualism, Cousin and Caro, more emphatically than ever. He lauded Littré, and flatly asserted that science and metaphysics are incompatible. But another part of him enthusiastically reverted to the quasi-religious humanitarianism of his youth, identifying Humanity again with the Great Whole, alluding to 'the universal prayer' of the peoples, the ascent towards progress and growing brotherhood of man. He was also attracted by the pantheism and all-embracing historical vision of the older Michelet – the aging poet-naturalist whom he personally knew and loved. He praised Michelet for having been one of the first modern thinkers to fall down on his knees before the Great Mother. He claimed that Michelet's poetic conception of the earth overflowing with life, new beings constantly appearing, all driven by the same First Force, all marching towards the same far-off goal of universal peace and love, the great final kiss, was scientifically true. 'Never,' he wrote in *La Tribune* of June 18, 1868, 'has any mythology invented a lie which gives us an idea of such a reality.'

On the morning of June 25, 1868, while rereading Michelet's *L'Oiseau, L'Insecte,* and *La Montagne* on a small, deserted island surrounded by rushes near Gloton, he had a mystical experience. It resembled somewhat the one that he had ascribed to his short-story character Jean Goujon. Half-reclining, he suddenly felt himself become attached to the earth like the nearby poplars. He felt coursing up through his flesh the same sap that he could hear trembling under their bark. He shared in their proud, free life. Motionless and mute like them, he became like them absorbed in the worship of the sun and long reveries about the secrets of the earth. He understood the language of the birds and insects.

79

X

In 1867, the year he wrote, much against his will, *Les Mystères de Marseille*, that unhappy piece of hack work, he also composed *Thérèse Raquin*, a truly superb novel. It was his first serious attempt to apply to his own fiction the new artistic principles that he had been hammering out for so long.

As he worked on it, he was particularly influenced by certain specific novels by his new masters. One of these was Flaubert's *Madame Bovary*. Another was the Goncourts' *Germinie Lacerteux*, an analysis of a curious case of hysteria provided by their old housemaid, transported just as she was into the book. Reviewing it for *Le Salut public* shortly after it had come out in 1865, he had praised it to the skies, expressing for the first time in print his taste for the revolutionary kind of literature it represented. 'It has the powerful interest of a physiological and psychological problem, of a case of physical and moral illness, of a story which just has to be true.' He was also thinking, of course, of *Le Père Goriot*, *La Rabouilleuse*, and other novels by Balzac – the Balzac of whom he had written in 1866, echoing Taine: 'He dissects man, studies the play of the passions, interrogates each fibre, analyzes the entire organism. Like a surgeon, he has no shame or feelings of aversion when he probes human wounds. He cares only about the truth.'

The original spark of inspiration had come from a mediocre novel by Adolphe Belot and Ernest Daudet, *La Vénus de Gordes*, serialized in *Le Figaro* in 1866. It recounts the murder of a husband by his wife's lover and concludes with the guilty couple's trial and execution. The theme fascinated Zola. He had jotted down his own variation in a brief short story published in *Le Figaro* of December 14, 1866, 'Un mariage d'amour.' Instead of having the lovers arrested, he had them destroyed by their own remorse. *Thérèse Raquin* grew directly out of the short story. He kept all its episodes, but in the process of developing them added a fourth major character for extra pathos, the murdered husband's mother.

'I feel that this will be the great work of my youth,' he wrote Arsène Houssaye on February 12, 1867. On May 29, he confided to Valabrègue that it was almost finished and that he was very pleased with it. 'I think that I have put myself into it, body and heart. I fear, indeed, that I have put into it a little too much of my body and I that I shall upset the Public Prosecutor. It's true that I'm not afraid of spending a few months in prison.'

First published in the August, September, and October, 1867 issues of *L'Artiste,* Houssaye's literary review, the novel was brought out in book form by Lacroix in November. Unlike *La Confession de Claude,* it failed to rouse the Public Prosecutor, but a number of critics were scandalized by it – or at least pretended to be. Louis Ulbach, who, besides being an old friend of Zola's, happened to have financial interests in Lacroix's business, obliged them with a particularly strong denunciation. It was printed in *Le Figaro,* of which he was then literary editor. The book, he said, was a 'puddle of mud and blood,' adding that it 'far too faithfully resumes all the putridities of contemporary literature.'

Zola was delighted. The sales of the book, which had been selling slowly, picked up. What was more important for his career, Ulbach and the other outraged critics had handed him a new opportunity to assert himself and the principles he stood for. 'Truth, like fire, purifies everything,' he righteously declared in his reply to Ulbach, also printed in *Le Figaro.* In the preface to the second edition, which came out in May, 1868, only six months after the first, he made the same point and stressed the novel's serious, scientific aspects. 'In *Thérèse Raquin,* I have decided to study temperaments, not characters,' he said. 'That is what the book is all about. I have chosen persons completely dominated by their nerves and blood, devoid of free will, let into every act of their lives by the fatalities of their flesh. Thérèse and Laurent are human beasts, nothing more.' In analyzing them, he concluded, he had 'simply performed on two living bodies the sort of analytical operations that surgeons perform on cadavers.'

In a famous essay published in 1858, Taine had called Balzac a 'naturalist.' In this same preface, Zola used for the first time the same term to designate all those contemporary writers, like the Goncourts, with whom he most closely associated himself: 'The group of naturalistic writers to which I have the honor to belong,' he wrote, 'is courageous and active enough to produce powerful works, works which are quite capable of defending themselves.'

He was quite aware that in *Thérèse Raquin*, he had by no means attained all his major artistic goals. The style lacked the simplicity that one would expect to find in a novel of scientific analysis. As Sainte-Beuve wrote him, words like 'wallow' and 'brutal' recurred too often. Despite his claims to scientific objectivity, he had occasionally strayed from the truth. The Passage du Pont-Neuf, an important part of the setting, was in real life by no means the dark, sinister hole that he had made it out to be. He had not been able to conceal his loathing for Thérèse and Laurent, referring to Camille's murder as a 'sinister comedy.' Nor had he always been consistent. He had more than once forgotten that Thérèse and Laurent were merely soulless human animals and endowed them with a moral sense, as when he had written of Thérèse at the outset of her liaison with Laurent that 'she knew she was doing evil.' The case that he had chosen to study in the novel was too exceptional. It lacked that broad representativeness that he admired in the classics. Real-life dramas were usually less rigid and did not contain so great an element of madness and horror. Moreover, he had to admit the truth of Taine's comment:

> To be sure, *Germinie Lacerteux* and *Thérèse Raquin* are true-to-life stories, but a book should always be more or less a depiction of a whole, a mirror of society in its entirety . . . . When you block all the vistas and imprison the reader, the windows tightly shut, face to face with a monster, a madman, or a sick person, the reader is afraid. He is often even nauseated. He cries out in protest . . . . In this kind of story, Balzac and Shakespeare are the great masters. There is in every accomplished artist a sort of encyclopedic philosopher with broad, complex views.

Nevertheless, Zola was right to be pleased with *Thérèse Raquin*. Although he had failed to live up to his literary ideal in some respects, he had done so very well in others. The style, while by no means, perfect, is vigorous and clear. The book possesses to a high degree the concreteness and color he admired in the romantics. It has a beauty of form reminiscent of the great classics. The drama is divided into six parts, each of which leads to the next with the sort of inevitability that one associates with

Greek tragedy: the animal-like passion of the lovers, their crime, their horror at what they have done, their resultant suffering, their fear and hatred for each other, and their suicides. Over this psychological composition, there is imposed a narrative composition in three parts, each consisting of about the same number of chapters and ending with a remarkable episode: Camille Raquin's murder. Thérèse and Laurent's marriage, and the final death scene.

Above all, Zola had succeeded in attaining his purely literary aim, as opposed to his scientific one; for he had wanted to write not only a valid physiological study but also a first-rate horror story. Few works surpass *Thérèse Raquin* in this respect. Whatever the scientific value of the book may be, it is a gripping nightmare. It has rightly been compared to Hawthorne, Poe, and a certain Dickens. There are no more gruesome scenes in literature than the one in which Laurent drowns his old friend Camille in a sham boating accident while Thérèse complacently looks on or those that take place afterwards in the Paris morgue, which Laurent repeatedly visits to inspect the corpses recovered from the Seine in the hope that Camille's will be among them. While there, Laurent is sexually drawn by the nude body of a young girl who has hanged herself for love. A well-dressed woman lets her eyes explore caressingly the muscular body of a mason killed in a fall. Camille's ghost, with its greenish, convulsed face, seems to haunt the guilty lovers everywhere. Laurent becomes convinced that Camille's spirit has invaded the family cat, François, and, after mercilessly torturing the poor beast for days and weeks, he finally kills it by hurling it at a wall. When he and Thérèse embrace, Camille's decomposed body seems to come between them. The scar left by the bite Camille gives Laurent during their struggle in the drowning scene assumes a life of its own, turning livid whenever he sees it in his shaving mirror, boring, biting into him, filling him with terror. Having become pregnant, Thérèse imagines that she is going to give birth to a drowned infant and that she can feel its icy, decomposed cadaver inside her womb. She provokes Laurent into beating her, and the next day has a miscarriage.

Since it is easier to sympathize with Camille's mother, Madame Raquin, a gentle, kind old lady, than with any of the other characters including Camille, a colorless, weak, sickly young man, her story may well strike the reader as the most horrible of all. Deceived by Laurent's apparent attachment to Camille's memory, she thinks that she has found in him a new son. Two years after Camille's death, she not only urges Laurent and her daughter-in-law to get married but invites them to live with her. When she finally learns the truth, she is incapable of doing anything about it except stare at them, hoping for vengeance, for she has by this time become completely paralyzed.

The novel's view of the world is just as nightmarish as the specific events it relates. The scientific realist in Zola provides the raw materials, but the pessimistic dreamer, the black poet of 'Doute,' transforms them into a frightening subjective vision. Scientific and dream motifs converge, resulting in a sinister ambiguity. From a scientific point of view, Thérèse and Laurent's extreme passivity must be interpreted as a reflection of Zola's scientific determinism. The mechanical interplay of temperament and environment, of instinct and externally applied stimuli, completely governs their actions. But this same terrible passivity may also be construed as an instance of that loss of control which is commonly encountered in nightmares and which is also exemplified by the paralysis of Camille's mother. The materialism of the novel, its attempt to apply, like Taine or Deschanel, the methodology of the naturalist to the study of human behavior, translates on the dream level into a nightmare image of degradation, the transformation of human beings into beasts. (The same theme of degradation is also developed through the repeated evocations of Camille's rotting corpse.) The narrator's positivistic refusal to provide the story with any metaphysical or religious framework creates the painful illusion of a world which is not only sordid and painful, but also meaningless.

It was indeed Zola's best work so far, just as he had been sure it would be. Even the critics who were revolted by it were unable to ignore it. The public was buying it. Those whose opinions really mattered to Zola, like the Goncourts, Gautier, Sainte-Beuve, and Taine, were impressed by it despite what, rightly or wrongly, they considered to be its shortcomings. Sainte-Beuve, perhaps the most respected literary critic of the day, found it on the whole remarkable and conscientious and expressed the opinion that it might mark the beginning of a new era in the history of fiction.

XI

Madeleine Férat, Zola's next novel, also published by Lacroix, came out in the bookshops in December, 1868. It had essentially the same plot as *Madeleine*, the three-act play that he had written in 1865 and twice failed in 1866 to get accepted. Both have to do with a woman who is happily married until her former lover, a close friend of her husband, who knows nothing about their relationship, suddenly shows up after an absence of many years. In both, the wife, unable to bear this situation, finally commits suicide under the vengeful eye of an old Protestant servant who imagines herself to be an agent of divine retribution. The chief difference between the play and the novel is that, in the latter, Zola is principally concerned with illustrating a physiological theory which he had discovered in Michelet. Michelet, in his turn, had got it from a treatise on heredity by a physician named Dr Prosper Lucas. According to this theory, or, more precisely, Michelet's version of it, once a woman has given herself to a man, she is his forever. She will always bear his mark. It is even likely that her child by another man will resemble him. (Lucas, much more cautious, was not at all convinced that this principle can be applied to higher forms of life.)

Madeleine Férat has some unforgettable scenes, including Madeleine's death. Madeleine herself – an essentially good woman destroyed by forces beyond her control – has a certain tragic grandeur. Geneviève, the half-mad, Bible-spouting old servant, who regards Madeleine as an incarnation of Lubrica, the temptress of St Anthony, is endowed with a nightmarish vitality. The book has biographical interest. Guillaume, Madeleine's husband, is another fictional projection of Zola. Like Zola, Guillaume was persecuted in his youth and, just as Zola found a strong protector in Cézanne, he has found one in Jacques, Madeleine's lover. Guillaume also reflects Zola's loss of faith in the redemptive power of romantic love. In contrast to Claude, who recalls an earlier Zola, he has never 'had the stupid idea of trying to redeem a sinful woman.' But neither as a scientific study nor as a work of art, does *Madeleine Férat* attain the power of *Thérèse Raquin*. Its central thesis, the theory of impregnation, is too implausible. So are the numerous coincidences in the plot.

Everything seems too contrived. The Public Prosecutor's threat to take action against Lacroix if certain allegedly immoral passages were not removed (Zola refused to permit this) and Zola's indignant reply, published in *La Tribune,* provided, however, some useful publicity, and the novel sold fairly well.

XII

During this same period, when Zola was in his late twenties, the moment when he felt that he was ready to write his masterpiece, the work that he hoped would bring him immortal fame, finally arrived. He had found his major themes, forged an aesthetics, nearly mastered his craft, tested his powers, discovered his limits. Especially since he had joined *La Tribune,* he had developed an extraordinarily powerful style, warm, passionate, torrential, but also remarkably concise and clear, with an enormous range. It could be as ironic and mordant as Juvenal or as lyrical or epical as Michelet or Hugo. He had also come to know better than most people the world he lived in. Through his rough daily struggle to survive in it, he had been molded by it, imbued with its traits. He had come to embody it, the way a tiger does the jungle or a whale the sea. When he spoke, he did so not just for himself but for millions of his contemporaries. He had not, it is true, managed as yet to piece together a stable, solid vision of reality (what serious thinker of his confused, questioning epoch had?), but he had amassed a rich treasure of values, intuitions, myths, dreams, hypotheses which possessed for these contemporaries as well as himself an enormous appeal.

What was just as important, he was by now fairly well known. He had already published six books. *Madeleine Férat* would be his seventh. He had a sympathetic publisher, Lacroix, who might be persuaded to bring out his great new work and perhaps even help support him with advances while he was writing it.

Throughout 1868, his magnum opus began to take shape in his mind, slowly at first, then more rapidly. If he was to crush the Goncourts – whom, in the privacy of his own thoughts, he was now coming to regard less as masters than as competitors – and prove himself the equal of such giants as Hugo or Balzac, it would, he realized, have to overwhelm the public not only by its contents, but also by its sheer mass. Once *Madeleine Férat* was out of the way, in late November, he began laboring on this new project in earnest. He now envisaged it as a single giant, multi-volumed novel. He feverishly drew up a series of plans each more or less different from the preceding ones. Day after day he went to the Imperial library (now the Bibliothèque Nationale), accumulating hundreds of notes. By December 14, he had already decided, as he confided to the Goncourts, that there would be a total of ten volumes. He had also already found by then a tentative title: 'L'Histoire d'une famille.'

The project had originated in the happy convergence of two vast themes, each of which had preoccupied him both as an artist and as a thinker since his adolescence: the theme of life, life's irrepressible power, life rushing on, forever renewing itself; and the theme of contemporary history. While composing *Madeleine Férat*, he had been fascinated not only by Prosper Lucas's theory of impregnation but also by the whole nascent science of heredity. He had devoured each of the two volumes of Lucas's *Traité de l'hérédité naturelle* from cover to cover. This massive, pedantic looking work not only appealed to his intellect. It fired his imagination. Through it he penetrated, or so he thought, to the very heart of the life process. Moreover, Lucas's conception of life had a lot in common with his own. Like him, Lucas revered universal life, equated it with nature, defined it as the divine creative principle of the universe, and regarded it as engaged in a continuous act of creation. He was also impressed by Lucas's belief that to study the elementary forms of human activity as manifested by heredity is to study the elementary forms of activity of nature herself.

In contrast to Lamarck and other naturalists who had hypothesized that only species are subject to heredity, Lucas thought that individual dogs, birds, or humans are also. Moreover, he belonged to a hardy group of theorists who held that hereditary traits are determined not only by 'the fatality of a destiny going back to the sources of life,' but also by 'the free, responsible activity of the soul.' Life not only 'imitates' and 'recalls,' he declared; it also 'invents' and 'imagines.'

The hundreds of concrete examples, many culled from history and mythology, marshaled by Lucas in support of his complex system, suggested to Zola a host of interesting characters and situations – enough, indeed, to fill the giant work of fiction that he had in mind. Intrigued, for instance, by Lucas's remark that in ancient Rome the most beautiful courtesans issued from the lower classes, he decided to include among his family members a ravishing whore born of working-class parents. Motivated by his urge to be exhaustive, he was determined to illustrate Lucas's system in its entirety.

Like many other mid-nineteenth-century scientists, Lucas, who had published his treatise between 1847 and 1850, years before Pasteur's famous discoveries, stoutly believed in spontaneous generation. He argued that the state of the parents during coitus could determine the character of the child – for example, that if Hephaestus was lame, it was because Jupiter had been drunk when he lay with Hephaestus's mother, Hera. But Zola drank in unquestioningly everything Lucas wrote. Had not Taine as well as Michelet cited Lucas as an authority? Had not a brilliant young zoologist, Fortuné Marion, an old friend from Aix, enthusiastically approved the plan for this new work? Even Lucas's theory of impregnation, unlikely as it seemed to some commentators, was quite solid, Marion had asserted.

But if one of Zola's objectives was to incorporate Lucas's system into his magnum opus, he was also motivated by his old ambition to write an epic account of the unfolding history of his own time. He saw that the members of his fictional family, besides illustrating Lucas, could help him achieve this other grand objective. By distributing these family members – his Rougons and Chantegreils, or should he call them his Rougons and his Sardats or his Rougons and his Macharts? – throughout society and involving them in the major events of contemporary history, he could focus on each level of society and each major moment or aspect of its collective life. He could also evoke the dominant traits of his age – its energy, democratic fevers, social mobility, unbridled ambitions, dazzling rewards, nervous tensions, murderous competition, transitional upheaval. 'These are confused, turbulent times. What I want to depict is precisely this confusion, this turbulence,' he wrote in one of his earliest plans.

What justified combining his physiological and historical objectives was his determination to provide a complete scientific explanation of human behavior. According to Taine's famous formula, human character was the product not only of race, but also of milieu and moment. Furthermore, had not Taine advised him to widen his horizons and to place his characters against a background encompassing the whole of society?

He had difficulty establishing just the right balance between his physiological and historical aims. He started out by favoring the former. But in his later plans, the physiological study and historical study assumed equal importance. He wanted each to be exhaustive and to complement and reinforce the other. On the one hand, he would bare 'the hidden springs, the strings moving the human marionette.' On the other hand, his family members would be representative social and historical types. The story of his family would resume the whole history of the Second Empire from its outset in the *coup d'état* of December 2, 1851, up to the present. His novel would be at one and the same time a work of in-depth analysis and a vast panorama. 'I am studying humanity itself, in its most intimate machinery,' he concluded.

While he was drawing up his preliminary plans, his imaginative, visionary, prophetic side was by no means asleep. He went on venting in *La Tribune* his hatred of the Second Empire and his longing for political and social reform. On November 29, 1868, he declared, 'When a society is rotting, when the social machine is getting out of order, the role of the observer and thinker is to note every new wound, every unexpected new blow.' Living in the ruins of a world, their duty, he went on to say, was 'to study these ruins, to study them boldly and candidly, without fear or prevarication, in order to draw from them the elements of the world of tomorrow.' He acknowledged the role that love, indignation, hatred and all the other strong emotions played in the creation of great works of art. But he was also as convinced as ever that the ideal novel of his time must be scientific and did his best to ensure that his new project would have those qualities that he most admired in scientists. At first he conceived of it as a work of pure, disinterested observation: 'I do not want to have a decisive impact on human affairs, to be a politician, philosopher, or moralist like Balzac. I shall be content with being just a scientist . . . . No conclusions.' Then, in a later plan, he relented somewhat. He decided that in a volume depicting the working class he would call out for certain specific social reforms – but only through the frank exposition of the facts.

In his preparatory notes he repeatedly cited Taine and used terms reminiscent of Taine: 'moment,' 'milieu,' 'logical,' 'deduction,' 'generative fact,' 'mathematically,' 'forces,' 'methodical.' In his effort to be scientific, he relied heavily, moreover, not only on Taine and Lucas, but also on other scientific writers. Chief among them was the then widely respected physiologist Charles Letourneau, whose *Physiologie des passions* he had reviewed in *Le Globe* of January 21, 1868. Lucas and Letourneau went together like oil and water. Lucas's system was largely based on a belief in free will. Letourneau resolutely denied free will. Lucas exalted man as the living symbol of divine universal life. Letourneau was convinced that what poets, philosophers, and theologians termed 'the unfathomable mystery of life' is nothing but a 'phenomenon of organic assimilation and disassimilation.' He maintained that man, 'envisaged sanely and not through the tinted glass of metaphysics, is, like all other organized beings, nothing but an aggregation of histological elements, fibers, or cells, forming a living "federal republic" directed by the nervous system and constantly renewing itself.' But the logical incompatibility of Lucas and Letourneau did not trouble Zola. He was particularly impressed by Letourneau's doctrine that man's moral and intellectual needs are as organic as his need for food, and that the need for food is the most imperious and indispensable of them all. He decided to make his novel to a great extent a novel about different sorts of hunger – hunger for food, wealth, power, all the benefits of modern civilization. 'I shall study the ambitions and the appetites of a family scattered throughout the modern world,' he told himself. Summing up his work in one sentence, he concluded: 'I want to portray, at the outset of a century of liberty and truth, a family which rushes in pursuit of all the good things the future promises and which stumbles and falls in its headlong race because of the troubled gleams of the moment, the fatal convulsions attending the birth of a world.'

His chronical skepticism, inability to settle permanently on any one vision of reality, and strong desire to conform to his scientific ideal made him reluctant to incorporate into the novel any particular philosophy. 'They say,' he wrote, 'that there is no great novelist who does not contain a philosopher. Yes, an absurd philosophy, like Balzac's. I prefer to be nothing but a novelist.' Nevertheless, he was convinced that he could not do without some philosophy or other, if only for the sake of consistency. So he decided to select the vaguest one he could think of: 'The best one would perhaps be materialism; by that I mean to say the belief in forces which I shall never have to explain.'

As for the overall structure, he wrote: 'Everybody is doing detailed analysis very successfully these days. It is necessary to react with solidly constructed masses, chapters; with the logic, the thrust, of these chapters, succeeding each other like super-posed blocks, locking into each other; with the breath of passion animating the whole, sweeping from one end of the work to the other.'

Despite its scientific foundations, the novel, as he envisaged it, would not be at all rigid or austere. Each episode, each volume, would contain a dramatic action based on some part or other of the physiological and historical study underlying the entire work. A thoughtful reader would, he hoped, be able to perceive in each of these actions the grand idea behind it all, but everyone would find them poignantly interesting. 'Don't forget,' he told himself, 'that a drama grabs the public by the throat. It gets angry, but it doesn't forget. Always give it, if not nightmares, at least excessive books which will stick in its memory.'

At the beginning of 1869, he submitted a detailed prospectus to Lacroix. He told him that he wanted to publish two episodes a year, thereby concluding the whole novel in five years. Lacroix liked the idea and bought it. He agreed to give Zola an assured income of 500 francs a month, provided that Zola consented to make over to him the profits he hoped to receive from the newspapers in which the episodes would be serialized in advance of publication. A contract was drawn up. Soon Zola was hard at work on the initial volume, *La Fortune des Rougon*. When, on September 15, Alexis, accompanied by Valabrègue, called on him for the first time, he had almost finished and was able to read them the first pages. *Le Siècle*, a moderate left-wing daily with a circulation of over 37,000, the largest of any newspaper in France at that time, had agreed to serialize it starting in October. His great work was under way at last!

[3]

The Continuing Struggle

I

On April 2, 1870, Zola turned thirty. He was again making enough money to live fairly comfortably and could reasonably expect to see his income go on rising thanks to the profits he hoped to reap from his books. The time had come to put his affairs in order. For over five years, Alexandrine and he had been living together, but they had not yet been married. At ten o'clock on the morning of Tuesday, May 31, in the *mairie* of the 17th *arrondissement*, they were legally wed. Roux, Cézanne, Alexis, and Solari witnessed the ceremony. The announcement cards send out by Zola's mother snobbishly omitted the bride's plebeian first name, Gabrielle.

That same spring, Zola's relationship with Edmond de Goncourt became more intimate. Jules had died from syphilis on June 20. In reply to Zola's letter of condolence, Edmond thanked him for the courageous support that he had always given his and his brother's novels. ' . . . during the final stage of his illness, when darkness had already begun to overtake him,' he wrote Zola, 'your articles on *Madame Gervaisais* brought him his last good days. I shall always be indebted to you, and my gratitude could become friendship if you would like that.' Zola promptly answered, warmly accepting Edmond's implied offer.

As before, he divided his time between his creative writing and his journalism. During the first eight months of 1870, he contributed thirty-six articles to *La Tribune* and three other journals: *Le Rappel,* a left-wing opposition daily founded by Hugo's supporters, *La Libre pensée,* a small left-bank anticlerical weekly, and *La Cloche,* the chief organ of the Parisian radical majority. Occasionally he wrote on literary subjects, but his main interest was now politics. Edging ever closer to the far republican left, he had become irrevocably committed to its struggle against the Second Empire. In article after article, he kept on attacking the Emperor's foreign and domestic policies, his personal power, the scandals of the regime, its worldly bigotry, and its insolent display of luxury in the face of working-class poverty. He compared the Second Empire to a Roman orgy or to a pack of hounds devouring a slain stag – a horrible *curée*. He evoked the revolutionary thoughts that a cold, hungry working-class girl might have reading newspaper accounts of a Tuileries ball. He made common cause with Hugo, Michelet, and other republicans in their efforts to persuade the military to desert the Empire and return to the tradition of the republican army.

II

On July 19, war was declared on Prussia. Despite France's woeful unpreparedness for this long expected trial of strength, the prevailing mood was jingoistic. War hysteria had been mounting for days. In Paris, crowds marched in the boulevards chanting: 'To Berlin!' Newspapers took up the cry throughout the country. Zola looked on sadly. Like most other members of the extreme left, he regarded the war as the final proof of the criminal folly of Napoleon III's policies. In an article entitled 'Vive la France!', published in *La Cloche* of August 5, he openly asserted that 'fifty thousand soldiers on the banks of the Rhine' had rejected the Empire, that they wanted nothing more to do with 'this terrible power that has placed in the hands of a single man the life and wealth of the nation.' Within forty-eight hours, he received a summons to answer the charge of attempting to discredit the government and incite civil disobedience. Only the the news of the disastrous French defeat at Wissembourg, which came through on August 6, prevented him from being brought to trial. The case was postponed, then forgotten in the turmoil of events marking the Empire's last days.

Although he was thus spared from having to serve the prison term which he had courted, the war profoundly altered his existence in other respects. The serialization of *La Fortune des*

Rougon, which had tardily begun in *Le Siècle* that June, was interrupted on August 10 'because of the gravity of the circumstances.' On August 18, *La Cloche,* the only paper he was then still writing for, suspended publication. 'This frightful war has made my pen fall from my hands. I am like a soul in torment,' he wrote Goncourt.

After the fall of the Empire on September 2, the war against the Germans continued under the new Government of National Defense. Bazille, Manet, Degas, Guillemet, Alexis and many of Zola's other friends had taken up arms, but as the sole support of his widowed mother, he had been exempted from military service. Alexandrine was terrified at the thought of remaining in Paris during the approaching siege. On September 7, twelve days before it began, he reluctantly fled with her and his mother and their dog, Bertrand, to Marseilles.

Two years earlier, Zola and Léopold Arnaud, who had published *Les Mystères de Marseille,* had discussed the possibility of founding a new newspaper there. With Arnaud's help, Zola and Marius Roux now attempted to do so. They christened it *La Marseillaise.* The first issue hit the streets on September 27. Printed in editions of 10,000 copies at Arnaud's press and distributed in Marseilles, Aix, and elsewhere, the paper seemed at first destined for success. It soon encountered financial difficulties, however, and on December 16, went out of business.

But meanwhile Zola had formed another project. It seemed to him that, what with all the connections he had made in the republican party, he had a good chance of obtaining a political appointment. He despised politics, but he needed the money. His eyes were set on the sub-prefecture in Aix in particular. With this in mind, he took the train to Bordeaux, the seat of the Government of National Defense, arriving there on December 12 in a cold, steady rain. The officials he counted on to help him were less cooperative than he had expected.'One would say that there has been a veritable conspiracy of silence,' he wrote Alexandrine and his mother, adding testily, 'If they're playing games with me . . . I will get back at them some day.'

On the 14th, he had only sixty-eight francs left in his pocket, enough to last barely a week. As time dragged on and nothing acceptable turned up, he became increasingly anxious. He also suffered from loneliness. The men he wanted to see were either out of town or hard to get hold of, and he had no wish to associate with the people in whose company he found himself, mostly petty government clerks and third-rate Parisian journalists. The rain kept on falling day after day. During his many idle hours, he paced back and forth under the arcades of the Grand Théâtre or retired to his hotel room and read books from a circulating library or wrote long, affectionate letters to Alexandrine and his mother. After all that the three of them had gone through together, they had grown extremely close. It was painful for them to be separated.

Using a penholder that they had fashioned out of paper (since they could not afford to buy one), they wrote him back at equal length, worrying about his health, wondering if he was eating properly, and exhorting him to be patient and have courage. Somehow they managed to send him an extra fifty francs.

Finally, when Zola had just about given up his quest for a government job and had, indeed, already secured his travel warrant for the return trip to Marseilles, his luck turned. Glais-Bizoin, a government minister, whom he had got to know when he had worked for *La Tribune*, hired him as his private secretary at 500 francs a month. The job was not what Zola had wanted, but it was respectable enough. 'It's the sort of position that imbeciles respect,' he wrote his mother and Alexandrine. As the news of his appointment spread, people were already doffing their hats to him. But what was more important, it kept him and his family from starving. On the 27th, after a frightful journey during which their train was held up for twenty-four hours by a heavy snowfall, he and his loved ones were at last reunited. Happily, he led them into the apartment he had been lucky enough to find in the overcrowded city.

At times, he wondered if his life would ever be the same as it had been before his flight from Paris. He had brought with him the manuscript of the first chapter of his second *Rougon-Macquart* novel, *La Curée*, and now and then he opened it and thumbed through it pensively, as if it were a document from a distant past. A report reached him that *Le Siècle* had lost the manuscript of the last chapter of *La Fortune des Rougon*. As long as he was trapped there in the depths of the provinces, there was nothing, however, that he could do about it.

On January, 1871, Glais-Bizoin nominated him for a prefectural office at Bayonne. He also tried to get him a similar post at Castelsarrasin. But nothing came of it. Soon afterwards the armistice was signed. On February 12, 1871, the Government of National Defense having been dissolved, his position as Glais-Bizoin's secretary was terminated. However, since the newly elected National Assembly had decided to meet temporarily in Bordeaux, he easily obtained a job as parliamentary correspondent. He wrote daily reports for *La Cloche,* which had resumed publication, and *Le Sémaphore de Marseille,* edited by A. Barlatier, an old friend of his father's.

III

The Assembly left Bordeaux for Versailles on March 11. Three days later, the Zolas arrived back in Paris. The ground floor of their little house on the Rue Condamine had been requisitioned during the siege and allocated to a refugee family with five children. Fortunately, Alexis had been there to look after things. Zola's papers were intact. None of the silver had been stolen. The furniture had not been seriously damaged. The trees, vine, and roses had been pruned and rid of caterpillars. The peony and dahlia roots were undisturbed. One of the first things Zola did, now that he was home again, was to run over to *Le Siècle's* printing office to hunt for the lost manuscript himself. Fortunately, he found it, lying on the proof-reader's desk, in plain view. Inexplicably, no one had thought to look for it there!

On the 18th, the civil war of the Commune broke out. The people of Paris had risen in revolt against the government of Thiers, which was now centered in Versailles. Within ten days, the Commune had seized control of Paris. Zola sympathized politically with neither side. In order to continue his coverage of the assembly, he had to travel back and forth every day between the two hostile cities. Pale, shabby, silent, and observant, he could easily have been taken for an enemy agent by either the Communards or their opponents. On March 20, in the Gare Saint-Lazare, just as he was leaving Paris to attend the Assembly's first session in Versailles, he was, in fact, momentarily arrested. Two days later, he was arrested again, this time by a Versailles police superintendent. He was imprisoned in the

Orangerie and might have been shot if he had not been able to give the name of a powerful acquaintance willing to vouch for him – Gustave Simon, the son of the Minister of Education, who had got to know him in the office of *La Cloche*.

In early May, the recently constituted Parisian Committee of Public Safety began rounding up hostages. There was a good chance that Zola might be one of them because of his tepid support of the Commune. He had, therefore, no choice but to flee Paris again. On the 11th, armed with Prussian passes, he and Alexandrine took the train from the Gare du Nord to Saint-Denis, where they found shelter in a transit camp set up for refugees. After his mother had managed to join them, the three of them went on to the house he had leased in Gloton, not returning to Paris until the end of the month, during the final bloody week of the Commune.

Although he never betrayed the least sympathy for the Communards' radical social and political objectives, he courageously maintained in his articles that their leaders were not bad men at heart, however much they might have been misled by their own propaganda. The brutality with which MacMahon's troops suppressed the Commune horrified him.

At thirty-one, he was as nervous and emotive as ever. He could not stand the sight of blood. The mere thought of death filled him with terror. Yet now he was confronted by death and destruction on a gigantic scale. He was overwhelmed by the horrible spectacle of the Commune's fall. 'All night long it was like a bloody dawn,' he reported in the *Sémaphore* of May 28.

> The sky was livid, as if coppered by the approach of a terrible storm, and traversed by crimson flashes lighting up large portions of it. The shooting went on and on. The fighting was taking place in this frightful setting, under this diabolical sky reminiscent of all the horrors of a Dantesque hell.

A day or so later, he made his way among the hundreds of corpses piled up under the bridges, observing, like a modern Dante, the mingled, grotesquely dislocated heads, arms, and legs and the horribly convulsed faces. He was among the first to venture into the Père Lachaise Cemetery, where the final battle had been fought. He gazed on the trampled ground, the blood-stained tombstones, the pools of blood, and the dead lying everywhere, just where they had fallen. A seventeen-year-old youth stretched out with his arms crossed on a slab of white stone caught his eye. A bit further on, a National Guardsman had been impaled on the pointed tips of an iron railing and was still hanging there, like an ox's carcass suspended in a butcher's shop.

In the *Sémaphore* of June 11 and 12, he reported further horrors: the mass incineration of the multitudes of bodies that had been hurled into the casemates of the fortifications, bloodcurdling tales of people who had mistakenly been buried alive along with the dead.

The pitiless repression that followed the defeat of the Commune angered him. He boldly defended Courbet, who had been blamed for the destruction of the Vendôme column. As, day after day, the military tribunals and firing squads carried on their ghastly work, he cried out for clemency.

IV

By now, Zola's own personal life, however, had resumed pretty much its pre-war course. The nearly three-quarters of a year that had elapsed between his flight from Paris to Marseilles and the fall of the Commune seemed, as it receded into the past, increasingly unreal. 'Here I am,' he happily remarked, 'safe and sound back in Les Batignolles, as if I were waking up from a bad dream.'

He was overjoyed to be reunited with most of his old friends. He and Baille, who was now also married and who had gone into his father-in-law's optical equipment manufacturing business, no longer saw much of each other. Bazille had joined the Zouaves and died in the battle of Beaune-la-Rolande in November, 1870. But Zola's relationships with his other old companions had taken up where they had left off. As before, Alexis or some other intimate would surprise him as, dressed in a sweater, a soiled old pair of pants, and big, heavy fur-lined shoes, he worked in his garden, trimming his lawn, weeding his rose beds, watering his lettuce, or pruning his trees. On warm summer evenings, he would move the dining room table out on to the narrow terrace, and the family would have supper outside. Afterwards, just as before the war, Alexis, Roux, Duranty, and one or more of the painters might arrive, and they would all sit around the table, leaning on their elbows, sipping the hot, steaming tea which was still all he could afford to serve them, and chatting under the stars until midnight.

The five months of enforced literary idleness in Marseilles and Bordeaux had, he suspected, been good for him. He felt young again, full of new energy and optimism – an optimism heightened by the advent of the new republic. 'Never have I been more hopeful or approached my work with greater zest,' he wrote Cézanne in July, 1871. 'Paris is being reborn. As I have told you so often, our reign is dawning. I'm a bit disappointed, it's true, that all those imbeciles aren't dead, but I'm comforted by the thought that each and every one of us is still alive. We can now resume our battle.'

In the same letter, he elatedly announced that the initial volume of the *Rougon-Macquart* series, *La Fortune des Rougon,* was at the printer's. (*Le Siècle* had finished serializing it in March.) 'You cannot imagine how much I'm enjoying correcting the proofs. It's just as if I were bringing out my first book.'

The novel was published on October 14. Appropriately, he had laid in it the foundation of the volumes to follow. Its scientific title, he declared in the preface, should be *Les Origines* – that is to say, the origins of the Rougon-Macquart family and the origins of the Second Empire.

He had set it in Plassans, a small Provençal town modeled on Aix. In two early chapters, he rapidly relates the first few decades of the family history beginning in the late eighteenth century. Adélaïde Fouque, an eccentric peasant, marries Rougon, one of her farm hands. They have a son, Pierre. After Rougon's untimely death, she becomes the mistress of a lazy, drunken smuggler named Macquart and has by him two more children, Antoine and Ursule. Thus the two main branches of the family come into being – the legitimate branch, the Rougons, destined to rise to the highest reaches of Second-Empire society, and the illegitimate branch, the Macquarts, condemned to remain mostly in the ranks of the exploited and oppressed.

The rest of the novel is taken up with three inseparable, yet partly independent stories: Pierre's rise to wealth and power; a republican insurrection in Provence caused by Louis Napoleon's *coup d'état* on December 2, 1851; and the charming love idyll of Ursule's idealistic adolescent son, Silvère Mouret, and an orphan girl, Miette Chantegreil.

As the title implies, the first of these stories is the central one. It is a grimly farcical tale. Pierre, based partly on Cézanne's *nouveau-riche* father, is the very model of a crass provincial opportunist. He starts out by cheating his mother and half-brother and half-sister out of their inheritance and using the profits to buy his way into a respectable, but financially distressed bourgeois family. His wife, Félicité, is just as greedy and socially ambitious as he is. For years, they struggle in vain to achieve their dream of success, but finally, after the Revolution of 1848, their big chance arrives. Félicité suspects that there is a fortune to be made in the political turmoil provoked by the revolution and pushes Pierre into politics. Alerted by their eldest son, Eugène, a Bonapartist agent, as to the probable turn of events, Pierre is the first in Plassans to support the future emperor. When, during the republican revolt, the mayor is captured, Pierre boldly takes possession of the town hall. Then, to enhance his heroic image as the town's savior, he bribes his dissolute half-brother, Antoine, a republican, to lead fifty of his like-minded drinking companions into an ambush, where two of them are shot. The gullible burghers think – just as Pierre intended – that he has singlehandedly stemmed a surprise attack. He is decorated and appointed Plassans' new tax collector, a post which cannot fail, if he properly exploits it, to make him one of the town's wealthiest as well as most respectable citizens. As for the illegitimate side of the family, only Antoine, the traitor, profits from these events. Silvère and Miette join the insurgents. Miette, wrapped in the red flag of insurrection, falls in battle. Silvère is captured and executed. His cousin, Aristide Rougon, Pierre and Félicité's youngest son, could have saved him, but declined to do so out of fear of being politically compromised.

While setting forth the early history of the family, Zola also recounts the origins of the Second Empire. But here his method is not so much that of an historian as it is that of a poet. The great historical events, beginning with the French Revolution of 1789, which made possible Louis Napoleon's rise to power are alluded to, but none of them takes place on the stage of the novel. Instead, they are evoked partly through their repercussions in Plassans, partly through the techniques of the *roman à clef*, partly through poetic imagery. Pierre's betrayal of his mother, Adélaïde, and half-brother and half-sister, Antoine and Ursule, is an obvious historical symbol. It stands for the French bourgeoisie's betrayal of France by its refusal to allow the lower classes to receive their rightful share of the revolutionary heritage. (Significantly, even Adélaïde's maiden name, Fouque, begins and ends with the same letters as the word *France* and has the same number of letters.) On another level, Pierre's character and career mirror those of Louis Napoleon and the greedy adventurers around him. Félicité's shoddy *salon*, with its dirty, yellow hues, drawn blinds, and conspiratorial atmosphere, symbolizes the moral milieu in which the Second Empire was hatched. Her furtive nocturnal trips to pour poison on the roots of the Plassans Liberty Tree and the glee with which the town's conservatives celebrate its felling are further historical allegories. When Miette is shot down, it is 'Virgin Liberty' herself who falls. Silvère's death symbolizes the death of idealism and the triumph of crass, cynical egoism. The blood flowing everywhere in the final chapter stands for all the blood shed by the Prince Président and his supporters on their way to power.

The novel conforms only partially to the formula that Zola had worked out in his preliminary *Rougon-Macquart* notes. Heredity and history are major themes. There is an abundance of documentary detail. The insurrection is closely modeled on the historical popular uprising that took place in Le Var after the *coup d'état*. Zola skilfully builds up the illusion that the novel is a predominantly naturalist work. Yet despite its scientific pretensions, it is in reality a passionately partisan republican tract. It is also a satire holding up to ridicule or scorn everything that Zola hated in the French bourgeoisie and especially the bourgeoisie of Aix, which had caused him and his family so much personal suffering.

Furthermore, it is impossible to read *La Fortune des Rougon* without recalling Zola's belief, going back to 1866, that the modern novel descends from the Greek epic via the Greek romance. Although the main story is essentially a modern realistic comedy reminiscent of Balzac, one of the two secondary stories, the ill-fated republican insurrection, is given epic treatment. The other, Silvère and Miette's innocent young love, recalls, as Zola himself repeatedly points out, the Greek romance. The narration of Pierre's vulgar victory feast faintly echoes Trimalchio's banquet in the *Satyricon*. This mixture of the satirical, epic, and idyllic, Balzac, Homer, Longus, and Petronius, produces a curious, yet powerful effect. It helps create relief, heightening the contrast between the betrayers of the republic, who are all treated satirically, and its defenders, all of whom are transformed into idealized modern counterparts of the old epic or idyllic heroes. What is more, by including these vestiges of antecedent genres, Zola assured that the very structure of this overture-like novel, like its principal characters, would illustrate his central *Rougon-Macquart* theme of life persisting and renewing itself, perpetuating old forms and inventing new ones through heredity.

Everywhere in *La Fortune des Rougon,* one finds evidence, moreover, of the dreamer and visionary in Zola, as well as the scientific realist. Along with the obvious symbols, the novel contains countless subtle ones. As in *Thérèse Raquin* and more than one of Zola's other earlier writings, realism and dream converge. Almost anything – a door in an old stone dividing wall, the window through which Félicité spends much of her time gazing covetously at the tax collector's mansion – yields complex symbolic meanings. The epic passages abound in poetic exaggeration and hallucinatory imagery. The country road up which the band of insurgents march becomes a torrent, the marchers, a human tempest. Their battle song, the *Marseillaise,* fills 'the sky, as though blowing from giant mouths through monstrous trumpets that hurled it, vibrating with the stridency of brass, into every part of the valley.' Inanimate objects come to life, as in the romantic poets and landscapists whom Zola so much admired. As in some of Zola's earliest stories, there is an obsessive intermingling of the themes of love and death. Silvère and Miette want 'to go to bed together in the earth.' The dead buried in the abandoned country graveyard where the two young lovers meet envy their love and try to bring it to fruition, so that they may share in it vicariously.

These plants that clutched them by the feet on fiery nights and almost made them stumble were thin fingers, narrowed and elongated by the tomb, protruding from the soil to retain them, to hurl them into each other's arms. The sharp, penetrating odor that the broken stems exhaled was the fecundating scent, the potent juice of life, that the graves slowly and laboriously produced and that made lovers straying on to these solitary paths drunk with desire. The dead, the ancient dead, longed for Miette's and Silvère's nuptials.

Zola threw himself heart and soul into the task of publicizing the novel, just as he had with all his previous works. Unfortunately, the critics paid it little attention. It fell far short of attaining the commercial success he had hoped for. One of the reasons was that the book trade was in a deep slump. Another was that the moment was one of extreme political reaction – hardly the right time to launch a book exalting radical republican ideals. However, several of the best writers of the day found *La Fortune des Rougon* impressive. Théophile Gautier hailed its author as a new master. Flaubert wrote Zola: 'I have just finished your atrocious and beautiful book! My head is still reeling. It is powerful, really powerful! . . . You have a splendid talent and you're a good, honest man.'

V

While doing his best to promote *La Fortune des Rougon*, Zola also composed the last four chapters of *La Curée*. *La Cloche* started serializing it in late September, but had to discontinue its publication after the Public Prosecutor, responding to charges of immorality, threatened to seize the paper if it went on printing it. The whole volume came out, unexpurgated, towards the end of the year.

Its main subject is the corrupt high society of Paris during the Second Empire. It follows the progress of Pierre and Félicité Rougon's youngest son, Aristide Rougon (*alias* Saccard), as he amasses a colossal fortune, largely through his ruthless exploitation of the opportunities for quick, shady profits created by

Baron Haussmann's reconstruction of the French capital. It is also about Aristide's effeminate, vicious son, Maxime, and his incestuous affair with his stepmother, Renée, Aristide's second wife. 'I wanted,' Zola explained in the preface,

> to depict the premature exhaustion of a race which had lived too fast and ends up with the man-woman of rotten societies; the furious speculation of an epoch incarnated in an unscrupulous, adventurous temperament; and the nervous breakdown of a woman whose innate appetites have been doubled by an excessively luxurious environment. With these three social monstrosities, I have tried to create a work of art and of science which would amount at the same time to one of the strangest pagest of our mores.

The three main characters are supported by a large cast of glittering Second-Empire types culled from society columns, gossipy books, or Zola's own glimpses of the Parisian upper crust of that time, mostly at Arsène Houssaye's lavish receptions – the top-hatted robber barons, the bejewelled, bare-shouldered society woman and demimondaines, the dissolute young fops. The whole crass, splendid, depraved world to which they belonged comes back to life, with its over-decorated new mansions in the Parc Monceau, the sleek millionaires' carriages in the Bois de Boulogne, the fashionable cafés, the lavish dinners, the theatre parties, the Tuileries balls. Even the Emperor briefly mounts on stage – to ogle Renée.

By far the most interesting character, however, is Renée herself. In his notes, Zola had envisaged her as nothing but a pretty, vain, weak-willed 'Parisian doll,' but as he wrote the novel he was led, happily, to make her more complex. Unlike Aristide, Renée comes from an old, upright bourgeois Parisian family. Her father, M. Béraud Du Châtel, is 'one of those Spartan republicans who dream of a government of perfect justice and sage liberty.' Up almost to the end of her brief existence, when she is granted a moment of enlightenment, she is entirely subjugated by her monstrously depraved way of life. Yet, even though she lacks the strength to resist its temptations, she never entirely loses the sense of dignity, honor, and moral obligation that her father instilled in her. This inner tension imparts to her, if not grandeur, a sharply poignant quality lacking in the other characters, most of whom arouse merely amusement or disgust.

The plot of *La Curée*, like that of *La Fortune des Rougon*, has all those features which Zola associated with modern fiction while containing elements reminiscent of Greek romance as well. It also presents parallels, if not with the Greek epic, with Greek tragedy. Furthermore, it is haunted from beginning to end by the myths of Narcissus and Phaedra. The resemblances between the novel and the myth of Phaedra, or, more precisely, the major Greek and French versions of it, are particularly numerous. Where his old, silly poet friend Pagès du Tarn had so ridiculously failed, Zola was determined to succeed. Not only is Renée Phaedra, Aristide Theseus, and Maxime Hippolytus; Renée's father, who embodies her conscience, clearly corresponds to Phaedra's father, Minos, King of Crete. Like Minos, M. Béraud Du Châtel dwells on an island – the Ile de la Cité. Like the dead Minos in Hades, he is a judge.

Even the setting of the novel and its motifs are strongly determined by these mythological themes. Béraud Du Châtel's dark, sober, quiet old house – so different from Aristide's gaudy new mansion – perpetuates a dead past corresponding to the classical underworld. Renée is repeatedly associated with the sun, Helios, the ancestor of Phaedra. In keeping with the Narcissus myth, the novel is full of evocations of mirrors, lakes, windows, and other glossy, reflecting objects. Maxime has a little mirror which he takes out of his pocket during class, sets between the pages of his book, and gazes into for hours on end. An immense mirror covers the wall of the first landing of the grand staircase of Aristide's house. As Renée goes upstairs, she examines herself in it, wondering, as she watches her image loom up before her, whether she is really as delightful as people say. Much emphasis is also placed on eyes: Maxime's eyes, for example – 'two blue holes, bright and smiling, coquette's mirrors behind which one could perceive all the void of his mind.'

Yet in all of this, Zola was not so much aiming at a translation of the old stories of Narcissus and Phaedra into modern terms, as he was at writing a modern-dress variation on them and compelling the reader to compare the new and the old versions. They coexist in a contrapuntal relationship, contrasting with and reinforcing each other. Above all, what is brought out is the nobility of the leading characters of the old myths and the corruption and degradation of most of their Second-Empire opposite numbers. Zola's bourgeois Theseus, for example, instead of being outraged by his wife's adulterous behavior, merely sees in it an opportunity to blackmail her into loaning him a large sum of money, which she is obliged to borrow from her father.

The theme of corruption is also served by the book's treatment of the Greek pastoral romance. The story of Silvère and Miette, except for its unhappy ending, is a Greek pastoral romance in modern dress, but the story of Renée and Maxime is an infernal distortion of that genre. Instead of the awakening of innocent young love, it treats of decadent passion in more than one of its most perverted forms. Appropriately, the bucolic setting of the old tales has been replaced by Aristide's ostentatious, sinister hothouse, full of rare, exotic, largely poisonous plants. In scenes going well beyond the limits of realism, it assumes an evil life of its own, tempting and abetting the guilty lovers.

La Curée is a superb piece of work, but, like its predecessor, it sold poorly. Again, the press showed little interest. Lacroix was about to go bankrupt and was unable to provide the usual publicity.

VI

Lacroix's business failure caused Zola considerable anguish. He was besieged by creditors demanding payment of the promissory notes he had signed in return for Lacroix's advance payments on his books. Not the least of his worries had to do with the future of the series. What would become of it now? His hands shook. He feared he was developing heart trouble, a bladder disease, rheumatism. Fortunately, an adventurous young publisher, Georges Charpentier, came to his rescue. The great poet Théophile Gautier, who had never met Zola but continued to be impressed by his budding genius, had recommended him to him. Charpentier bought from Lacroix for 800 francs the right to republish the first two volumes of the series. He also drew up a new contract, in which Zola agreed again, as he had with Lacroix, to provide two novels a year. Unlike Lacroix, Charpentier would buy the manuscripts directly from Zola, at 3,000 francs apiece, and would thus own them outright. As before, Zola would receive 500 francs a month in advances.

Not long after this latest financial crisis, Zola drew up a new general plan for the series. Instead of the original ten novels, he now envisaged seventeen.

The third novel, *Le Ventre de Paris,* was published by Charpentier on April 19, 1873. It was a logical sequel to *La Curée.* After having depicted the shady, thriving world of high finance during the Second Empire, he now portrayed the complacent, materialistic *petite bourgeoisie* of the same period. The chief dramatic theme of *Le Ventre* is the never-ending war between the fat and the lean – a war from whose battles the fat always emerge victorious. The novel is set in and around what was then the crowded central food market of Paris, Les Halles, sheltered by a soaring complex, now dismantled, of gigantic iron and glass pavilions largely erected during the Second Empire. Antoine Macquart's daughter Lisa has married a prosperous pork butcher, Quenu. Both belong very much among the fat. Her brother-in-law, Florent, however, belongs very much among the lean. A naive, idealistic republican, Florent was arrested in 1851 by Louis Napoleon's police and deported to French Guiana. When the story begins, in June 1858, he has recently escaped and returned to France. He hides out in the market quarter, which he knew as a boy. Lisa shelters him for a while, but in the end she betrays him to the imperial authorities. 'What scoundrels respectable people are!' is the book's last sentence. 'The general idea,' Zola wrote in his preliminary outline,

is the Belly; the belly of Paris, Les Halles, into which food flows and accumulates for distribution in the various quarters . . . . the belly of humanity and, by extension, the bourgeoisie digesting, ruminating, and sleeping off its pleasures and quite ordinary virtues; finally, the belly in the Empire – not the insane erethism of Saccard racing after millions, the sharp thrills of financial speculation, the formidable dance of golden coins, but the full, solid contentment of hunger, the ox crunching hay at the rack, the bourgeoisie secretly supporting the empire, because the empire supplies its mash day and night, its full, happy paunch distending in the sun and rolling all the way to the charnel house of Sedan.

But the novel is first and foremost a vast, animated description of Les Halles. Zola had long been fascinated by the artistic possibilities of this motif. In 1872, when he and his disciple Alexis were both working for *La Cloche*, he would often lead him after they left the newspaper's office, at no. 5, Rue Coq Heron, into Les Halles. 'What a fine book could be made with this rascally monument!' he had exclaimed. 'And what a truly modern subject! . . . I'm dreaming of an immense still life.' They had explored the market together. One evening, when they had arrived at a certain spot on the Rue Montmartre, he had suddenly halted and said, 'Turn around and look!' Seen from that point, the markets were a spectacular sight. In the sunset, they resembled nothing so much as a great, airy jumble of Babylonian palaces. He had noted the effect, and he had kept coming back with paper and pencil, taking numerous other notes, visiting the area at every time of day and in every type of weather. Once, he had spent a whole night there. He had even persuaded a guard captain to take him down into the basements and up on to the glass roofs. All his observations had gone into the novel. It contains hundreds of light and atmospheric effects. He had spent so many years associating with artists that he had come to see like them. He vividly evokes, for example, the iridescent, flesh-like tones of shellfish, the opal of whitings, the nacre of mackerel, the gold of mullets, the lamé of the herrings, the silver of the salmons glistening in a shaft of sunlight – or feathers flying like dancing snowflakes in a bright golden haze surrounding women plucking chickens. Numerous passages recall Jongkind, Pissarro, or Monet.

The novel is frequently also reminiscent of Hugo's *Notre-Dame de Paris*. It brings Les Halles alive, much as Hugo had the cathedral. Just as Hugo had poetically transformed the concerted sounds of the church bells of Paris into a spectacular display of light, Zola transforms the smells of cheeses displayed in the market into a musical symphony. (In *La Curée* he had already done the same thing with the perfumes of the flowers in

Aristide's hothouse.) Marjolin, the monstrous yet pathetic hero of the story's love idyll (still another variation on the Greek pastoral romance), plays a role analogous in several ways to Quasimodo's. In *Notre-Dame de Paris,* Paris is repeatedly seen through the eyes of the poet Gringoire, a character based partly on Villon, partly on Hugo himself. In *Le Ventre de Paris,* the market is often seen through the eyes of Antoine Macquart's grandson, the painter Claude Lantier, a character based as much on Zola himself as on Cézanne. But if *Le Ventre de Paris* presents certain striking parallels with *Notre-Dame de Paris,* it also contrasts with it, proclaiming not only Zola's debt to Hugo, but his break with Hugo. *Notre-Dame de Paris* is, among other things, a romantic manifesto. *Le Ventre de Paris,* as the text makes very clear in Chapter IV, is a naturalistic manifesto exalting positivism, materialism, progress, and the dawning twentieth century, symbolized by the architecture of Les Halles. The crowded, thriving modern market place is contrasted with Saint-Eustache, whose gloomy, deserted nave is dwarfed by its giant pavilions.

Yet despite Zola's naturalistic pretensions, the imaginative poet in him dominates this novel. Fact is constantly transformed through the consciousness of its viewpoint characters into hallucination, as when Les Halles, in the first chapter, seem to submerge and digest Florent. Moreover, the world of the novel significantly differs in some respects from the real world. That Quenu should have come, after years of plying his trade, to look like a pig or that Lisa, reflected in the mirrored walls of their prosperous pork-butcher's shop, should, in Florent's eyes, resemble a belly – the metaphorical symbolic belly she incarnates – are details that the realistic mode can afford to tolerate. But more than one of the other characters of the novel, including some of the most central and memorable, are delightfully fantastic – the stuff of dreams, allegory, and myth. The best example is Lisa's chief rival, the beautiful fishwife Louise Méhudin. Louise is not so much a realistic character as she is a mythical embodiment of the sea, the Sea herself. Colossal, heavy, with her gigantic bosom, strong fishy odor, violent, changeable humor, overwhelming vitality, titanic, statuesque grace, she could never have made her way into a typical Balzac novel or most of Zola's other realistic models.

When her bodice opened [Florent] thought he could glimpse emerging from between two whitenesses a haze of life, a breath of health . . . . It was a persistent perfume attached to her fine, silky skin, a fish grease flowing from her superb breasts, her royal arms, her supple waist, adding a rude aroma to her womanly scent . . . . Then, the swing of her skirts exuded a mist; she walked in the midst of an evaporation of slimy seaweed; with her great goddess's body, her admirable purity and pallor, she was like some beautiful antique marble rolled by the sea and brought back to the coast in the net of some sardine fisherman.

The novel was a great success. After ignoring the first two *Rougon-Macquart* volumes, the critics now seemed to rediscover Zola. Even *La Revue des deux mondes,* which had so disdainfully rejected his youthful verses, conceded that he was 'not without certain literary qualities.' A second edition came out in May.

VII

He had hardly finished *Le Ventre de Paris* before he began *La Faute de l'abbé Mouret* – towards the beginning of 1873. Then he put it aside and dashed off *La Conquête de Plassans,* which thus became the fourth *Rougon-Macquart* novel. Part of the overall narrative structure of the series was beginning to emerge. Each new volume both complemented and contrasted with the preceding one. After having depicted the *nouveaux riches* and the trades-people of Paris during the Second Empire, he had now returned to the provincial middle class of that same period. After having indulged in an orgy of description giving full rein to his love of color, crowds, vast panoramas, elaborate metaphor and symbol, he had felt the need of writing a novel of psychological analysis placed in a restricted setting and written in a sober style. His mood, in short, was once again less romantic than classical. After having emulated Hugo, he was moving back once more toward Molière.

The result is a gruesome horror story about a sinister, cold, worldly, brutal, and ambitious priest named Ovide Faujas and his briefly successful struggle for power. Like Pierre Rougon's eldest son, Eugène, now Minister of the Interior, Faujas is a typical representative of the little band of unscrupulous men-on-the-make who had profited from the *coup d'état* of December, 1851. After having been discharged from his diocese because of some shady business in which he had been involved, he offers his services to Eugène. Since the *coup d'état*, Plassans has become a stronghold of the clerical party with its strong legitimist leanings. Eugène charges Faujas with winning the town back for the government. He does so brilliantly but in the process ruins the Mourets, in whose house he has rented rooms. Little by little he takes it over. Marthe Mouret, Pierre and Félicité Rougon's daughter, is completely subjugated by him. Under his influence, she undergoes a religious conversion, develops a guilty love for him, and no longer feels anything but loathing for her husband (and cousin), François Mouret. Finally, after a series of increasingly grave nervous attacks, she dies. François, thought to be crazy thanks to Faujas' machinations, is confined in an asylum. In the end, he really does go mad, escapes, and sets fire to his former dwelling. Both he and Faujas are consumed by the flames.

The novel has a certain interest as an illustration of the belief which Zola entertained at the time he wrote it that religious piety is a form of insanity to which women in particular tend to be prone; but it is memorable above all for its central character. Although Faujas resembles in some respects Balzac's Troubert, in *Le Curé de Tours*, he recalls above all Molière's Tartuffe. But he is also in many ways a product of Zola's own peculiar imagination. As soon as Marthe sees him, she is strangely troubled by the way he looks at her, like a bird of prey. 'It seemed that in the depths of his eyes, ordinarily a mournful gray, a flame suddenly passed, like the lamps one sometimes glimpses passing behind the sleeping façades of houses.' From that page on, Faujas becomes a pure creature of nightmare.

Published just when the reactionary movement that dominated the early years of the Third Republic was at its peak, the novel sold even more poorly than the first two volumes of the series. But the great critic Brunetière, writing in *La Revue des deux mondes,* praised its exact, true-to-life qualities. So also did Anatole France. Flaubert was especially impressed by the ending and found the novel even better than *Le Ventre de Paris*.

VIII

Although Zola's main preoccupation was now more than ever with his fiction, he still dreamt of conquering the stage. In 1873, his theatrical version of *Thérèse Raquin* had enjoyed only a brief run even though the great actress Marie Laurent had agreed to take the part of Mme Raquin. He spent part of the following year composing a new play, *Les Héritiers Rabourdin,* inspired by Ben Jonson's *Volpone.* The first-night audience applauded it, but the critics tore it apart, and it too folded after only a few performances.

That November, he published, under the title *Nouveaux contes à Ninon,* a selection of the chronicles, satirical fragments, reminiscences, and happy or sad tales that he had written since 1866. In the preface, he expressed his nostalgia for his youth in Aix. He recalled above all his strolls throughout the Provençal countryside and the calm faith in the forces of life that his contacts with nature on those occasions had inspired in him. He recalled the struggles that he had been caught up in for the past ten years – 'ten years of forced labor, ten years of bitterness, of blows given and received, of ceaseless combat.' He evoked his wounds, his scars. He expressed his disgust with the steady flow of journalistic articles he had had to turn out in order to support himself. He confessed how tired he was sometimes and how the only thing that kept him going was the memory of the vows he had made to Ninon, his ideal, imaginary childhood love. 'My passion for the absolute suffered in the midst of all these stupidities, so freighted with importance in the morning, and so forgotten by the close of the same day.' He spoke of his obsession with realism, his determination to portray the truth, no matter how unpleasant, his love of exact, probing analysis. He boasted that he had managed to make a living without compromising any of his beliefs. He admitted how dissatisfied he was with what he had accomplished so far.

Ah, Ninon, I have done nothing yet! I weep over this

mountain of blackened paper. I am distressed at the thought
that I have not as yet been able to quench my thirst for truth,
that my arms are too short to embrace the whole of nature in
all her vastness. I am consumed by a keen desire to take the
earth, possess her in a tight embrace, see, know, say
everything. I want to set down all humanity on a white page,
all living beings, all things, to create a work which will be the
immense ark.

Some day, he promised Ninon, he would return to her, Aix,
and the bucolic reveries of his youth. Meanwhile, he said, he
would need all his virility to continue his struggle to accomplish
his serious literary objectives.

The volume included 'Les Quatre Journées de Jean Gourdon.' Among the other pieces there were numerous real or
imagined reminiscences. By the time he had written them he
had transformed many of the people, places, and events from his
past into symbols. He could still vividly recall, for example, the
colorful penitents, gilded saints, chanting priests, out-door altars,
flower-strewn streets, and other details of the Corpus Christi
processions in which he had participated in his boyhood – even
the faint, silvery tinkle of the censers, as clear as if he had just
heard them the day before; but they had become in his
imagination a bitter-sweet poetic figure of the decline of
Catholicism:

> The sun is setting. Rosy gleams of light are extinguished on
> the roofs. With dusk, a great, delicious peacefulness settles
> over everything. And in the limpid air of Le Midi, the
> procession recedes into the distance with its dying voices, the
> melancholy demise of a whole age descending into the earth.

In another piece, Calvaire Levasseur, the blacksmith whom he
had come to know in Gloton, has metamorphosed into a modern
Hercules, the hero of the quasi-religious cult of work that Zola
had come to share with many of his contemporaries:

> He was bare to the waist, his muscles bulging and taut, like
> one of those great figures of Michelangelo, standing erect with
> supreme effort . . . . In my eyes, he was the consummate
> hero of labor, the indefatigable child of this century, cease-

lessly hammering out on his anvil our tools of analysis and fashioning in fire and by fire the society of tomorrow . . . . It was there, in his shop, in the midst of the ploughs, that I recovered forever from my disease of laziness and doubt.

He kept on with his journalism even though he had by now come to regard most of it as sheer drudgery. He still needed the money that it brought him and relished the opportunities it occasionally gave him to express and impose his personality and ideas upon the public. As before, he kept on insisting that art was life, or, as he now put it, 'the eternal efflorescence of humanity.' He went on giving vent to his passion for truth, science, reality, his hatred of aesthetic absolutes, his rejection of any one arbitrary ideal of beauty, his passion for the present, his faith in progress. In an especially moving paragraph, he confessed more eloquently than ever before his love and veneration for Paris, the city of progress:

> Its immense drama is what attaches me to the great unfolding drama of our times, the lives of its bourgeois and working-class people, its whole restless, floating population whose every grief and joy I burn to record. It is my brother, my big brother, whose emotions touch me and who cannot cry without bringing tears to my own eyes. I feel it rocked by the immense labor of the century; I see it about to give birth to a new world, and my proudest wish would be to cast it, all warm and full of its titanic task, into some gigantic work of art.

More than ever, he felt a need to ally himself with other like-minded writers. In *La Cloche* of November 8, 1872, he went so far as to express publicly his regret that there was nothing at that time comparable to the tight-knit literary brotherhoods that had flourished among the romantics in the 1830s. Journalism and the deadly competition it had instigated were largely to blame, he said. 'I mean that journalism which has cast into the streets a whole swarm of fine little gentlemen at so much the line.' But the lack of any great name to cluster around was, he surmised, another reason. In any case, the result was, he complained, exaggerating a little, 'an absolute solitude.'

> We labor alone, mistrustful, exchanging greetings on the sidewalk, taking refuge, some in their wounded pride, others

in their stubborn devotion to work. In all of Paris you will not find a single salon where thirty-year-old writers can feel at home.

Thirsting especially for more companionship with other men of letters whom he revered or could at least regard as more or less his peers and mindful as always of the benefits they could all derive from fighting side by side, he worked harder than ever to remedy the situation.

As early as 1869, he had already established a cordial relationship with Flaubert, sending him copies of his latest novels along with respectful letters addressing him as his master. But it was not until after the war that they had become close friends. Although they disagreed on many things, they warmly admired each other. Through Flaubert, he met Turgenev and Maupassant. At Flaubert's and Goncourt's, he also renewed his acquaintance with Alphonse Daudet, whom he had met at *L'Evénement,* for which they had both worked, in 1866. Towards the end of 1874, he and Mallarmé got to know each other at Manet's.

He spent as much time with his literary friends as possible. He could almost always be found at Flaubert's regular Sunday afternoon receptions in his modest bachelor apartment on the Rue Murillo. After throwing a red silk cloth over the manuscripts on his worktable, the old Viking, dressed in his loose pants, flowing robe, and small silk skullcap, would answer the door himself. Often the first to arrive would be Turgenev. Then others would enter, including Taine and Daudet. Zola, followed by his faithful disciple Alexis, would show up in his turn, panting hard after trudging up the five flights of stairs. Goncourt would generally appear last, squeezing into the crowded room. Often Maupassant had been there since before the reception began. Zola, as always, was generally timid and awkward in conversation. When the discussion became more animated and lyrical than usual, he would occasionally become uneasy, shift his legs, and try to break in with a 'But! But!' But his voice would be drowned out by the din. Only after it had subsided would he venture to speak again, making some sober remark in a calm voice.

He and Flaubert, Goncourt, Daudet, Turgenev, and other

friends would also see each other at his own Thursday evening at-homes or at the Daudets' or, among other places, in the salon of Zola's new editor, Charpentier, with whom he had become very friendly too. The Charpentiers' receptions tended to be large and worldly. They were attended not only by men of letters, but also by painters, including Manet, musicians, politicians, and other socially prominent people, indeed, anybody who was anybody in Paris.

Starting out on April 14, 1874, Flaubert, Goncourt, Turgenev, Daudet, and Zola began to meet once a month for an elaborate gourmet dinner which, since they had all suffered the indignity of having their plays hissed, they dubbed the 'Dinner of the Hissed Authors.' Flaubert had had the idea after the failure of *Le Candidat*. The first of these feasts took place at the Café Riche. They would drink a lot and indulge their mutual taste for good food. Flaubert satisfied his appetite for Normandy butter and *canards rouennais à l'estouffade*. Goncourt ordered preserved ginger, Turgenev caviar, Zola sea urchins and shellfish. The diners' faces would redden and glow. Their voices could be heard throughout the building. Flaubert had a particularly thunderous laugh. The conversation would become more than usually Rabelaisian. The first night, it had begun with a great dissertation on the special aptitudes of constipated and diarrhetic writers. Zola loved every minute of these occasions. The wine, the affection he felt for each of his four companions, their mutual respect, if not agreement, loosened his tongue, and he would end up shouting with the rest of them, loudly debating points of theory – much as he had once done with Cézanne and Baille or with his artist friends at the Café Guerbois. Or he would talk plaintively about his impoverished youth, his present problems, the insults he had been forced to put up with, the mistrust people had of him, the critical conspiracy to ignore his works, his fears that his talent would never be acknowledged, that he would never be decorated or elected to the Academy, that he would always be a pariah. He confessed his ambition to dominate, to crush Paris with his prose, to take revenge on all those who had treated him badly.

Toward the end of 1874, another series of dinner parties was inaugurated, with the peculiar name 'dîners du Boeuf nature.' Zola presided alone, surrounded by Alexis, Solari, and other young admirers and disciples. Occasionally Cézanne, Roux, or some other old friend from Aix would join them. Slowly but surely, Zola was coming closer to his goal of being the head of a school.

'We must stand together, side by side,' he wrote Daudet on November 9. 'The battalion is small, but it will be strong.'

IX

La Faute de l'abbé Mouret, the fifth volume in the *Rougon-Macquart* series, came out on March 27, 1875. Like its predecessor, *La Conquête de Plassans,* it is set in Provence, has to do with a priest, and is violently anticlerical. But in most other respects it differs from *La Conquête de Plassans* even more strikingly than that earlier novel does from *Le Ventre de Paris.* Its hero, Marthe and François Mouret's second son, Serge, a high-strung, intensely devout, otherworldly young *curé,* sharply contrasts with the diabolical Faujas. Moreover, it goes beyond mere anticlericalism to present in a dubious light several of the major doctrines and practices of the Catholic Church itself.

Furthermore, the chief underlying theme and, for that matter, the whole mood, style, and structure of *La Faute de l'abbé Mouret* set it apart from all Zola's other earlier novels. While writing it he had for the first time been primarily concerned with a subject appertaining to the history of ideas – the conflict between Catholicism and the revived pagan cult of nature which had become a major feature of nineteenth-century French secular religious thought. He had also been motivated by a desire to champion certain religious concepts and attitudes that had long appealed to him. The result is a work which, despite its wealth of true detail, is only in the most superficial sense realistic. From the outset, the reader is faced by patent allegory. Quite rightly, *La Faute de l'abbé Mouret* has been called the first great symbolist novel.

What is more, the pastoral romance, or, more exactly, Zola's own generally tragic variety of that traditionally happy genre, either excludes or absorbs in this book all the other genres encountered in Zola's earlier fiction. The book also contains parallels with the mediaeval mystery play, for it is in large part a modern dress variation on the Biblical story of Adam and Eve.

In a remote, arid, sun-scorched corner of Provence, Serge, a young parish priest, is reduced by his excessive piety to a state of delirium bordering on madness and death. He cannot even remember who he is. His uncle, Doctor Pascal, takes him to Paradou, a vast, ruined eighteenth-century garden largely based on Zola's memories of the ruined garden he had in his youth discovered on the banks of the Durance. Here, Serge is nursed back to health by the caretaker's daughter, a beautiful, half-savage girl, Albine. A new life begins for Serge. As he regains his health and consciousness, the episodes of the story of Genesis find their counterparts in his story one after the other: Adam's delight in creation, his dream, the creation of Eve, the temptation, disobedience, shame, expulsion, suffering and death.

The novel repeatedly evokes the ancient Biblical tale, but even as it does so, it distorts and revises it. For this nineteenth-century Adam and Eve, the temptation is to make love. Paradou is the Garden of Eden transformed into the natural paradise of eighteenth-century philosophers. Endowed with a single, all-inclusive life and moved by a single will, Nature, as represented by Paradou and Albine, plays the role of the Biblical Satan. The tree of the knowledge of good and evil becomes the tree of life, an unmistakable fertility symbol:

> It had a giant height, a trunk that breathed like a lung . . . .
> It seemed good, robust, potent, fecund; it was the dean of the
> garden, the father of the forest . . . . From its green vault
> descended all the joy of creation; fragrances of flowers, songs
> of birds, drops of light, cool awakenings of dawn, drowsy
> tepidities of dusk. Its sap had such great force that it flowed
> from its bark, bathing it in a mist of fecundation, making of it
> the very virility of the earth.

As Serge and Albine recline in its deep shade, they are compelled to make love at last. In doing so, they find perfect bliss and become one with the supreme forces of nature. Serge is at last a man, Albine a woman. His cure is complete. The whole garden applauds and copulates along with them. The birds, bees, and even the atoms that constitute matter join together in ecstasy. Like Eve, Albine discovers that she is naked and is overwhelmed with shame. But only Serge, whose memory has suddenly come back at the sight of the outside world glimpsed through a breach in the wall, is expelled from this modern Eden. Jehovah, transformed into an evil tyrant, is represented by Archangias, a brutal, sadistic monk in charge of the local school. It is he who yanks Serge out of Paradou and tries to prevent him from returning. Yet unlike the Biblical deity he never enters the garden. Like Adam and Eve, Serge and Albine are condemned to die. But they do so in different ways. Albine, heartbroken first by Serge's refusal to come back to her, then, when he weakly relents, by his impotence (for his resumed vocation has by now utterly destroyed his virility) commits suicide. As for Serge himself, he has not when the novel ends as yet died literally, but the text makes it clear that he is already as good as dead – physically a mere eunuch, spiritually a cipher, neither a good Christian nor a good pagan, a man reduced to a state of morbid nothingness. His black cassock has, in effect, been transformed, as Zola puts it, into a shroud.

La Faute de l'abbé Mouret is also more ambiguous than any of Zola's earlier works. What exactly is Serge's sin? Is it his having indulged in sexual intercourse? Or is it, rather, his ascetic exaltation of abstinence, virginity, and sterility, his rejection of Eros, life, fecundity, and all the forces of nature? Or is it his abandonment of Albine after he has promised to remain forever faithful to her – that is to say (assuming that fidelity to one's beloved is not a natural, but a human virtue) a sin not against nature so much as humanity? Why does Albine feel shame after having made love with Serge? Must one see here, like some critics, a symptomatic expression of a fundamental ambiguity in Zola's attitude towards sexual love – an ambiguity deeply rooted in Western thought, which both exalts sex and condemns it as sinful? Or can one not perceive here, on the contrary, a reflection of Michelet's belief, familiar to Zola, that every virtuous woman experiences shame after she first makes love because she fears that she has not pleased her man? No matter how closely one scrutinizes the text of the novel, one will find nothing that absolutely prevents any of these interpretations.

Nor can one definitively read into the text any single philosophical or religious bias. Although at first sight the novel would appear to be an unmitigated attack on Catholicism, it is quite possible that it does indeed, as another critic has suggested, reveal through its priestly hero Zola's long sublimated desire to fall on his knees before the Church. Or it may be read as an exposition in fictional terms of many of the ideas Michelet had set forth in *L'Amour* and *La Femme*. Or the novel may be seen as an expression of the bitter nihilism voiced after Albine's death by her uncle, the old atheistic philosopher Jeanbernat, the caretaker of Paradou: 'Well, I was right; there is nothing, no, nothing, nothing at all . . . . It's all a big joke.' Or, to mention still another possibility, the novel may just as easily appear to some readers to reflect all these clashing attitudes concurrently, thus expressing something of the ambiguity of Zola's thought itself and indirectly, through Zola, the thought of his confused, questing age.

In any event, *La Faute de l'abbé Mouret*, despite its ambiguity, or possibly in part because of it, is an exceptionally powerful novel. Even the excessively long catalogues of plants, flowers, and trees included in the descriptions of Paradou and the book's other shortcomings have not prevented it from being one of Zola's more popular works. Barbey d'Aurevilly, always the champion of Catholicism, could not contain himself: 'It's the naturalism of animals placed shamelessly and indecently above the noble spiritualism of Christianity! . . . I do not believe that, in this time of vile things, anyone has written anything more vile . . . . ' Taine wrote Zola: '*La Faute de l'abbé Mouret*, in its style and its proportions, breaks out of the fictional mold; it's a poem. The park has a perimeter of twenty leagues; it's Eden, a valley in Kashmir. There is nothing more intoxicating; I am reminded of a Persian poem, of certain passages in Indian epics.' Maupassant had, in part, the same reaction: ' . . . your book made me drunk and, what is more, strongly excited me!' Before 1875 was over, it had already gone through four editions.

X

The sixth volume of the *Rougon-Macquart* series, *Son Excellence Eugène Rougon,* was published in February, 1876. A political novel, it transports the reader back to Paris. Its hero is Pierre and Félicité's eldest son, Eugène, whose overriding motive is his insatiable longing to dominate and manipulate other men.

When the story begins, Eugène has already become president of the Council of State. His fall from power and successful struggle to regain it, involving his ambivalent relationship with the ambitious young Italian beauty, Clorinde Balbi, provides the chief dramatic interest. The plot is in part a modern variation on the tale of Samson and Delilah. For a time at least, Eugène, like Samson, is a strong man undone by his sexual vulnerability and the machinations of a seductive woman intent on destroying him. But above all *Son Excellence Eugène Rougon* is of value as a psychological study of raw political ambition in the context of the corrupt politics of the Second Empire.

Zola had based its characters, incidents, and settings partly on numerous journalistic and literary sources and on information furnished him orally by Flaubert, Goncourt, and other friends who had been closer to the imperial court than he. Flaubert, who had once spent two weeks as a guest of the Emperor at Compiègne, had even gone so far at one of his Thursday receptions as to mimic the Emperor for Zola's benefit. Dressed as usual in his lounging robe, he had imitated the Emperor's dragging gate, one hand behind his bowed back, another twisting his mustache, while emitting characteristically inane remarks. But Zola had also drawn heavily on his own direct observations of the political world. As Glais-Bizoin's secretary in 1870 and as a parliamentary chronicler for *La Cloche* and *Le Sémaphore de Marseille*, he had watched the political animal at length and from up close. All that he had learned about the psychology and mores of politicians he injected into his portrayal of the novel's characters, imbuing them in their turn with the same intense life that he had given most of his earlier characters.

Not only the Emperor but dozens of the other leading political figures of the Second Empire, some undisguised, the others only thinly masked, come alive again in the novel's pages. For example, Eugène is obviously modeled in large part on Eugène Rouher, sometimes referred to as Napoleon III's 'vice-emperor.' Clorinde, who ends up in the novel as the Emperor's mistress, recalls the irresistible Countess de Castiglione, who really was for a brief time the Emperor's mistress.

As in his earlier novels on social and political subjects, not to mention the many political articles he had fired off for *La Tribune, La Cloche,* and other opposition newspapers, Zola sees everything from the radical republican point of view. He is portraying people he hated. Once again, he is at his satirical best – cruel, cold-eyed, a would-be modern Juvenal, complacently exposing everything that was despicable in his hapless targets. The novel was not, however, a great popular success. Its subject, despite the effort Zola had gone to to make it as appealing as possible, failed to excite the public. Furthermore, it had barely appeared, after months of delay caused by difficulties beyond Zola's control, before the immense scandal provoked by his next novel, *L'Assommoir,* broke out, totally distracting the public's attention.

[4]

First Great Triumphs

I

With *L'Assommoir,* Zola's dream of fame, so long nurtured, came true at last. This novel is, without any doubt, one of the most powerful ever written. Its impact has always been due in large part to its sociological subject: the working class, or more exactly the working class of mid-nineteenth-century Paris, as it really was. This is still a fascinating theme even though the books that have been written about the world of the modern proletariat are now legion. But in France in the 1870s, there was no more original, timely, or audacious fictional topic to be found.

The modern French industrial proletariat was being born – a fact of which politicians, journalists, and writers, barely aware of it at first, were now increasingly taking note. Since the last years of the Second Empire there had been major strikes in Le Creusot, La Ricamarie, Aubin, and elsewhere, all brutally suppressed. Under the pioneering leadership of such militants as Eugène Varlin, Benoît Malon, Henri Rochefort, Jean-Baptiste Millière, and Adolphe Assi, the working-class revolutionary movement had been gaining momentum. The workers were organizing into unions. The First International, banned in France in 1872, had become an internationally feared force. In Paris, Baron Haussmann's alterations had forced the common toilers out of the heart of the city into the grimy suburbs, creating what was in effect two distinct cities, one for the haves, the other for the have-nots. The Parisian bourgeoisie eyed this new community encircling their own with a mixture of curiosity, contempt, guilt, and fear.

Hugo, George Sand, Eugène Sue, and other romantics had written novels about the suffering of the poor of their day, but their depictions had been hopelessly sentimental and, by realistic standards, quite false. Balzac had barely touched on the subject. In 1864, the Goncourt brothers had boldly proclaimed: 'Living as we do in the nineteenth century, in a time of universal suffrage, of democracy, of liberalism, we have wondered if what one calls "the lower classes" do not have the right to be treated in fiction; if this world below a world, the common people, should remain excluded from literature and disdained by authors who have till now said nothing about the soul and the heart that it may well possess.' Yet *Germinie Lacerteux,* the novel that the Goncourts wrote to fill this void, is not really so much a portrait of the working class as it is a study of a special case of hysteria. When Zola undertook to treat the subject in his turn, it was still, at least from the naturalistic point of view, almost untouched.

As he himself saw very well, it was also a subject extremely rich in the raw material of drama and epic. Not only was the working-class world full of fresh colorful motifs, as contemporary painters – Courbet, for example, with his *Stonebreakers,* or Daumier and Degas, with their studies of laundresses and other working-class figures – had discovered. The way working-class people behaved had an earthiness, a primitive simplicity and vigor, about it that infinitely appealed to the dramatist and poet in Zola. The Hellenistic revival that had been going on throughout his lifetime had affected him too, and it seemed to him that anyone who wanted to write a work directly inspired by the Greek epic and Greek tragedy should choose workers or peasants as its leading characters. Only they still acted like the heroes of Homer or Euripides. Upper-class behavior had become too refined, too complex, too full of nuances, too artificial, in a word, too civilized, to fit the epic mould. For a while, he had toyed with the idea of composing a modern *Andromache* in a peasant setting. He had even drawn up a preliminary plot outline, together with summaries of Euripides' and Racine's tragedies on the same theme. The subject of *L'Assommoir* appealed to the same classicizing side of his nature.

But the novel's power also comes, of course, from what Zola did with his great subject. He knew the world of the Parisian working class as well as any other author of his time. His mother was from it. He had himself lived in it. He knew what it was like to be ill-clothed, cold, and hungry. In his contacts with working-class people, he had noted everything, forgotten nothing. What he did not know, he had gleaned from Denis Poulot's widely read book on the subject, *Le Sublime,* and other relevant studies. The novel attests to this familiarity on every page. It is a masterpiece of detailed, scientific observation. It is also remarkable for its brutal realism, its rejection of all the old middle-class myths about workers, its insistence on showing the common people of Paris exactly as they were during the Second Empire, its refusal to omit anything relevant, no matter how unpleasant it might be: the narrowness and meanness of spirit that poverty too often brings about, the promiscuity, squalor, violence, drunkenness. In *Le Ventre de Paris,* he had described the effects of hunger in detail – the sort of stomach-wrenching hunger that he himself had known during his Bohemian days; and in *L'Assommoir* he does so at even greater length. He does not even hesitate to include scenes of child abuse or to evoke the stench and feel of vomit in a drunkard's bed or the stink of rotting corpses.

The dramatic plot is immensely beautiful and moving. At the outset, he had decided that the central character would be Gervaise Macquart, the second daughter of Antoine Macquart and Joséphine Gavaudan. He had also made up his mind early in the planning stage that one of his main aims would be to illustrate the evil effect of the slums on those condemned to live in them. But it was only in the summer of 1875, when he had first started working on the novel in earnest, that the main outline of the plot had occurred to him. He had wanted something very simple. He and his family were spending three months – his first long vacation in years – in Saint-Aubin, on the coast of Normany, and one day, as he and Alexis were sitting by the ocean, he was struck by the immense curve of the horizon between the sea and the sky. 'Look here, I must find something like that,' he said. 'Something completely simple, a beautiful line proceeding straight ahead . . . . The effect will perhaps also be very great.' He was right. The central action of the story, Gervaise's career in Paris, her rise and fall, does indeed follow the line of a huge arc, the sea at Saint-Aubin, its cleanness and grandiose simplicity contrasting with the sordidness, the pettiness, and disorder of the slum setting in which the story takes place. It also reinforces the impression that he wished to give of the inexorability of Gervaise's fate, beginning with her lover Lantier's abandonment of her and their two children, Etienne and Claude, her marriage to Coupeau, a zink-worker, her momentary success as a laundress, then, following the fall of her husband, crippled by an accident, into a life of idleness and drink, her own decline as she takes the same path, losing everything including her self-respect, turning into the butt and laughing stock of her neighbors, and finally starving to death in a dark niche under a tenement stairway.

The tale, as Zola tells it, is extremely gripping. By the time he wrote it, his story-telling genius had at last fully matured. All the characters are intensely alive. Most of them are also memorable. Lantier, Gervaise's faithless love, who, after running off with another woman, slinks back to live with her and Coupeau, forming with them a ménage à trois, leading, like Coupeau, a life of ease at her expense, is one of the most memorable cads ever imagined. Goujet, the hardworking blacksmith, who faithfully loves Gervaise without ever attaining the object of his passion but is always there when she needs help, vainly trying to save her, is also an unforgettable figure. So also is Coupeau and Gervaise's daughter, Nana, alluring with her golden locks and light blue eyes, but already hopelessly depraved long before she reaches adolescence and leaves home to become a prostitute. Virginie, with whom Lantier takes up after he has sucked Gervaise dry and whom he devours in her turn, is the perfect paradigm of the treacherous false friend, winning Gervaise's affection and trust, only to help destroy her.

Even most of the numerous secondary figures of the novel go on living in the reader's mind long after he or she has finished the last page: for example, Gervaise's malicious, selfish, gossipy relatives envious of her prosperity when the laundry shop she has opened with a loan from Goujet is going well, close-fisted with her in her decline, secretly relishing her misfortunes; Bru, the worn-out, unemployed old worker dying of hunger, little Lalie, the saintly martyred child, brutalized by her drunken father after he has kicked her mother to death; Colombe, the placid, strong-armed proprietor of the tavern after which the novel is named; or old Bazouge, the tipsy undertaker's assistant, who lives next-door to the Coupeaus in their tenement house on the Rue de la Goutte d'Or and who, at the story's end, seizes Gervaise's already green corpse in his big black hands and, as he tenderly lays her in her coffin, burbles on, between hiccups: 'Listen, dear, . . . you know . . . it's me, Bibi-la-Gaieté, known as the ladies' comforter . . . . There, there, you're all right now. Night-night, my lovely!'

As for Gervaise herself, she may not be in the forefront of the world's great literary characters – the Hamlets, the Goriots, the Emma Bovarys, the Anna Kareninas (Zola's genius lies more in the portrayal of crowds, communities, and other collectivities than the creation of individual characters); but few would deny that she follows not far behind. Certainly, none of the characters in Zola's earlier novels, not even Thérèse Raquin, quite comes up to her as a literary creation. Bandy-legged, delicate, sensitive, good natured, blond, pretty enough in her youth, then increasingly ravaged in the years of her decline, she gradually crumbles morally as well as physically. Yet there is nothing really evil about her. She is at first a thoroughly decent, loving, hard-working, ambitious woman, a faithful wife, a good mother. Her main 'faults' – the ones that start her off on her long, heart-breaking decline – are her affectionate and trusting nature, her occasional inertia, her inability to say no, her excessive kindness and tolerance, her desire to please, her love of good food. It is all very ironic. Even her affection for her husband contributes to her undoing. Instead of letting Coupeau be taken to the hospital after his accident, she insists on nursing him herself, depleting their savings, and spoiling him in the process, encouraging his laziness, putting up with his bad temper, and condoning his increasingly frequent drinking.

All Gervaise really wants of life is to work steadily, always have something to eat, have a decent place to live in and bring up her children, not be beaten, and die in her bed. Her failure to achieve any of these goals must, in the last analysis, be blamed not on her, but on her heredity and environment. She is, in every respect a victim. Conceived in a moment of drunkenness during one of those nights when her parents had been beating each other, she is from the outset the product and object of violence. Her congenital lameness is the 'hereditary reproduction,' as Zola puts it in his archaic physiological terminology, of her father's brutal treatment of her mother. From the age of eight on, she is put out to work. Constantly mistreated by Macquart, unprotected in any way, exposed to every sort of temptation, she becomes pregnant for the first time when she is fourteen. If she runs away with Lantier to Paris, it is only to get away from Macquart. The slums complete her undoing. When she meets Goujet, the one man who could have saved her, it is too late.

As her end approaches, she becomes increasingly repulsive – filthy, ugly, lazy, irascible, confused, drunken, altogether dotty. When she is forced by hunger to go out into the streets in the middle of winter to try to sell herself, no one will have her. Like her husband, who dies of delirium tremens, she frequently shakes all over, emitting little involuntary squeals. Her ape-like grimaces make urchins in the street throw cabbage-stumps at her. For months, she sinks lower and lower, doing dirty jobs for a few coppers, which she spends on liquor. One evening somebody bets that she will not eat something disgusting, but she does, to earn ten sous. Yet even now, the reader cannot help sympathizing with her quite as much as with the noblest tragic heroine – an Andromache, a Phaedra. This is something quite new in French literature. The Goncourts had thought that they were writing a working-class tragedy in *Germinie Lacerteux,* but their attempt was spoiled by their irrepressible aristocratic condescension towards their working-class heroine, Germinie, their tendency to depict this character, whom they had based on one of their housemaids, as a kind of animal. Intended to be tragic, Germinie is merely horribly heart-rending, like a run-over dog. Gervaise, despite her lowliness, is always fully human. Even at the end, when she has sunk as far as anyone could ever go, the reader cannot help sympathizing with her and sharing Goujet's inextinguishable love for her.

Zola expertly pumped his subject matter for all the pathos and humor it contained. *L'Assommoir* is the sort of book that constantly makes the reader laugh or cry. Despite its predominantly grim character, it has many hilariously funny passages – the account of Gervaise and Coupeau's wedding party, for example, including a trip to the Louvre, in chapter three, or those episodes involving Gervaise's sister-in-law, Madame Lerat, who reads dirty meanings into everything yet cannot abide 'rude words.' Zola's language itself is occasionally quite comical, as when, during a description of Gervaise's preparations for her feast-day party in chapter seven, he says that 'the soup was still snoring like a pot-bellied friar asleep in the sun.' He also, with

Homeric honesty and lack of prudishness, explores the whole realm of working-class sexuality, from the pure, self-effacing devotion of Goujet, to the utter lasciviousness of Nana and her fellow artificial flower makers.

One of the great novelties of the book is to be found in the language in which it is recounted. In writing *Madame Bovary,* Flaubert had faced the problem of how to incorporate the pedestrial, cliché-ridden speech of his bourgeois characters into his own prose without losing artistic unity. Zola, wrestling with an analogous problem in *L'Assommoir,* solved it beautifully by composing the whole text in the language of the common people it was about – exploiting all the rich, colorful vocabulary of this language, its slang, powerful, expressive rhythms, earthiness, concreteness, embedded folk wisdom, marvellously vivid metaphors. In the process, he purified it in the fire of his own genius, bringing out all its literary potentialities, much as Dante had with his native Tuscan.

At the same time, Zola gave full vent once again to his own astonishingly fecund poetic imagination. As in most of his earlier novels, there is nothing in the fictional world of *L'Assommoir* that could not actually have existed – no Spenser-like fairies or dragons; yet it is a world seen through the eye of a great poet. Not only is it a work of truth, like all great poetry. Dreamlike allegory and symbol lie in wait everywhere, much of it all the more effective, perhaps, for being unexpected like the Greek warriors hidden in the Trojan horse. The water from the dyeworks in the courtyard of Gervaise's tenement house on the Rue de la Goutte d'Or changes color to reflect the stages of her life, first pink, then blue, and finally black. In one of the novel's most poignant passages, a love-scene between Gervaise and Goujet, the dandelions in the sooty, city-enclosed field in which they meet – the closest they ever get to nature – are apotheosized into paradisaic flowers, symbols of the sun. The big iron rivets hammered out by Goujet on his blazing anvil acquire, for Gervaise, as she watches him admiringly, an unmistakably Freudian quality. Colombe's tavern is metaphorically transformed into an infernal church. The tenement house is metamorphosed into a vision of hell, complete with hellmouth (the large gaping entrance), Oceanus (the dyemaker's stream), and the chorus of the damned (the moans and groans of the tenants). The slaughterhouse and hospital that enclose the space of the novel stand for the violence, sickness, and death of the world in which Gervaise is imprisoned. Even Gervaise's trade takes on symbolic significance, for what could be more appropriate in this novel bent on airing the dirty laundry of society and concerned with the problem of sin and salvation than that its heroine should be a laundress?

Lantier, without ever ceasing to be a man, takes on the characteristics of a demon, the very embodiment of everything that Zola detested, especially ignorance, hypocrisy, falsehood, sloth, and the sexual and economic exploitation of women. Goujet, Lantier's exact opposite, is transformed, metaphorically, into a god. The ideal worker, he reincarnates the superhuman blacksmith of Zola's short story 'Le Forgeron.' He is Hercules, Vulcan. He also embodies another major recurrent figure of Zola's personal mythology, the redemptive lover; and as such he is given Christlike attributes and associated with cleanliness, whiteness, light, true love, self-sacrifice, even the sacramental bread and wine. Old Bazouge, needless to say, personifies Death. Gervaise, whatever else she may be, is, as modern criticism has shown, a modern incarnation of the pariahs, criminals, and cripples that, in ancient seasonal rites, were first treated royally, then killed as emissary victims.

As in Zola's earlier novels, things assume a sometimes frightening life. The steam engine of the big, crowded public laundry Gervaise visits in the first chapter snorts and puffs like a living monster. The windows of the tenement house stare down like real eyes. Colombe's still becomes a noxious beast with a poking, twisting snout and a belly round as that of a tinker's fat wife. Even shadows become alive – the shadows of the still, transformed into obscene shapes, figures with tails, monsters opening their jaws to devour the whole world, Gervaise's grotesque shadow looming and wheeling as she staggers past the street gaslights in her search for help in the final chapter. Reflecting Zola's materialism and determinism in general and, in particular, his emphasis on the baleful influence of the working-class environment, things are also invested with an irresistible power. Sometimes people and things completely change roles. Gervaise and her fellow washerwomen in chapter one are turned into mere puppets dominated by the routine of the mechanized

130

washhouse. In one of the pub scenes, Gervaise, unable to hear what the drinkers are bawling at each other, is amused by the sight of their mechanically waving their arms about, thrusting out their chins, their eyes popping out of their heads. In the final chapter, Coupeau, still shaking from the DTs for a moment even after he is dead, also becomes nothing but a mechanical doll.

On the one hand, it rejects the old, traditional religious solutions to the ills of society. In particular, it is, quite as much as any of his previous writings, not only anticlerical but anti-Christian. It scathingly depicts the indifference of mid-nineteenth-century Catholicism to the plight of the urban poor. It demonstrates how little Christian charity counts for in the modern world. As Gervaise wanders in search of help through the icy streets she encounters many fashionably dressed ladies and gentlemen, yet, 'not one single soul,' Zola remarks pointedly, 'guessed at her plight and slipped ten sous into her hand!' He contrasts the rising tide of luxury of Napoleon III's Paris, symbolized by the lofty brand-new buildings, with the desperation and squalid hovels of the slums. He points out among the advertisements stuck on an iron parapet which Gervaise passes a small one in a pretty blue offering a fifty-franc reward for a lost dog. What is more grave, he goes out of his way to attack the doctrine of Divine Providence. Gervaise's world is very definitely not one in which God has his eye on the sparrow or, as Psalm 146 has it, 'executes justice for the oppressed . . . gives food to the hungry . . . lifts up those who are bowed down . . . upholds the widow and the fatherless.' When, at Gervaise's feast-day party, Madame Lerat sings in her nasal voice what amounts to a loose paraphrase of the same psalm,

> The poor little waif, by her mother forsaken,
> Finds shelter at last in the house of the Lord,
> God sees all from heaven, and vengeance hath taken,
> The motherless child is the child of the Lord,

Gervaise cannot help bursting into tears. She feels she is the lost, abandoned waif whom God is going to defend. Yet the whole story of her life is there to prove that she is wrong, and Zola drives the point home in the final scenes when, during her final quest for help, she prays God not to let it snow and the snow starts falling, mercilessly stinging her on the face.

On the other hand, the novel suggests very discreetly some of the ways in which social improvements some day just might, in Zola's opinion, be attained. That is to say, it preaches in an eloquent yet wholly undidactic sort of way the saving grace of some of Zola's sacred values, above all nature, work, love, and the self-renewing and purifying power of life. Coupeau is almost cured from his sloth and alcoholism by an extended stay in the country. Gervaise is never happier than when she is busily washing or ironing away, and Goujet, the ideal worker, is the only character in the story exempt from the general degradation. Moreoever, Goujet's love for Gervaise, if it does not save her (any more than the young Zola's love saved the prostitute Berthe), comes very close to doing so, providing Gervaise with her happiest moments, and it does indeed save her son, Etienne, whom Coupeau takes on as his apprentice and protégé. The circle games played by Nana and her friends in the tenement house courtyard during Mama Coupeau's wake must probably be interpreted as a symbol of life's eternal renewal, the main philosophical theme of the entire *Rougon-Macquart* series. Throughout the whole novel, moreover, Zola is obviously serving the cause of social justice, another of his supreme values, by depicting so graphically and movingly the evil effects of its absence in Napoleon III's France.

The serialization of the novel had barely begun, on April 13, 1876, in *Le Bien public*, before people were already heatedly discussing it. What shocked the public above all was the crudeness of its language, but there were also objections to its extreme realism and what numerous readers regarded as its gross obscenity. Some disliked what they imagined to be its political bias. *Le Bien public*, a journal of the far republican left, discontinued printing it in early June, for political reasons, finding it insufficiently radical. The remaining chapters had to be printed elsewhere, in a little literary weekly, Catulle Mendès' *La République des Lettres*, not without harrassment by the public authorities.

Zola finished the manuscript towards the end of November. A slightly modified version, including the parts that had been omitted in *Le Bien public* and *La République des Lettres*, was brought out in book form by Charpentier at the end of January. The uproar now became thunderous, recalling the battles fought over

Hugo's *Hernani* in 1830.

A writer named Pontmartin characterized the novel as 'disgusting filth.' The respected critic and scholar, Edmond Scherer, a former Calvinist professor of theology in Geneva, contemptuously termed Zola 'the Balzac of the pot-house.' Others accused him of slandering the people, of treating it with 'Neronian contempt.'

Hugo himself, the Hugo of *Les Misérables,* joined in the chorus of blame. 'It is a bad book,' he told a friend. 'It shows, as if wantonly, the hideous sores of the privation and degradation to which the poor have been reduced . . . . I went into all that as a moralist, as a physician, but I am opposed to anyone's doing so in an uncaring way or merely out of idle curiosity.'

Other commentators praised the work. Anatole France defended its language, noting that it was impossible to render faithfully the thoughts or sensations of a human being without doing so in his or her own tongue. Mallarmé was wildly enthusiastic. 'Here's a truly great work,' he wrote Zola in a long laudatory letter, 'and worthy of an epoch in which truth has become the popular form of beauty!' As for Zola's fellow realists and naturalists, the older ones failed at least at first to come to his support. Champfleury was as shocked as anyone by its revolting subject matter. Edmond de Goncourt was jealous of the novel's success and expressed in his journal a suspicion that some of the things in it had been filched from him. Flaubert's first reaction was negative. He disliked the style, perceiving in it a kind of critical preciosity. Maupassant, Huysmans, and the other younger writers of the same general tradition, however, were exultant. They all agreed that (in Maupassant's words) it was 'truly beautiful and prodigiously powerful.'

The hubbub caused by *L'Assommoir* astonished everyone, including Zola himself. There were innumerable parodies, caricatures, songs, pamphlets, brochures. The public was buying it like hot cakes. It was the most widely read novel in Paris. Edition after edition rolled off the press: thirty-eight in 1877, twelve more in 1878. In less than five years, the total would surpass one hundred. Even the Parisian working people, whom it was said to libel, purchased over 40,000 copies of a cheap popular illustrated edition in the course of 1878 alone.

II

Ironically, *L'Assommoir*, this novel about the poor, made Zola a rich as well as famous man. It is true that for several years before it was published, his financial situation had already very much improved. Thanks to Turgenev, who had made the arrangement, he was now writing regularly for an influential Russian monthly, *Viestnik Evropy,* as well as *Le Sémaphore de Marseille* and, starting out in April, 1876, *Le Bien public,* a radical republican Parisian daily. After *La Faute de l'abbé Mouret,* Charpentier, who had become one of his dearest friends as well as editor, had torn up their original contract and replaced it with what that good man had been the first to admit was a more equitable one, stipulating a simple royalty of forty centimes per volume. By the early part of 1876, before the serial publication of *L'Assommoir,* Zola's income had grown to more than 25,000 francs a year. The proceeds from his contributions to the Russian review alone amounted some months to 800 francs.

As his prosperity grew, Zola had at last been able to indulge fully his taste for shellfish and other good food. He was putting on weight. Alexandrine and his mother were dressing better. In 1874, the three of them had moved to a modest, but comfortable three-storey house with a garden on the Rue Saint-Georges (now Rue des Apennins) – another step up in the world. They had furnished it in the romantic style, which, to be sure, was no longer in fashion, but which Zola clung to because it was the style he had associated with success in his impoverished youth. Instead of a charwoman for only a few hours a day, they had been able to afford first a live-in manservant, then a live-in couple. They had also been able to take long summer vacations for the first time in years, at Saint-Aubin, in 1876, and at Piriac, on the Bay of Biscay, in Brittany, the following year.

But now money was gushing in in a golden torrent. On April 21, 1877, they moved again, this time to an apartment on the Rue de Boulogne (now Rue Ballu). They furnished it in the same outmoded romantic style as their former dwelling, but much more sumptuously. Zola was now able more than ever to satisfy his passion for antiques and knick-knacks: mediaeval stained glass, a Henri II bed, Aubusson antiques, Italian and Dutch furniture, 1830 casseroles. Flaubert, always the old romantic, was in ecstasy. 'I've always dreamt of sleeping in a bed like that,' he exclaimed when he saw the bedroom. ' . . . It's the chamber of Saint Julian the Hospitaler!'

Then in May, 1878, Zola bought, for 9,000 francs, a little farmhouse at Médan, in the Seine valley, about twenty-five miles from Paris. Hidden in a nest of verdure, it was separated from the rest of the hamlet by a magnificent alley of trees and, on the other side, it looked down across railway tracks at the river. As he wrote Flaubert, there was not a single bourgeois in the whole vicinity. A few weeks later, the whole place was swarming with masons, painters, upholsterers, and they were never to leave. After they had finished working on the little house, Zola had them build a new one next to it costing ten times as much. An imposing tower, it contained on the top floor a spacious study, fifteen feet high and thirty square, with an immense antique carved-oak writing table, a great chair, and a colossal fireplace inscribed with the gold letters: 'Nulla dies sine linea.' There was also a great bay window fronting the river and, opposite, an alcove with a divan. The terrace overhead commanded a magnificent view of the whole surrounding countryside.

Like the apartment on the Rue de Boulogne, Médan was a realization of Zola's youthful fantasies, only more so. The whole interior was draped and furnished in the same romantic manner – Indian Buddhas, silk-upholstered modern chairs, Venetian chests, a vast profusion of gewgaws. With the passage of time, the estate, which he soon tended to regard as his principal abode, grew larger and larger. He kept on adding new structures, all imagined by himself. He bought up the surrounding fields, transforming them into a wooded park. He acquired a sizable island in the Seine opposite his property, named it Paradou, and embellished it with a small chalet. Indulging his love of plants and animals, he added gardens, a greenhouse, and a farm. The stables were made of marble and were traversed by a gallery of carved oak with a peep-hole through which he could peer down at his cows and horses and other beloved animals without disturbing them.

With his new acquired wealth, he was also able to entertain on the scale he had always aspired to. During the many months he spent at Médan every year, the guest pavilion was rarely empty. The friends of his youth, Cézanne, Solari, Roux, frequently came to visit him. Flaubert, Goncourt, Daudet, Charpentier, and the painter Guillemet, were always welcome. So were Zola's disciples, who now included, in addition to Alexis, Maupassant, who had met him through Flaubert, and three other young men: Henry Céard, who had introduced himself to Zola, Joris Huysmans, introduced by Céard, and Léon Hennique, introduced by Alexis.

III

It was a heady time. On April 16, 1877, at the Restaurant Trapp, these younger admirers together with another, Octave Mirbeau, held a banquet which amounted, in effect, to the official founding of the naturalist movement. They acclaimed Flaubert, Goncourt, and Zola as the three masters of modern literature. As Goncourt noted in his journal, it was 'an exceptionally gay, cordial dinner.' The menu consisted of Bovary soup, salmon-trout *à la fille Elisa,* chicken stuffed with truffles *à la Saint-Antoine,* artichokes *au coeur simple,* parfait *naturaliste,* Coupeau wines, and *Assommoir* liqueurs. All Paris was talking about it.

But Zola was not so foolish as to suppose that the campaign that he had been waging for so long to conquer the world, help shape the course of history, and capture enduring fame was over. The spectacular success of *L'Assommoir* encouraged him. His picture was prominently displayed in the front window of every book store. Henceforth, everything he did was news. He had won a great victory, but he realized that he needed more and ever greater ones if he was to achieve his true, infinitely ambitious goal. He also knew that if he was to profit from the position he had already gained, his first task was to consolidate it. So, instead of resting on his laurels, he fought on harder than ever.

He passionately defended *L'Assommoir* in the press, protesting among other things his respect for the common people and his devotion to the cause of social justice. He redoubled his efforts, moreover, to assure the triumph of naturalism. The word, which he never clearly defined, had by now accrued, in addition to its original scientific meaning, other, vaguer, philosophical and literary connotations. In the broadest sense, it now stood for all those theories and practices that he wanted the public to associate with his name and which he felt would assure the success of himself and his school. It meant, he asserted, truth in art, and, as such, went back to Plato and Aristotle. It was a method of capturing nature, humanity, the eternal ground of being, as it was, in its ever-changing forms. It meant applying science to art. It was positivism, respect for fact, mistrust of metaphysics and religion, the modern analytical method. But it was also the freedom of the artist to give vent to his individual temperament in the expression of the truths he had found. But what is truth? What is nature? What is the eternal ground of things? Could Zola and his disciples really claim that they had come closer to capturing reality than Racine or Hugo? Faced by such questions, Zola could only answer that 'naturalism' would 'end up with the meaning that we will give it.' Essentially, it was no more definable than 'romanticism.' When Flaubert, who knew how empty words could be, criticized him for going to what seemed to him such absurd lengths to assure the victory of naturalism, he replied, 'Yes, it's true that I'm no fonder than you are of the word "naturalism"; and yet I will go on repeating it ceaselessly, because things have to be baptized with a new name, if people are to think them new.'

In 1875 he had published only nine pieces, in 1876, forty-nine, mostly theatrical reviews. In 1877, he dashed off seventy articles, in 1878, sixty-nine, in 1879, one hundred. They were a strange and wonderful mixture of Joan of Arc and P. T. Barnum. Much of what they said reflected what he had thought for years – his most firmly held literary principles, his abiding literary loves and hates, his passion for truth, science, life, nature, humanity, progress, the nineteenth century. But, in the heat of battle, he used whatever ammunition came to hand. He said with passionate conviction things he had not really thought through. Profiting as much as ever from his command of the art of publicity, he shocked, goaded, provoked screams of pain as well as cheers – and also some raised eyebrows and disdainful grins. He knew that the literary world was a jungle in which the sons had to kill their fathers if they were to take their places; so he brutally lit into the romantics, especially Victor Hugo, the idol of his youth, but also the embodiment of romanticism and the one author, more than any other, whom he dreamt of succeeding. 'He has crossed this epoch without seeing it, his eyes fixed on his dreams .... He has never been anything but a rhetorician.' He made fun of Hugo's most recent poems, characterizing them as senile. He contrasted Hugo with Balzac, expiring 'stoned and crucified, as the messiah of the great school of naturalism.'

Not surprisingly, he also praised Flaubert, Goncourt, and Daudet, and had kind things to say of such 'descendants of Balzac' as Champfleury, Duranty, and Hector Malot. In a long article titled 'Les Romanciers contemporains,' he also (what had he to lose?) said exactly what he thought of the other best-known novelists of his day: Jules Sandeau, Octave Feuillet, Victor Cherbuliez, Louis Ulbach, Edmond About, Erckmann-Chatrian, Jules Verne, and all the rest. His judgements, delivered with compassionate irony, would all be ratified by posterity. The article created, however, a terrible uproar. Needless to say, it made him many new enemies, but it also won him some new admirers and solidly established him as one of France's leading literary critics.

He did not even hesitate to attack such luminaries as Renan, still one of the two or three most influential intellectual leaders of the age. He criticized Renan for having halted halfway between religion and science, neither a true believer nor a true scientist, but only a poet, like Lamartine. He turned up his nose at Renan's cloudy, romantic pantheism. He made fun of Renan's style, 'voluptuous as a caress and unctuous as a prayer,' the sentences 'genuflecting and swooning in a cloud of incense.' He poured scorn above all on Renan's attempts to reconcile science with idealism.

As for himself, he had by now gone beyond Taine's pseudo-positivism, to embrace the pure positivism and rigorous experimental method of the great physiologist Claude Bernard. Bernard had done more than even fellow scientists like Marcelin Berthelot and Pasteur to popularize the notion of experimental science. His *Introduction à l'étude de la médecine expérimentale,* published in 1865, had become a widely read classic – the *Discours de la méthode* of the nineteenth century. When Bernard died in Paris on February 10, 1878, he was accorded a public funeral – an honor never before bestowed by France on a man of science. At about the same time, Zola read a copy of the

Introduction loaned him by Henry Céard. In a long essay published the following year, 'Le Roman expérimental,' he identified naturalism with both Bernard's method and his underlying assumption that the only kind of knowledge available to man was scientific knowledge. He accepted Bernard's scientific determinism and his positivistic conviction that we shall never know ultimate causes, only the laws governing the succession of phenomena. He applied Bernard's distinction between observation and experimentation to what he and his fellow naturalists were doing in their pursuit of truth and even went so far as to assume that the results of the 'experiments' that he and his fellow naturalists conducted on their human guinea pigs had quite as much scientific value as those conducted by experimental scientists like Bernard. This is, of course, absurd, as Brunetière and a host of other earnest critics delightedly pointed out. Zola himself was never to repeat it again. But the furor it created had at least provided him with further publicity.

IV

While waging this newspaper campaign, he also went on with his creative writing. When Céard wrote him that Huysmans had put aside a half-finished novel, *Les Soeurs Vatard,* he worriedly replied:

> But tell him that he has to go on working. He is our white hope; he doesn't have the right to abandon his novel, when our whole group needs works. And you, what are you doing? I am well aware that you are publishing some of your older pieces; but that's not enough. You must write new ones – dramas, comedies, novels. In the next few years we must overwhelm the public with our prolificness.

He himself had never worked harder – or more productively. In 1875, he had written one of his best short stories, 'L'Inondation,' about a flood of the Durance that completely ruins a good man and his family. Between 1876 and 1880 he churned out fifteen more stories, including some very good ones and at least one more masterpiece: 'L'Attaque du moulin,' about the Franco-Prussian war. A three-act farce, *Le Bouton de rose,* put on at the Palais-Royal in the spring of 1878, flopped like all his previous plays, but the theatrical version of *L'Assommoir,* prepared under his direction by a previously unsuccessful minor playwright named William Busnach and produced at the Ambigu, was a smash hit. It lasted for two hundred and fifty-four performances, not counting those put on in the provinces, and, all in all, contributed considerably to the diffusion of naturalism.

The eighth *Rougon-Macquart* volume, *Une Page d'amour,* came out on April 20, 1878. Zola had composed it partly at L'Estaque, a fishing village on the outskirts of Marseille, where he had spent a five-month working holiday in 1877. Whereas the preceding novels in the series are primarily sociological or religious in theme, this work is first and foremost a psychological study. It is also, in contrast to what he had done so far, very sweet and tender. Set in Passy, an elegant Parisian suburb, it is about a good, pure-hearted woman, Hélène Grandjean (Ursule and Mouret the hatter's daughter) and her violent, but short-lived passion for Dr Henri Duberle, a respected, essentially decent married man. When the story begins, Hélène is a well-to-do young widow. She lives with her daughter, Jeanne, a sickly, neurotic child. Jeanne is jealously attached to her, and, to keep her happy, she devotes herself completely to her, seeing no one else except Abbé Jouve and his half-brother, M. Rambaud. Then one night Jeanne falls gravely ill. Since their regular doctor is away, Duberle, whom they have never met is prevailed upon to come in his place. Hélène and he are attracted to each other and before long they fall deeply in love. In a moment of weakness, they make love for the first and only time. Jeanne, tortured by the realization that she is no longer the sole object of her mother's affection, becomes, once again, gravely ill and dies soon afterwards. Crushed by grief and guilt, Hélène breaks off her relationship with Duberle and, two years later, marries M. Rambaud. By then, her love for Duberle has completely died. As the title implies, it was only a page in a book, a day in a lifetime.

Among the most remarkable features of the novel is the series of panoramic descriptions it contains of Paris, one at the end of each of the five parts. All in all, they are an amazing artistic feat. Through an exceptionally skilful use of simile and metaphor to evoke fleeting effects of light and shadow, they create a literary equivalent of the cityscapes that the Impressionists were doing at the same time. The bird's eye view concluding the opening chapter of a Paris first drowned in mist, then slowly emerging under a rosy-white springtime sun is one of the finest pages, artistically, that Zola had written. Not even Chateaubriand or Hugo, who were masters of this sort of thing, could have done better. Moreover, Paris is made to perform in these passages a very special function, not very different, as Zola himself pointed out in a preface, from that of a classical chorus: 'From my twentieth year I dreamt of writing a novel in which Paris, with its sea of roofs, would be one of the characters, something like the chorus in classical antiquity. I needed an intimate drama, three or four creatures in a small room and then the immense town on the horizon, always present, watching these creatures laugh and weep, with its eyes of stone.'

He was worried that the public might find the novel a bit tame after *L'Assommoir* and perhaps a bit too cozily domestic and goody-goody, despite the spice that he had naughtily injected here and there. The critics were for the most part pleased, however. One called it 'the work of a master': 'I sincerely admire this true and very poignant poem.' Another admired its 'penetrating beauty.' Some readers, it is true, found the descriptions of Paris and some of the medical details somewhat boring, but they welcomed the surprising 'purity' of the book with relief, and the sales, while not spectacular, were better than Zola had expected. Cézanne, for his part, was impressed by the controversial descriptions. So was Mallarmé. Among Zola's closest colleagues, Goncourt was jealous once again. Daudet, also jealous, said rather spitefully of the Rougon-Macquart family tree which Zola had had drawn up and published with the novel that if he had thought up such a thing he would immediately afterwards have flung himself from the highest branch. But Flaubert enjoyed the book:

Don't be afraid; I don't understand your doubts about its value. But I would not advise my daughter to read it, if I were a mother!!! Despite my advanced age, the novel troubled and *excited* me. I desired Hélène

enormously and I understand your doctor very well.
The two-fold scene of the rendez-vous is SUBLIME.

V

Then came *Nana*. With *Une Page d'amour,* Zola had softened the
public up for the next big blow, and when it arrived it was a
blockbuster. After a brief stop on the heights of Passy, he had
plunged once again into the infernal regions of the Second
Empire, leading his readers with him into a part of it that he had
briefly evoked in *La Curée* and *L'Assommoir* but never as yet
explored in its entirety: the demimonde, the world of imperial
gallantry, Offenbach, the cancan, masks, back-stage corridors,
race horses, and fast women – not the sentimental, consumptive
'grisettes' of the July Monarchy, but the 'biches,' or 'cocottes,'
that had dominated Parisian gossip sheets in Zola's youth:
Hortense Schneider, Blanche d'Antigny, La Païva, Cora Pearl,
and all the others, half-artist, half-prostitute, bejeweled, applauded, sometimes lethal, reigning like queens over their madly
jostling top-hatted, caped, and cane-holding admirers.

Nana is all of these glittering, hip-swaying temptresses – and,
if the truth were told, several of the 1870s too – all rolled into
one. From one point of view, the novel is her story, much as
Zola had envisaged it in his original notes for *Les Rougon-
Macquart:* 'The poignant drama of a woman destroyed by her
appetite for luxury and easy pleasures.' In *L'Assommoir,* he had
recounted her childhood and early adolescence. When this new
work begins, she has turned eighteen and already has had a baby.
She is introduced to the reader just at the moment that she is
making her debut at Les Variétés as Venus in a farcical comic
opera titled *La Vénus blonde.* Her voice is nasal, off-key, completely
untrained. She has no acting talent. When the audience laughs
at her, she starts laughing herself. But her good humor, street-
urchin airs and gestures, boundless energy, blond hair, blue eyes,
red lips, dimpled chin, flaming cheeks, and luscious figure with
its round shoulders, Amazonian breasts, and broad, powerful
hips – all fully visible under the most transparent of gauzes –
create a sensation. There is not a man in the house that does not
yearn to go to bed with her. Her career as a great courtesan is

launched, and in the following pages, Zola recounts it step by step in lurid detail: her venial liaison with a shady banker, Steiner; her unhappy love for a poor actor, Fontan, who lives off her earnings from prostitution, beats her, and finally abandons her; her subsequent spectacular rise to the zenith of her profession, leaving one ruined life after another in her wake, squandering the immense riches laid at her feet, insatiable, tranquilly audacious, giving no thought to the morrow, essentially good hearted, not consciously malicious, but stupid, lazy, always blaming others, never herself, self-pitying, mindlessly preparing her own destruction even as she zestfully causes that of the rich pleasure seekers surrounding her; and, finally, her equally spectacular downfall and death from smallpox in a sordid hotel room.

But the novel is not only the story of Nana and her rise and fall. In his preliminary outline, Zola had jotted down: 'The philosophical subject is this: a whole society racing after a piece of ass. A pack behind a bitch, who is not in heat and who doesn't care a bit about the hounds pursuing her. *The poem of male carnal appetite,* the giant lever that moves the world. That's all there is, just ass and religion.' The dramatis personae include, besides Nana, some other women, mostly prostitutes like her, procuresses, hangers on, or wives or mothers of Nana's victims. But most of the novel's hundred or so characters are men, whose literary function is to represent the male society of the Second Empire – and, whether Zola admitted it or not, of the moment he was writing, less than a decade after Sedan – in general. They are a varied lot, most notably: Steiner; Fontan; Bordenave, the fat, crass, cynical manager of Les Variétés; Vandeuvre, an elegant aristocrat, race-horse owner, member of the imperial court; La Faloise, an unintelligent, pedantic, fast-living young man who has come to Paris from the provinces to finish his education; Captain Hugon, who steals for Nana; Hugon's timid, awkward younger brother, Georges, who dresses up like a girl at her command and after she refuses to marry him commits suicide; Fauchery, a dissolute journalist and playwright who offers actresses publicity in return for their favors; Chouard, an old, debauched Marquis; Muffat de Beuville, Chouard's son-in-law, the Empress's chamberlain, a Napoleonic count, one of the most haughty, respected and, until he sees Nana, devout and upright men in Paris; Daguenet, one of Nana's pet lovers, whose marriage she helps arrange with Muffat's daughter, Estelle, and who returns to Nana's bed on his wedding night; even 'the Prince of Scotland,' who visits Nana in her dressing-room – not to forget Venot, a former lawyer, a religious bigot, churchwarden at La Madeleine, and friend of the Muffats, who helps hush up the scandal caused by their excesses and reconverts Muffat to Catholicism. All of them are interesting characters, but none more so than Muffat, who occupies almost as important a place in the novel as Nana and becomes in the end perhaps even more human and pitiable. Desperately struggling against his passion, torn between sex and religion, temperament-ally a mystic, he is, nevertheless, her abject slave, exhausting his vast fortune to help defray her limitless expenditures, putting up, sometimes reluctantly, sometimes gladly, with every sort of humiliation, swallowing her infidelities, even letting her kick, whip, or ride him as he goes on all fours like a bear, a horse, a dog, naked or attired in his official court uniform, sword, opera hat, short white breeches, red frock-coat embroidered with gold, and symbolic gilded key attached to the left skirt.

As was his want, Zola had gone to a great deal of trouble to achieve trueness to life. His unhappy experiment with Berthe had taught him much about common whores, but the private lives of the great actress-courtesans had remained for him largely a closed book. It had been necessary, therefore, in composing the novel, to rely heavily on what he had picked up from newspapers and books or learned from friends and acquaintances like his disciple Céard, Edmond Laporte (a friend of Flaubert and Maupassant), or Ludovic Halévy, one of the authors of the libretto for Offenbach's *La Belle Hélène*. Like the eighteenth-century realist, Restif de la Bretonne, he had gone out at night to observe prostitutes selling their wares. Accompanied by Halévy, he had also attended the premiere of an opera bouffe at the Variétés and been received by the leading lady, Anna Judic, in her dressing-room. After doffing his spectacles, he had closely examined it, plying her with questions about its powder-puffs, jars, brushes, and make-up applicators. As in most of the previous *Rougon-Macquart* novels, the characters, objects, and events in *Nana* largely reflect specific real-life prototypes. For example, Nana, while representative of actress-courtesans as a class, recalls Blanche d'Antigny and Hortense Schneider in particular. *La Vénus blonde* is Zola's pastiche of *La Belle Hélène*. Fontan is the actor Coquelin cadet, La Faloise, Antony Valabrègue. The Prince of Scotland is the future Edward VII, who, as is well known, had visited Hortense Schneider in her dressing-room while she was starring in *La Grande-Duchesse de Gérolstein*. Nana's splendid mansion, a present from Muffat, recalls the town house of another great courtesan, Valtesse de la Bigne.

In setting out to show the prostitute exactly as she was, brutally, realistically, Zola was doing somewhat the same thing that he had in *La Confession de Claude*. He still wanted to destroy what seemed to him to be the dangerous myths perpetuated by most of the best-selling earlier treatments of the subject – Prévost's *Manon Lescaut*, for example, or Hugo's *Marion de Lorme*.

But Nana, while remaining very much a woman and effectively destroying these earlier myths, assumes in her turn not only symbolic, but also, as Flaubert was the first to point out, mythic dimensions. On one level, the most general, she is woman, lust, sex, bestiality, the omnipotence of the flesh incarnate. As the very structure of the novel, whose plot mirrors *La Vénus blonde*, emphasizes, Nana and Venus are one. On another level, she embodies the Second Empire, which, as Zola points out in *L'Assommoir*, Napoleon III had turned into a giant bordello. Her history and that of the Empire both recall an imperial fireworks display, the giant rockets exploding in immense, bright, breath-taking showers, then fading away as their embers streak down towards extinction in the night. Her rise to fame occurs during the same year as the final apotheosis of the Empire, in the Paris Exhibition of 1867. Nor is it just coincidental that she is born at the same time as the Empire, in 1852, and dies precisely at that moment when the ailing Empire's own agony, the Franco-Prussian war, commences. The silence of her deserted death chamber is broken by shouts rising from the boulevard outside: 'To Berlin! To Berlin! To Berlin!' Her decomposing face is the face of the Empire at Sedan:

a charnel-house, a heap of humor and blood, a shovelful of corrupt flesh cast down there, on the pillow. The whole face was covered with pustules . . . One eye, the left one, had

145

completely sunk in the boiling purulence; the other, half open, was going under, like a black, decayed hole. The nose still suppurated. An entire reddish scab dangled from one of the cheeks, invading the mouth, stretched in an abominable laugh. And on this horrible and grotesque mask concealing the abyss, the hair, the beautiful hair, kept its sunlike flame, streaming down in golden waves.

But on another level, Nana is a retributive force of nature, Gervaise's vengeance, the vengeance wreaked quite unconsciously by the slums upon the rich and powerful who have allowed them to develop – or, as Fauchery, the novel's fictional journalist, puts it, a fly, 'a sun-colored fly that has risen from the dung, a fly that sucks in death on the carrion left to rot on the roadside and then, buzzing, dancing, glittering like a precious stone, flies in through the windows of palaces and poisons the people inside merely by alighting on them.'

On still another level Nana embodies not so much the Venus of the old myths as the degraded, sullied Venus of *La Vénus blonde*. She symbolizes the soulless exploitation of women as sexual objects, which, so many years before, fresh from his adolescent readings of Michelet's *La Femme* and *L'Amour,* Zola had blamed for everything that was wrong with society and dreamt of combating. Not surprisingly, the novel strikes, for the first time in the series, an apocalyptic note. The disasters it recounts prefigure the destruction of the evil world over which she has reigned. Astride Muffat's back as he lurches about on all fours (a scene inspired by a similar one in Otway's *Venice Preserved*), Nana is the Red Whore of Babylon sitting on the scarlet beast which is full of blasphemous names.

Like *L'Assommoir, Nana* provoked a tremendous uproar. Even before the serial publication began, in *Le Voltaire* of October 16, 1879, the public, its curiosity aroused by articles and posters announcing the event, was discussing it excitedly. Then, after the first few instalments had come out, the din increased. All those many critics and writers who could not abide Zola's subject matter, aesthetic theories, and art furiously attacked the novel without even waiting to find out how it ended. Employing the same terms they had used for *L'Assommoir,* they called it a 'sewer,' 'a cesspool,' 'a quadruped novel.' They accused Zola of being a Peeping Tom. They compared him to the Marquis de Sade. Here and there, however, there were shouts of praise. One reviewer was impressed by its apocalyptic qualities. Another lauded its portrayals of Paris 'whose form one must admire even when one finds the subject annoying or irritating.'

Despite the thick skin Zola had developed over the years, he was a bit taken aback by the ferocity of many of the tirades. He knew the reasons for it. A good deal of jealousy was involved, not to mention the hatred provoked by the polemical articles he had been turning out in his campaign to support naturalism. Louis Ulbach, one of the novel's most acerbic critics, was among those authors whom he had pitilessly torn apart in 'Les Romanciers contemporains.' But that did not make any of this abuse any easier to take. He relished, however, all the publicity. As always, he defended himself, in the process expertly pouring fuel on the flames. Meanwhile, in the snowy fastness of Médan, he was rushing to finish the final installment in time for it to appear as scheduled, on February 5, 1880. (Somehow he also managed, in the midst of all this, to write, out of friendship for Flaubert, an excellent article on *L'Éducation sentimentale*, prompted by the new edition marking its tenth anniversary.)

When *Nana* came out in book form, on February 14, the barrage of criticism, which had died down for a while, resumed, more strident than before. The scandal caused by *Nana* was turning out to be even worse than the one provoked by *L'Assommoir*. Most if not all of the fashionable, right-thinking critics of Paris competed to see who could demolish Zola completely. More than one, posing as an authority on the demimonde, delighted in pointing out little factual errors or sins against verisimilitude. But the public loved the novel. The first edition, consisting of 55,000 copies – a very large number in those days, was gobbled up in no time at all. Before the year was over, ninety editions had been sold out. By the following fall, the number had already surpassed one hundred. Once more there was a flood of caricatures by André Gill and other cartoonists. Part of the book's immense appeal lay in precisely those qualities which a great part of the vast public shared with Zola and instinctively perceived reflected in it. It was not the work of a saint. It was rooted in Zola's own erotic dreams. The writing of many passages had violently excited him. He was clearly just as vulnerable to Nana's beauty as any other male, but he was also a predominantly good, even puritanical, man. The reformer in him was as alive as ever. One could see on nearly every page that he was repelled by his subject quite as much as he was drawn by it, that the novel was first and foremost a long cry of pain and indignation at the evils it portrayed – the 'cry of a decent man disgusted,' as one sympathetic critic put it, 'by the sight of human degradation and the gradual collapse of all those proud things society is built on.' *Nana* showed the ugliness as well as the appeal of vice. It proclaimed quite as fervently as any religious tract that the wages of sin are death. At the same time, it expressed Zola's lingering hatred of the Second Empire, his hostility to Catholicism, his loathing of the aristocracy – still other traits widespread among Zola's contemporaries.

Once again Goncourt, as jealous as ever, played down Zola's achievement. He turned up his nose at those characteristics which *Nana* had in common with other serialized novels. He privately accused Zola of stealing again from his works and expressed the opinion that Zola's genius was assimilative, not, like his own and his brother's, creative. But most of Zola's other closest literary friends were as enthusiastic or at least supportive as they had been with his best earlier works. Huysmans, who had himself written a novel about a prostitute, wrote: 'I am emerging from *Nana* in a state of utter amazement. Confound it! . . . A beautiful book, a new book, absolutely new in your series and in what has been written on the subject up till now.' Flaubert was equally ecstatic: 'I spent all yesterday until eleven thirty at night reading *Nana*. I could not go to sleep all night, and I am still in a state of stupor . . . . The characters are marvellously true . . . . At the end, the death of Nana is Michelangelesque!' The same day, he wrote Charpentier: 'What a book! . . . Our good Zola is a man of genius . . . . '

VI

He was world famous. He was rich. But was he happy? He could not really say that he was. Nothing in his manner had changed very much from what it had been before. His fat face, now embellished by a mustache and short beard, still wore the pained, anxious expression that it had assumed in his childhood. There were, of course moments of exultation. Yet there were even more dark and painful ones. In 1875, Alexandrine had been gravely ill and since then frequently ailing, nervous, and depressed. He too was having health problems, no less painful for being largely psychosomatic. Towards the end of 1875, the nervous disorders he had suffered from since the age of twenty had suddenly grown much more severe. He was plagued by colics. He was obliged to urinate frequently – a necessity that made train travel difficult, since there were as yet no toilets in railroad cars. In late January, 1880, once the manuscript of *Nana* was completed, he had been so exhausted that he had had to take to his bed for three days, tortured, as he wrote Céard, by 'abominable nervous aches.' On February 1, at a dinner hosted by Turgenev, he showed up with a cane, suffering from severe pains in the thigh, which he suspected were sciatic.

Sometimes he wondered if he would ever have the strength to finish the *Rougon-Macquart* series, which, he had by now decided, would consist of twenty volumes. His marriage with Alexandrine was sexually a failure. She was no longer able to give him the physical love he longed for. They remained close friends, but sexual intercourse with her had become little more than a duty to be performed perfunctorily every ten days. 'Imagine a sick man, tossing in bed from one side to another without managing to find a comfortable position,' he remarked to a German admirer. 'Well, that sick man is humanity in wedlock.'

Moreover, the relationship between Alexandrine and his mother had soured. There had always been some tension, but now it never seemed to cease. Independent by temperament, gay, emotional, his mother found it hard to put up with the younger woman's goodhearted, but authoritarian ways. After all that she had been through, she was tired of fighting. Instead of facing down her daughter-in-law, she became more and more retiring. Alexandrine, for her part, resented the way, now that she and Zola were rich, members of the Aubert family were constantly pestering them for loans, which, of course, were never repaid. When she tried to put a stop to it, the two women almost had a falling out. In the end, Émilie, more determined than ever to live just as she wanted to, had left them, moving into a small apartment on the Rue de Boulogne, not far from her son's Paris dwelling.

He was too busy to give much thought to the grave philosophical and religious problems that had always troubled him. He admitted in his polemical essays that his and his fellow naturalists' ultimate objective was to find God through their scientific analyses of the world. (How he reconciled this aim with his new, purer positivism, he could not have explained.) As before, he inveighed against metaphysics and religion. 'I can understand why practicing Catholics dislike us,' he wrote in April, 1879; 'for we are trying to chop down their beliefs.' He still had his sacred values; but his optimism, his utopian reveries, while by no means dead, were less insistent. He was more than ever convinced that to win out in life it was enough to be strong. He exalted the religion of force. In his more positivistic moods he advised his naturalistic followers to adopt evolutionism as their philosophy if they had to have one. At other times, he was troubled, as he had been during certain periods in the past, with melancholia. In his short stories as well as novels, the cruelty of nature and fate and the horrors of life in general were a constant theme.

Now that he was approaching forty, his old obsession with death had grown stronger. Via the hero of one of the best short stories of the period, 'La Mort d'Olivier Bécaille,' he eloquently expressed his old dread of being buried alive, swallowed up in a black void. He became more consciously aware than he had been before that his supreme motive for writing was to vanquish death, to achieve a kind of immortality, perhaps the only kind that he could ever have. 'Good God! Where would we get the courage to go on working,' he exclaimed in *Le Voltaire* of September 25, 1878,

> if the lowliest of us did not harbor the dream of living on throughout the centuries? That is the only thing that gives us the strength to go on. Perhaps we are wrong, but it is glorious to fool oneself in this way, and the worst misfortune that can befall us is to think, after having written a page: 'here's a page I shall survive.'

Alexandrine's father, Edmond-Jacques Meley, died on September 13, 1877. Zola's dear old friend Duranty died on April 9,

1880. Then on May 8, four days after Zola had moved into his new house in Médan, a telegram arrived from Maupassant bearing the two words: 'Flaubert dead.' The next day Zola wrote Céard: 'I am crazed with grief.... Ah, my friend, it would be better for us all to pass away! To get it over with once and for all! Decidedly, there is nothing but grief, and nothing makes life worth living.' That autumn there came another terrible blow. On October 17, his mother died in Médan of a heart ailment complicated by dropsy. When the moment came to transfer the heavy coffin, borne by ten men from the house to the village church, he wept uncontrollably. At the beginning of the funeral service, he collapsed on to the prie-dieu and remained there prostrate until the service was over. Alexandrine and he accompanied the coffin to Aix, where a crowd met them at the station. Once again, he had to endure, as he wrote Céard, 'the frightful pain of a religious ceremony,' after which his mother's body was placed beside his father's in their vault.

[5]

Full Summer

'As for myself,' he wrote Mme Charpentier, on October 30, 1880, less than two weeks after his mother's funeral, 'I shall try to drown myself in work.' He knew that the pain of bereavement would pass, but this was small comfort. The thought that his mother and he would never see each other again, that she had gone for ever, tortured him.

As the months went by, he remained profoundly troubled. Goncourt, observing him in December, described him as 'more unhappy . . . more disconsolate . . . more gloomy than the most disinherited student who has failed to qualify for a profession.' The Italian critic, Edmondo de Amicis, who called on him three months later, was struck by his extreme lassitude. His nerves were tauter than ever. He considered himself a sick man, despite his usual good health. The realization that he was no longer young continued to torment him. He now had a small bald spot, like a monk's tonsure. He had to wrestle with atrocious self-doubt. He could never summon the courage to reread his books, for fear of finding unexpected blunders. Each morning, as he sat down at his work table, he was afraid that his creative powers would fail him. He wanted to give up his series, forget it, go away, become a recluse in some remote spot, and undertake some work which would enable him to retire from the everyday battle and which he would never be able to finish, a colossal history of French literature, for example.

His awareness of life's sadness, the universality of pain, continued to haunt him. So did the spectre of death, sometimes strangely attractive, but usually too horrible to contemplate. He had always been somewhat superstitious. Had he not divided

152

L'Assommoir, his novel on misfortune par excellence, into thirteen chapters? Now, with more desperation than ever, he would often at night reopen and close his eyes seven times to prove to himself that he was not going to die. He was afraid that if he did, the world would expire with him. He and his wife, who shared his necrophobia, kept a light burning all night in their bedroom. Sometimes, troubled by the thought of death, he would suddenly leap out from under the covers and stand quaking beside the bed in a state of indescribable terror. In October, 1882, he had a nervous breakdown, with chills and nausea, and had to take to his bed for several days and be dosed with morphine.

His physical and psychological suffering was aggravated by the spiritual and intellectual anarchy reigning within him. During these first years of his forties, he was also going through another major metaphysical and religious crisis. It was quite as grave as the one he had undergone in his early twenties after reading Montaigne. He went on characterizing himself as a confirmed positivist, but positivism, with its rejection of all but scientific truth, was less than ever capable of satisfying his spiritual needs, heightened as they were now by the multiple bereavements of 1880. His thought, groping for solutions, reached far beyond it. The old, never-ending inner struggle within him between faith and doubt, hope and despair, had become, once again, almost unbearably violent. His mother's death had, as he put it, 'ripped a hole in the nihilism of his religious convictions.' He longed for the comfort of religion. Despite his skepticism, he had not always been able during the first flush of grief to repress the childish prayers rising spontaneously to his lips.

When he was caught up in conversation or engaged in his literary campaign, which he stubbornly went on waging until the fall of 1881 (when he gave up journalism altogether), he would become very dogmatic, militant, even sacerdotal. The would-be prophet in him momentarily dominated the cautious skeptic and the pessimist. His optimistic faith in science, progress, humanity, work, and life reasserted itself. On January 17, 1881, he proclaimed in *Le Figaro*: 'My credo is that naturalism, I mean the return to nature, the scientific spirit extended into all our realms of knowledge, is the very agent of the nineteenth century.' Five months later, in the same newspaper, he asked rhetorically,

'Why not have faith in life, in humanity?' and went on to
formulate another, more expansive creed:

> People reproach us for our lack of faith. I would like to stand
> up and in a loud, firm voice make my confession of faith. I
> believe in my century, with all my modern sensibility. Only
> those who have faith are strong. Whoever, in politics and
> literature, does not have faith in his time falls into error and
> impotence . . . . I believe in science, because it is the tool of
> the century, because it is bringing us the only solid for-
> mula . . . . Only science can save humanity. I believe in
> today and I believe in tomorrow, certain of an ever vaster
> enlargement, having committed myself with all my heart to
> the forces of life.

But when the conversation ended or the pen had fallen from
his hand, he would sink back into black doubt and despair, and
his obsession with death and the nothingness of everything would
return.

Since January, 1880, when a translation of some extracts from
Schopenhauer's writings had come out in France, this German
thinker's philosophy had had a profound impact on the thought
of many French avant-garde intellectuals. It was at once darkly
pessimistic and, for many, strangely comforting. Among Zola's
disciples, Céard and Huysmans, as well as Maupassant, were
studying Schopenhauer and frequently spoke highly of him.
There was much in his thought that repelled Zola, much also
that struck a responsive chord.

II

During this time of physical exhaustion and spiritual crisis, hard
work was Zola's only solace, as he had known it would be. He
had originally planned to write, after *Nana*, a novel with only a
few characters, little description, and a severely simple, almost
classic style. It was to revolve, he confided to a journalist in
April, 1880, about the ideas of suffering and goodness. It would
have as its central figure Pauline Quenu, the daughter of the

well-to-do pork butcher in *Le Ventre de Paris*. Towards the middle of 1880, he started planning it. It tended from the outset to be highly autobiographical. After his mother died, he included the death of a mother among the major episodes. But then he put the whole project aside. The subject had grown too painful. He could not summon the courage to go on.

Instead, he wrote *Pot-Bouille*, a dryly satirical novel on the theme of middle-class licentiousness, a companion piece to *L'Assommoir*. Whereas *L'Assommoir* features a large working-class tenement house reeking with poverty and vice, this book focuses on a new, luxurious middle-class dwelling, very respectable-looking on the outside, but a den of iniquity inside. One of the tenants is a Rougon-Macquart family member Octave Mouret, the elder son of François Mouret. Octave, a darkly handsome, ambitious young man with the morals of an alley cat, has come up to Paris and found a job in Au Bonheur des Dames, a draper's shop. It is managed by the daughter of one of the owners, a widow named Caroline Hédouin. Towards the end, Octave marries her purely out of self-interest. (In his heart of hearts, he still thinks of her as Madame Hédouin.) However, the novel is concerned not only with Octave's sordid story but also with the equally sordid daily lives of all the house's various other tenants, the Vabres, Duvreyiers, and Josserands among others, including their foul-mouthed servants. It lays bare in clinical detail the depravity hidden under their hypocritically virtuous exteriors – the shameful intrigues, gossip, dodges, sexual encounters.

Above all, it concentrates on the theme of the immoral use of sex for pleasure and profit. In one memorable scene, Adèle, one of the much-courted maids in the apartment house, is graphically shown solitarily giving birth to an illegitimate child in her room and then abandoning it in the Passage Choiseul. In other scenes, the reader is treated to disillusioned views of the inner workings of the nineteenth-century French middle-class marriage market. It is evident that, if the plebeian girls of Zola's time were propelled by their upbringing and environment into a life of prostitution, the daughters of the bourgeoisie were pushed by theirs into a life of adultery. To those members of the middle class of Zola's day who smugly regarded themselves as the champions of honor, morality, and the family, the book responded: 'That is not true. Here! Look at yourselves as you really are. You are actually even more immoral than the common people.'

The apartment house with its showy, sculpted exterior and sinister, garbage-strewn courtyard, assumes symbolic value, but, other than this, evidence of Zola's poetic imagination is little in evidence. The text consists mostly of rapid, racy summary and dialogue. The descriptions are all very short. The various stories are expertly interwoven, yet not as well perhaps as they might have been, for there is something almost too mechanical about the novel's structure. The demonstration of the central thesis proceeds too neatly. Real life is more complex, more ambiguous. Moreover, the compassion tacitly expressed in *L'Assommoir* is conspicuously absent. In portraying the working class, Zola had shown the good as well as the bad. In *Pot-Bouille*, he was obsessed almost solely with the evil side of his subject. All the details are based on reality; yet the novel lacks that intense, impartial truthfulness that he had achieved in *L'Assommoir* and more than one of his other works. Still, if not a great novel, *Pot-Bouille* is better than most. Once begun, it is hard to put down. It marvellously satisfies the universal human craving for something to be indignant about. The characters are well drawn. More than one is unforgettable.

Its reception was what one might have expected. The critics, indignant bourgeois all, generally damned it, using much the same terminology as they had for *L'Assommoir* and *Nana*. The public, mostly from the same class, this time seemed to agree. The sales were modest, nothing like those of *L'Assommoir* and *Nana*. Even Zola's friends and disciples, while supportive, had reservations.

III

The next novel, *Au Bonheur des Dames*, came out on March 2, 1883. It has a fascinating historical theme: the rise of modern big business in France during the Second Empire, at the expense, of course, of many small traditional merchants. The hero is again Octave Mouret. Following his marriage with Madame Hédouin, he has greatly expanded their draper's shop. His ambition is to rival the Bon Marché and the other huge department stores that had been built up during the same epoch. After his wife's accidental death, he continues to prosper. His employees, some of them former competitors whom he has ruined, come to number many hundreds. By the end of the novel, he has fully realized his dreams of commercial grandeur.

The book is chiefly given over to portraying, along with the conflict between Octave and his unfortunate competitors, the life of a great, thriving department store. As always, Zola was concerned with achieving the maximum amount of realism. He visited two big Parisian department stores, Le Bon Marché and Le Louvre, took notes, consulted with various authorities, including the architect Frantz Jourdain, a pioneer designer of this sort of establishment. But the painter and poet, as well as the sociologist, in Zola was entranced by his subject. The book is full of colorful, wonderfully animated descriptions – a view of construction on a new addition going on feverishly at night in the glare of giant electric arc lamps, for example, or a big, fantastic white sale to celebrate the opening of this new addition. The store is envisioned as a cathedral of one of the many new religions competing to fill the void left by the decline of Christianity – the religion of materialism, of salvation through consumption, of the commercial glorification (and exploitation) of woman. At the same time, it is transformed metaphorically into a giant beast, a vast living organism, gorged with gold.

The love interest is supplied chiefly by the story of Octave's relationship with one of his employees, a pretty, ambitious, talented young girl from the provinces, Denise Baudu. In the end, after resisting his advances for some time, she agrees to marry him. This is, as Zola was perfectly aware, a variation on the story of Pygmalion and Galatea. He even referred to it in his notes as 'the struggle with Pygmalion.' 'Decidedly,' he commented in his preliminary plot outline, 'the whole story resides in this twofold movement: Octave making his fortune from women, exploiting women, speculating on their coquettishness, and at the end, when he triumphs, finding himself conquered by a woman, a woman who has not schemed to do so, but who does so purely with her femininity.'

'What I want to do in *Au Bonheur des Dames,* Zola had also jotted down in his notes, 'is write the poem of modern activity. Hence, a complete shift of philosophy: no more pessimism, first of all. Don't conclude with the stupidity and sadness of life. Instead, conclude with its continual labor, the power and gaiety that comes from its productivity. In a word, go along with the century, express the century, which is a century of action and conquest, of effort in every direction.' The novel conforms with these objectives. Despite the social imperfections and heart-rending financial disasters recounted in it – the bankruptcies of the small neighborhood merchants, including Denise's uncle, put out of business by Octave – the dominant tone, in contrast to that of the earlier *Rougon-Macquart* volumes, is exuberantly positive and optimistic. *Au Bonheur des Dames* is first and foremost a hymn to modern business, a lyrical affirmation of the joy of existence, a glorification of the entrepreneurial spirit, a salute to the victors in the struggle for survival, a social Darwinistic tract.

He finished it towards the end of January, 1883. He was vastly relieved. Writing it had been a terrible tour de force. Not long after starting it, he had lost interest in it. Then, in October, 1882, he had had his nervous breakdown. After he had recovered sufficiently to take up his writing again, he had had to summon all his resolve to continue where he had left off. 'How heavy is the pen!' he had exclaimed. ' . . . I have become such a coward that the prospect of having to finish my book terrifies me.' Published in volume form on March 2, 1883, it was fairly well received by most critics but sold even more poorly than *Pot-Bouille*. Dining on April 20 with Goncourt, Daudet, Huysmans, and Céard, he observed sadly but resignedly: 'Our big sales are all over.'

IV

The subject of *La Joie de vivre*, his next novel, on which he had already started working, was, however, hardly the sort that makes for best sellers. It was the same project that he had begun, then cast aside, before writing *Pot Bouille:* the novel on the themes of suffering and goodness.

Towards the end of July, Alexandrine and he left for an extended holiday in Bénodet, a tiny, isolated Breton village near the bleak, wild coast of Finistère, near Quimper. While they were there, the news came first of Turgenev's death, then of

Manet's. Two more blows. He kept on working. There was something compulsive about his new book. And enormously difficult. It was his way of trying to resolve the new spiritual and emotional crisis that he had been going through during the past few years. In first planning it, then writing it, he was engaged in one long act of introspection, externalizing his own inner intellectual and spiritual turmoil, examining his feelings and ideas, exorcizing his personal demons, trying to get his values straight. Of course, he was also, as usual, doing his best to impart general significance to what he was recounting, to make it a social as well as a personal document, to prove and if possible heal the wounds of society as well as his own.

What made it so difficult was not only the extreme painfulness of the subject but also the instability, contradictions, and ambiguities in his own thought. As he composed it he was obsessed with the question: is life worth living? He could not come up with any single, certain, unequivocal answer, only wildly clashing ones. First one set of attitudes would prevail, then another. He had much more trouble planning it than he had his earlier novels, repeatedly revising the plot, changing the setting, altering the action, adding or subtracting characters. He had difficulty deciding which of the two central characters, Pauline Quenu and Lazare Chanteau, would assume the leading role. First it was to be Pauline. Then it was to be Lazare. Then, in the final version, it was Pauline again. His growing familiarity with Schopenhauer's philosophy, to which Huysmans and Céard had introduced him, also led him to make major changes. The ideas that he ascribed to Pauline and Lazare, especially the latter, took on a Schopenhauerian coloration. He made Lazare into a fervent disciple of Schopenhauer. At the same time, he added to the novel's functions that of commenting on Schopenhauer's thought as he and many of his fellow French intellectuals (very imperfectly, one must admit) understood it. In particular, he wanted to express his reactions to Schopenhauer's affirmations regarding the evilness and pointlessness of existence and the ideal of universal suicide.

The story takes place in Bonneville, a small, grim, remote Norman fishermen's village slowly crumbling into the sea. The village is, as Zola remarked in his notes, 'the abominable world in miniature.' Five of its families, the Houtelards, Prouanes,

Cuches, Gonins, and Tourmals, symbolically resume all the major sins – including covetousness, lust, anger, gluttony, envy and sloth – and all the principal ills besetting humanity such as hunger, ignorance, poverty, natural disasters, disease, and death. After the demise of her parents, Pauline, then sixteen, arrives in this community to live with her guardian, Chanteau, her father's cousin, and his family. It is not long before the Chanteaus begin to take advantage of her. As the years pass, they eat up most of the 185,000 francs she has inherited. When she falls in love with their son, Lazare, her second cousin, Mme Chanteau encourages it as long as Pauline's fortune remains intact. But after Pauline is nearly ruined by the failure of one of Lazare's madly speculative industrial enterprises, in which most of her small fortune had been invested, the good woman's affection for her turns to hatred. Her engagement to Lazare is broken off, and with his mother's blessing he marries another girl, Louise Thibaudier, the daughter of a rich Caen banker.

Lazare is a naturalistic version of Goethe's Werther, Chateaubriand's René, and Flaubert's Frédéric Moreau rolled into one: an intelligent, sensitive, but extremely neurotic, pessimistic, bored, proud, selfish, unstable, and ineffectual young man. He represents, furthermore, certain traits that Zola had observed in some of his contemporaries, especially in the younger generation. He is keenly aware of modern culture, willing to go along with and exploit science, conversant with the experimental method. He has a fairly good knowledge of modern literature. Yet he tends to deny everything and succumbs to despair, partly out of narrow-mindedness and impotence, but also partly out of bewilderment and discouragement caused by the inability of science, still only in its infancy, to fulfill the great expectations he has placed in it. He turns to Schopenhauer for solace. 'Romanticism created the despairing melancholic,' Zola wrote in his preliminary sketch of Lazare. 'Naturalism creates the skeptic who believes in the nullity of all things and denies progress.' But at the same time, Lazare is another of Zola's own fictional avatars. He not only reflects the neurotic, superstitious, pessimistic, intellectually troubled side of Zola. He is also a projection of one of Zola's nightmarish self-images – the flawed, ineffectual, abortive genius that Zola in his frequent moments of self-doubt and despair feared he might be.

The character of Pauline was largely determined by the overall dynamics of the *Rougon-Macquart* series. Having originally planned to write the novel just after *Nana*, Zola had wanted it to be as different from *Nana* as possible. Pauline, born the same year as Nana, 1852, is her exact opposite. Instead of giving herself to everyone, she is devoted to only one man, Lazare. She is intelligent, dutiful, selfless, charitable, self-disciplined, and virtuous in every other way. Whereas Nana degrades and destroys all that she touches, Pauline makes everything better. There is, as Zola himself put it in his notes, something 'hieratic' about her, even though she is not at all religious. She gives alms to the poor. When Madame Chanteau, now bitterly hostile, is dying, she tenderly cares for her. Despite her love for Lazare, or, more precisely, because of it, she encourages him to marry Louise for his own good. She helps deliver their sickly infant, Paul, and agrees to become his godmother. With the consent of his helpless parents, now estranged, she takes charge of the infant, gradually turning him into the picture of health. She ultimately sacrifices everything for those she loves – and is perfectly happy. Several of these traits also contrast, needless to say, with Lazare's. So also do her robust constitution, common sense, pragmatism, never-failing courage, and ever-resurgent optimism. She possesses, above all, a marvellous capacity to see life as it is, with all its horrors, and still love it passionately. But like Lazare, she also represents Zola himself as he was, or at least, wanted to be.

Among the secondary characters of the novel, old Chanteau, Lazare's father, the retired lumber merchant, also corresponds, in a way, to Zola's personal ideal. A hopeless cripple, relentlessly tortured by his gout, often crying out in pain, Chanteau, too, passionately loves life. When the news comes, in the final chapter, that the family maid, Véronique, has hung herself, he exclaims in a voice shaking with indignation, 'How stupid one has to be to commit suicide!' And with these words the novel ends.

In none of the works of fiction that he had written so far is Zola's capacity to create fully round, complex characters when he wanted to more in evidence. The same may be said of his gift for psychological analysis. Lazare's pessimism, including his fear of death, is convincingly motivated and dissected. So also is the all-too-human psychology of the mother, with her gradually crumbling conscience. Pauline, at first sight, may seem almost too good to be true – a figment of the hagiographic imagination. Yet on closer inspection, she also turns out to be profoundly and convincingly human.

La Joie de vivre is, moreover, the most philosophical, autobiographical, and confessional of the first eleven *Rougon-Macquart* novels. It is also more difficult to interpret on the intellectual and spiritual levels than any of them, except perhaps *La Faute de l'abbé Mouret*. The majority of its early commentators saw it as a frightfully sad work, despite its undoubtedly ironic title (literally translated, *The Joy of Living*). Some of the most intelligent regard it as a reflection not only of Zola's personal pessimism, but also of the troubled, gloomy mood that characterized French thought in general at the moment they were writing. 'This strange book,' wrote the journalist Edouard Drumont,

> which may seem so indelicate and contrary to traditional
> notions of what a work of art should be, is, nevertheless, a
> singularly powerful work . . . . The idea of expressing
> pallid, leaden, dismal things is in the air . . . . Zola, with his
> frankness, has described this spleen . . . . He has held up to
> modern man a mirror in which he can see himself. That is
> why the book will endure.

On the other hand, some recent critics have tended to regard the title as not at all ironic, contrary to what the older critics assumed. Studying the novel in the context of Zola's life and his preparatory working notes and other writings, they have been inclined to interpret it as an affirmation that it is possible to be happy, no matter how painful or evil life may be. Or, impressed by the up-beat ending, they have regarded the novel as an expression of Zola's belief in life. But one may also, if one wishes, construe it as an essentially ambiguous work, a work mirroring a still unresolved inner intellectual and spiritual conflict on Zola's part, a work at once desperately sad and full of hope, dark and bright like a storm cloud viewed at the same time from different angles.

V

La Joie de vivre is, in its own curious fashion, a great book, perhaps even, as one respected contemporary critic has suggested, a masterpiece. But its appeal has always been limited to a small public. Zola, taking cognizance in the spring of 1884 of how slowly the first edition was selling after it had appeared in the bookstores that March, had good reason to wonder whether he would ever again write a work that would have anything like the spectacular worldwide success of *L'Assommoir* and *Nana*. Moreover, it would be foolish to presume that he had already achieved his highest goal, of joining the immortals, of being admitted to the blessed company of those great authors whose achievements would endure for ever.

It was at this moment that he finished planning and started writing a new study of the working class which would be not only one of his most profitable novels, but also one of the greatest and most powerful novels of all time: *Germinal*.

The idea of including a second working-class novel in his series went back to the years immediately following the Commune, but until fairly recently his conception of it had been vague, tentative, and, in some respects, very different from what he had ended up with. All he had known for sure, was that, if his portrait of the working class was to be complete, he would have to depict, in addition to the aspects examined in *L'Assommoir*, the political and social side of working-class life. A number of fictional works about coal miners, including a novel entitled *Scènes de l'Enfer social* by a friend of his, Yves Guyot, had brought coal mines and coal miners to his attention. More than one of these works also involved strikes. By the middle of January, 1884, he had definitely decided that his new novel would recount a strike in the coal mines.

The subject fascinated him. It was timely, a matter of growing national concern. Since 1877, France had turned more progressive. The exiled Communards had returned. The socialist party had been formed in 1879. The national elections of 1881 had been a victory for the left. Violent confrontations between capital and labor were multiplying. Like most other thoughtful Frenchmen, he had become increasingly aware of the emergence of the new industrial proletariat as a separate class and of the rise of socialist militancy. He commiserated with the economically oppressed. He shared their hatred of the evils of the socio-economic system and their longing for social justice. Morover, he recognized as well as anyone else the historic magnitude and importance of the social questions involved. Indeed, he foresaw that the labor problem would be the most important problem of the twentieth century. Like many of his middle-class contemporaries, he even tended to view the vast social changes that would inevitably result from economic class warfare in apocalyptic terms (although, unlike many of them, he wanted to think, at least in his more optimistic moods, that these changes would be beneficial).

At the same time, the artist, the poet, and the would-be prophet in him were deeply stirred. The subject was just right, in short, for a writer with his particular talents and aspirations. It was colorful, dramatic, epical. There could be descriptions of the strange, black world of the coal mines. There could be crowd scenes, mine disasters. He could easily inject elements of romance, of fantasy, everything that he and his public liked. He could also serve his sacred values, fight for the things he believed in, truth, justice, work, progress, France, the nineteenth century, and all the rest.

On February 10, he had begun drawing up a first, very general and tentative plot outline based on his growing, but still second-hand knowledge of coal regions and the big strikes that had taken place in French coal mines since the last years of the Second Empire. Then, on the 19th, another major conflict, involving 12,000 miners, broke out at Anzin, near Valenciennes, in northern France. Four days later, he rushed up to the scene of action. During his summer vacation in Brittany in 1883, he had, as luck would have it, established a friendly relationship with Alfred Giard, a Lille professor who also happened to be a left-wing Deputy from the constituency of Valenciennes. Posing as Giard's secretary, he had been able to attend strike meetings in Anzin, visit miners' dwellings and cafés, question miners and their wives, form an idea of their mores, interview Émile Basly, one of their leaders, and inspect from close up the miners' behavior during the strike. He had also managed, during the little more than a week he stayed in the region, to familiarize himself with actual mines. Accompanied by an engineer, he had, despite his fear of the dark and of being buried alive, descended into the bottom of one of them, the Fosse Renard.

Armed with the hundreds of fresh, precise observations he had brought back with him to Paris, he resumed his outlining of the novel. His memory, as always, retained everything. He worked rapidly and expertly. His art of composition had, by now, fully matured. As usual, he divided his voluminous preparatory notes into separate folders: one for his successive rough drafts of the plot, another for brief profiles of the characters, another for his chapter plans, others for his reading notes, newspaper clippings, possible titles, and other documents.

If one could have observed him in the midst of this process, it might have seemed, at least to someone imbued with a romantic conception of how great artists create, disconcertingly methodical, even mechanical. He had begun, as always, with a paragraph summarizing the new novel in a few words: ' . . . the rise of the working class, the shove given society, which cracks for a moment: in a word, the conflict between capital and labor.' Then he had very logically deduced from this how he could best represent capital and labor within the limited dramatic frame of the novel. The main characters would stand for capital or labor as a whole. The secondary characters would stand for all the main varieties of bourgeois and workers, the scab, the firebrand, the labor leader, and so on. He almost invariably put first things first, proceeding from what was most central to what was less central in the plot. He carefully defined the chief principles that would govern his development of his characters. (For example, he specified to himself that he must make his bourgeois characters as human as possible. He also wanted to bring out the various degrees to which they were aware of, or indifferent to, the suffering of the miners and the injustices of the economic system.) He decided that one of his paramount artistic aims would be to achieve extreme relief through the use of violent contrasts. Another would be to frighten his bourgeois readers as much as possible.

The sociologist in him was determined to make the work into a complete social study of the proletariat and include an equally thorough portrait of a typical mining community. The physiologist wanted his way. The geologist – the Zola who had once, long ago, tried to found a new secular religion on geology – was set on taking the reader on a tour of a big mine. The skilled professional novelist in full command of his craft was bent on putting together a story that would fully exploit the dramatic and epic possibilities of the subject. Although very little that Zola jotted down in his notes would lead one to think so, the less conscious, more driven part of him, the imaginative poet, dreamer, reformer, would-be prophet, was very much involved too. Each of these different, frequently clashing Zolas wanted to accomplish his own peculiar objectives completely, without compromise, and the planning process went on until this was done.

Despite all Zola's efforts to act as logically as possible and to retain conscious command of this process, his subconscious played an increasingly important role, ultimately taking it over. He had the impression that an invisible hand was guiding his hand. 'As for me, I try to work as calmly as possible. But I no longer try to understand what I am doing,' he wrote Huysmans on May 20, from Médan, 'for the older I get, the more convinced I am that we have absolutely no control over what goes on in our works in gestation.'

He had deliberately written the first line on his birthday, April 2. It was appropriate that his novels – these, he would like to think, immortal incarnations of himself, his 'flesh and blood,' as he had repeatedly said – should be born on the same date as he. It was especially proper in the case of this novel, whose very title, reminiscent of spring and the month of Germinal on the Revolutionary calendar, evoked the leap of the old world into yet another April. (This image, suggested by the title, which he had at first rejected as too poetic, was among those that haunted him as he wrote, partially illuminating the higher meanings that the novel was assuming largely, it would seem, of its own accord.)

The serial publication began on November 26, in *Le Gil Blas*. He was still far from finished. On December 1, he wrote Goncourt from Médan: 'I am here in complete solitude and full of doubts about this cursed book which is giving me so much trouble.' He added that he thought he still had about six weeks of hard work ahead of him. Actually, he did not finish it until January 23, 1885.

The events recounted in the novel begin in early March, 1866. The setting is Montsou, a fictional northern French coal mining community based on Anzin. The leader of the strike and hero of the chief romantic subplot is Etienne Lantier, Gervaise's son and Nana's half-brother. The story also largely centers on a typical miner's family, the Maheus. Their daughter Catherine is at first torn between Etienne and another miner, a brutal fellow named Chaval. For a time, she is Chaval's mistress, but, in the dénouement, ends up briefly, before she dies, in Etienne's arms. But the real hero is a collective one, the Montsou miners themselves and the whole proletariat, which they represent.

The novel is marvellously constructed. From the overture-like opening chapter, in which the reader is introduced to Montsou along with Etienne as he strikes through the icy, stormy pre-dawn darkness in search of work, on to the enormous catastrophes recounted in the final chapters, the suspense builds up. One is swept along as if in the grips of a mighty current. The text is divided into seven parts, each consisting of from five to seven chapters. The first three parts are primarily devoted to familiarizing the reader with the coal country setting and portraying the life of the miners; but more and more the reader's attention is focused on the events leading up to the strike. Part IV has to do with its commencement and the admirable self-discipline and restraint that characterize the strikers during the first few weeks. Part V recounts the outbreak of violence provoked by their increasingly intense suffering, Part VI, the brutal repression of the strike by the Army, and Part VII, the anarchist Souvarine's deliberate flooding of the immense Le Voreux mine just as the strikers are about to capitulate. The novel concludes with scenes relating the agony of the miners trapped at the bottom, the heroic but almost completely ineffectual rescue efforts, the grim resumption of work, and Etienne's departure for Paris, where he plans to continue the battle for social justice.

Each part is distinct from all the others, like a panel of a giant fresco. One of the chief artistic peculiarities of the book is its painterly use of color, reminiscent in some ways of Cézanne's and anticipating the Expressionists. The novelist's palette, except for the ending with its vernal tones, is largely restricted to blacks, reds, and whites. Each of the seven parts has its distinctive color scheme. So do most of the chapters. In the first half of the novel, black dominates, in the second half, red. Most of the action takes place at night or in the inky depths of the mine. Numerous scenes are illuminated by reddish flames. As a rampaging mob of marchers thunders across the snowy plain in Part V, the last crimson rays of a setting sun turn the plain 'blood-red'; the road seems 'awash with blood' as the men and the women, 'besplattered as butchers in a slaughter-house,' keep coming on.

In none of his other writings, moreover, does Zola make more effective use of rhythmic repetition, Wagnerian leitmotivs, or techniques anticipating the modern film. The major scenes of the novel – the scenes of the marching mob just mentioned, for example, or the collapse of the flooded mine's surface structures in Part VII – are all extraordinarily cinematic in character. As in the cinema, the illusion of being face to face with reality with nothing in between is at times overpowering. Once again, as in one after another of Zola's earlier novels, it is only upon reflection that one realizes to what an enormous extent the apparently real world of the novel has been transformed by a powerful imagination. (The effect is somewhat like that of waking from an intensely realistic dream which, in retrospect, seems in many ways curiously misshapen.)

More than one of the secondary characters has violently exaggerated physical traits, like La Mouquette, one of the ore-carters, with her Gargantuan buttocks mockingly bared to the bourgeois spectators in the marching-crowd scenes. Human characters assume animal characteristics and, through metaphor, turn into beasts, plants, or things. Over and over again the plodding or stampeding miners are compared to herds of cattle. A boy has the features of a monkey. The enormous breasts of Maheu's wife, La Maheude, hang 'free and bare, like the udder of a huge cow.' An old miner becomes 'an old tree twisted by the wind and the rain.' An old woman, her breast torn open by a soldier's bullet, falls forward 'cracking like dry firewood.' The dead Chaval becomes a boss of coal. Animals, on the other hand, possess human traits. The blind mine horse Bataille, 'the old philosopher,' condemned to end his days in the black depths of the earth, wistfully dreams of sunlight and green fields. For Trompette, his companion horse, he is a tender, loving friend. Even so-called 'inanimate' objects are invested with an intense life. In the kaleidoscopic metaphorical universe of the novel, Le Voreux mine is 'an unknown, glutted, and crouching god to whom 10,000 starving people fed their flesh.' It is also a frightening marine monster, a living labyrinth, and, towards the end, a gigantic womb. As the superstructure of Le Voreux goes down into the abyss, the mine engine, 'torn from its stationary base, its limbs outspread,' struggles 'against death': it moves, stretches 'its connecting rod, its giant knee, as though to rise,' and then it dies, 'shattered and engulfed.'

As in most of the earlier *Rougon-Macquart* volumes, archetypes and modern historical forms coalesce to form a reality at once universal and particular, ephemeral and timeless. *Germinal,* like *L'Assommoir,* like so many other great modern novels (Balzac's *Le Père Goriot,* for instance, or Proust's *A la Recherche du temps perdu*) is, whatever else it may be, a variation on the ancient epic theme of the descent into hell. As in *L'Assommoir,* there is a persistent use of infernal imagery reminiscent of traditional Christian or Greco-Roman conceptions of hell. The opening chapter, with its black gloomy night, wailing, buffeting winds, and sea imagery, is a variation of verses 25-33 of Canto V of Dante's *Inferno:*

> Now I began to hear the doleful notes.
> I had at last come to the place
> Where a great lamentation beat against me.
> I had come to a place where light was mute,
> A place that bellows like a stormy sea
> When it is battled by contrary winds.
> This storm of Hell which never is at rest
> Drives forward all the spirits in its fury,
> Beating, overturning, molesting them.

The miners are repeatedly referred to as 'shades.' Like the looming gate of Gervaise's tenement house, the pit head of Le Voreux is transformed metaphorically into a hellmouth. A nearby burning mine stinks 'of the devil's foul kitchen'.

As Zola wrote *Germinal,* he was, moreover, haunted by Greco-Roman myths of the Creation, the War of the Gods, and the origin of man: the primordial cosmic struggles between Uranus and Cronus, Cronus and Zeus, the story of Deucalion and Pyrrha. Repeatedly, one encounters allusions to personages or places figuring in these ancient myths, or parallels with them: not

169

only Hades and Tartarus, but also Gaea, Cronus, Titans, Furies, Oceanus, the Vale of Enna, the golden age, and so on. Enraged women break into a 'stampede of furies.' Le Voreux is not only the voracious god capital, a hellmouth; it is also Cronus devouring his children. Mme Henebeau, the mine director's barren and unfaithful wife, is a wintry Ceres, the pit engine sinking into the abyss, a Titan. That burning mine, Tartaret, is Tartarus, that profound void where Uranus thrust his fearful children the Hecatonchires and Cyclopes, released by Zeus at the advice of their mother, the earth-mother Gaea, to take part in his war against Cronus. The inundation of Le Voreux recalls the classical as well as the Christian flood. Etienne's vision, with which the novel ends, of a new generation of strikers pushing up through the earth, like wheat, recalls mankind growing up from the stones that Deucalion and Pyrrha cast over their shoulders after the flood at Zeus's command.

Like most of the preceding *Rougon-Macquart* novels, *Germinal* is a fascinating mix of contrasting fictional modes and genres. Whereas the proletarian characters are largely endowed with, one might almost say, an expressionistic quality, the bourgeois characters are portrayed in a much more realistic manner. The part of the novel centered on the Hennebeaus and Hennebeau's nephew, the mining engineer Paul Négrel, a banal story of adultery, is, in style as well as content, predominantly realistic. The romantic subplot involving Catherine, Chaval, and Etienne partakes both of the melodrama and the Greek idyll. The main story, the story of the strike, however, derives from tragedy and the epic. Once again, as in *L'Assommoir*, working-class characters provide us with the modern equivalents of the noble heroes of Shakespeare, Euripides, or Homer. Even scenes that a century before *Germinal* was written would have been considered proper only for low farce – such as miners on a holiday drinking and dancing in a tavern – assume a tragic quality. Above all, *Germinal* is an epic. Not only is the principal theme, economic class warfare – a theme of vital interest to a whole people, a whole civilization – about as epical as any subject can be; so also is the setting: the vast, treeless plane, the underworld of the mines. So also are the metaphorical theme of a descent into hell, the crowd scenes, the heavy, insistent rhythms of the miners' picks or the mob's shouts for bread, the exaggerations, the repeated epithets, the sharp contrasts, the metaphorical mingling of gods and men, the very banality of the images, rooted in the common poetry of the French language – the extended metaphor of the Unknown God, the hell, storm, and seed metaphors.

Just as in most of Zola's earlier novels, furthermore, the realistic characters, objects, and events that constitute the fictional world of *Germinal* invite symbolic interpretation. As Zola himself put it, in a letter to Céard commenting on his fiction in general, but on *Germinal* in particular:

> We all lie more or less .... Now I may be wrong, but I think that I lie in the direction of truth. I have an abnormal attachment to true detail, a leap into the stars from the springboard of exact observation. Truth soars with a single stroke of the wing all the way up to symbol.

But it is just as difficult to determine with any certainty what the symbolic meanings and underlying world view of this novel are as it is those of any of Zola's earlier works. Once again, the would-be explicator is faced by the same sort of difficulties that are inevitably encountered in the interpretation of dreams or oracles. Not even Rimbaud, Mallarmé, or Lautréamont, among Zola's contemporaries, presents a greater challenge in this respect. Nor do any of Zola's other novels, including *La Faute de l'abbé Mouret* and *La Joie de vivre*. The truth is that *Germinal*, shaped, as it was, just as much by his subconscious as by his conscious mind, is constructed in such a manner that it is perfectly possible to read into it any number of different overall visions of reality or messages, some of them violently contradictory. It has an almost miraculous capacity to mean almost anything the reader wants it to.

Those pessimists who would like to perceive in it a vision of reality more or less confirming their own will find much in it that not only tolerates, but would even appear to encourage, even demand, such an interpretation. Even the glorious prophetic vision ascribed to Etienne on the final page – of the springtime sun rising, wheat burgeoning, the sound of seeds spreading in a great kiss, a new avenging army growing up through the soil – presents in this respect no great problem. For it may quite logically be argued that if Zola chose to conclude the novel in this way, he did so only because the very brightness of this dream, which, he intimates elsewhere in the novel, is nothing but a dream, serves to bring out through contrast the darkness of the reality of the miners' defeat.

Those, on the other hand, who hold more optimistic views of man, nature,and history will have little trouble in discovering in this same great novel strong reflections of these views. Romantic humanitarians can read it as a romantic humanitarian tract, anarchists as an anarchistic tract, Marxists, as a Marxist tract. Those familiar with Zola's youthful proposal for a new religion based on geology may, if they wish, regard it as a tardy recapitulation of the catastrophic, pantheistic, progressive, vision of reality inherent in this religion. Still others may see it as primarily an expression of one or another of Zola's other favorite cults: the predisposition of the optimistic dreamer and reformer in him to trust in nature, love, work, truth, science and the forces of life.

Read in the context of Zola's naturalistic theories, *Germinal* may appear to be an illustration of them. An anthropologist, on the other hand, may be struck above all by the evidence it contains of a much more primitive mentality. He may be impressed by the degree to which it would seem to reflect an apocalyptic vision of history or, if not that, something approximating primitive myths of eternal return. It is even possible to interpret the novel ritualistically, that is, to discern in the various stages which the colliers in general, and Etienne, their leader, in particular undergo reflections of the various stages of primitive fecundity and initiation rites and liberating exploits.

Still others may, as in the case of *La Joie de vivre*, for example, see in this extraordinary, almost limitless ambiguity still another symptomatic expression of Zola's own inner hesitations, incoherences, and contradictions, rooted in the intellectual and spiritual chaos of his time. It is somehow right that the *Divine Comedy,* the supreme poetic product of a great age of faith, should reflect in its underlying philosophical ideas the relatively strong spiritual and intellectual harmony of that age. It is, no doubt, also somehow right that *Germinal*, this superb prose epic about a world in the full throes of transformation, should project a poetic vision of reality reflecting the spiritual and intellectual chaos engendered by this process.

When the novel came out in book form, a few days after the

last installment of the serialized version had appeared in *Le Gil Blas,* on February 25, 1885, it was greeted with intense interest. Most of the conservative critics predictably accused Zola of having portrayed his subject in too somber colors or of having made factual errors (charges that, for the most part, he successfully rebutted). Brunetière was disdainfully silent, persuaded that lower-class characters like Catherine Maheu were hardly worth writing about, since they were not sufficiently complex. One reviewer claimed that Zola dirtied everything he touched. Another called the novel powerful and well-constructed, but badly written – 'in short, not very interesting.' But the great majority of critics admired the novel despite whatever reservations they might have, and more than one recognized it as the supreme masterpiece that it was. Some were impressed by its socialistic thrust and by its humanitarianism. 'His true glory,' wrote one commentator, 'will always come from his having heaved the most terrible cry of distress that humanity has ever heard.' Many more were impressed by its artistic, imaginative, poetic qualities. Considering the characters, one critic exclaimed: 'What prodigious relief he has given them! With what an intense life, in all its violent reality, he has made them live!' Jules Lemaître greeted the novel as a great epic, comparing it in some respects to Homer. Several were struck in particular by its Shakespearean, Dantesque, and Hugolian qualities. One made analogies with Delacroix. A large number, including Lemaître, were moved by what they considered to be its terrible pessimism – a pessimism which Lemaître defined in terms compatible with the fashionable Schopenhauerianism and von Hartmannism of the day: 'Men appear, like waves, on a sea of shadows and unconsciousness.' Gustave Geffroy, a reviewer for *La Justice,* hailed 'the poet that one generally refuses to see, the pantheistic poet with a superb gift for augmenting and idealizing things.' One commentator after another dwelt on the book's extraordinary artistic power. Few would have disagreed with the remark made by one of them: 'Monsieur Zola is a force.'

Huysmans and Maupassant wrote Zola enthusiastically praising the novel. For Huysmans, it was 'a damned good book.' Maupassant thought it the most powerful of all Zola's novels. Goncourt was livid with jealousy. Hearing that Zola had remarked apropos *Germinal* that his role had been 'to restore man

173

to his rightful place in creation,' the older writer exploded: 'He is becoming, upon my word, mad with pride.'

VI

On May 22nd, that same year, Hugo, whose once extraordinarily robust health had long been failing, finally died. By far the most revered Frenchman of his time, he was given a state funeral worthy of a Roman emperor. On the night of the 31st, all Paris kept vigil around his coffin lying under the Arc de Triomphe. The next day, two million Frenchmen followed the hearse from the Étoile to the Panthéon, now restored to its position as the resting place of France's greatest men. Although Zola had ferociously attacked Hugo's ideas in his campaigns for naturalism, he had never questioned Hugo's poetic genius. He sent the master's grandson, Georges Hugo, a note of condolence, assuring him that in his bereavement all hearts were broken along with his. To Goncourt, he remarked of the dead hero: 'I thought that he would bury us all. Yes, I really thought so!' Goncourt, recording the words in his journal, went on to report with what was now his usual malevolence: 'After saying this, he paced across the studio as if he was relieved by his death and as if he expected to inherit the papacy of letters.'

He had by now already started writing his next novel, *L'Oeuvre*. It had become his custom, after completing a major work involving a great deal of arduous research and study, to undertake something less demanding in this respect, and *L'Oeuvre* was no exception. Its theme was the world of art and letters. More specifically, he wanted to bring back to life in it the Parisian art world he had known so well during his youth and young manhood, just when modern art was being born: the Café Guerbois, Bennecourt, the studios, the salons, his friendships, Cézanne, Manet, Solari. But that was not all. 'With Claude Lantier,' he had jotted down that April, concerning the novel's hero,

> I want to portray the artist's struggle with nature, the creative effort that goes into a work of art, an effort of blood and tears to give one's flesh, create life: always battling with truth, and

always defeated, the struggle with the angel. In short, I will recount my own personal life of production, this perpetual, painful act of giving birth.

The plot in its final form had largely grown out of his attempt to reconcile these various historical, biographical, and psychological objectives.

As his pen scratched away, his heart overflowed with emotion. 'I'm recounting all my youth,' he wrote a Dutch critic and admirer, Van Santen Kolff. 'And I am putting all my friends in it; I am putting myself in it.'

He finished the novel on February 23, 1886. It was serialized in *Le Gil Blas* and came out in book form early that spring. The story focuses primarily on Claude: his relations with Christine Hallegrain, his model and mistress; his artistic and literary friendships, mostly with the novelist Sandoz and other former schoolmates from Plassans; the revolutionary artistic theories that they have hammered out together; his early artistic failures; his self-doubts and discouragement; his sickly short-lived son, little Jacques; and, above all, his heroic, but futile – and ultimately tragic – efforts during the last years of his life to create a masterpiece.

Conceived of on an immense scale, Claude's impossibly ambitious project starts out as an attempt to express not only the soul of Paris, but also the whole of nature, the whole of reality, through a realistic portrayal of the city as viewed downstream from the Pont des Saints-Pères. But, years later, it ends up as a gigantic picture of a woman – a fantastic symbolic creation, the idol, made of metals, marble, and gems, of an unknown religion, her thighs, the gilded columns of a tabernacle, her belly, a star, her sex, a mystic crimson rose. Christine (now Claude's wife) pleads with him to give up the whole insane undertaking, which has become, in effect, her rival. Yet he stubbornly keeps on working on it year after year, sacrificing to it everything including his small inheritance from a benefactor in Plassans, his peace of mind, his marriage, the happiness of those who depend on him. He is hard on Jacques. He neglects Christine, turning her into a mere servant. His sanity, always fragile due to his inherited flaws, finally shatters. One morning, overcome by despair, he hangs himself in front of the still unfinished work.

Christine, not long after discovering his body, dies of a congestion of the brain.

L'Oeuvre is a curious novel. Those readers who expect it to conform to Zola's naturalistic doctrines or faithfully mirror the French art and literary worlds of the late 1860s and 1870s will be disappointed. While superficially realistic in style, it is anything but a reliable documentary study of the mid-nineteenth-century French art world. Although Zola had known this world better than almost any other writer, he wrote with total disregard for many facts. Unfortunately, he seems not to have understood the theories of Chevreul regarding the nature of color and light. Nor did he appear to have grasped what for Cézanne and his other painter friends constituted the soul, or inner logic, of painting: the logic imposed by the colors and the painter's peculiar optics. Moreover, the novel is only partially and imperfectly a *roman à clef*. Claude, for example, is not a veiled portrait of Cézanne, as many critics have assumed. While largely composed of traits borrowed from Manet and other painters and from Zola himself, as well as Cézanne, he remains in the last analysis a creature of fiction. Zola's commingling in Claude's canvases of features reminiscent of both Cézanne and Manet (who could not abide Cézanne's works and refused to be shown together with him) is hard, furthermore, for art historians to stomach.

Yet even many of those readers who have been disappointed or even revolted by the novel in these or other respects have, nevertheless, found it fascinating. There is always the hope that a careful reading will turn up clues leading to a better knowledge and understanding of the historical figures, places, and events it imperfectly reflects. Separating what is true from what is merely fiction in it has always been for many readers an absorbing game. Anyone who has struggled to create a work of art cannot help but sympathize with Claude, Sandoz, and many of the other artists or writers included in the novel. In *L'Oeuvre*, Zola remains a powerful storyteller. For example, the account of the public's derisive reaction to Claude's first major painting, reminiscent of Manet's *Déjeuner sur l'herbe*, is tremendously exciting. The deep emotion with which Zola wrote the story comes through. It is impossible not to share it.

Moreover, those readers interested in Zola himself will always find *L'Oeuvre* an intriguing novel because of its extensive autobiographical and confessional elements. In none of his previous works, not even *La Confession de Claude* or *La Joie de vivre*, had he portrayed himself more completely in fictional guise. Although his main preoccupation in this respect had been, for the first time, to depict himself primarily as an artist and friend of artists, he had not been able to resist the temptation to put much else in besides. Much of his youth is evoked, barely fictionalized – the College Bourbon, his bucolic excursions with Cézanne and Baille, *La Genèse, Les Contes à Ninon,* his youthful dreams and struggles. His artistic evolution, some of his major artistic and philosophical contradictions, and his ideas at the time he wrote the novel are there too. Not only does he put much of himself into Claude; he also projects himself into the fictional world of the novel through Sandoz (whom he repeatedly refers to as 'I' or 'me' in his preliminary notes). He gives Sandoz his own horror of death and longing for immortal fame, his cults of science and work, his positivism, his Darwinism, and his literary naturalism. He ascribes to him his mood of world destruction and renewal, his awareness that he and his fellow artists were living in a time of transition, and his sporadic, all too fragile optimism about the future of society. He attributes to him his realization, born of his failure to complete *La Genèse,* that it is impossible to depict the whole of nature directly in a single work of art, that this can be done only indirectly, though some well chosen frame.

He also endows Sandoz with some of those old quasi-religious ideas to which he had again turned for comfort and strength as he continued to recover from the depression of his late thirties and early forties: most notably, his old mystical, pantheistic cult of nature and life. Sandoz's vision of reality is the same one that had come to him, Zola, in the summer of 1868, on a hidden, deserted little island in the Seine off Gloton. Just as he had then, Sandoz lies on his back in the grass, arms outspread, trying to enter the earth and drawing, like Antaeus, on its power. Sandoz's prayer is Zola's own prayer:

> Ah! Good Earth, take me, thou who art our common mother, the unique source of life! Thou who art eternal, immortal, in whom circulates the soul of the world, that sap which extends even to the rocks and which makes of the trees our immobile

brothers! . . . Yes, I would lose myself in thee. It's thou I feel there, under my limbs, embracing and inflaming me. It is thou alone who wilt be in my work like unto the first force, the means and the end, the immense ark where all things draw their life from the breath of all beings!

Perhaps the most curious aspects of the book, however, are those having to do with its symbolism and the relationship between its symbolism and its realism. The equation that Zola had made in his preliminary notes between the Biblical story of Jacob's struggle with the Angel and his own artistic struggle with nature was not a merely passing figure. In Zola's youth, one of the most talked about paintings in Paris had been, for a moment, Delacroix's fresco on this theme in the church of Saint-Sulpice. Zola had already, in *La Confession de Claude,* identified himself with Jacob. In one of his best youthful essays, he had, moreover, compared the futile, yet heroic, efforts of Pascal and the other great French moralists to capture truth to the same story. Jacob was, in short, one of Zola's major heroes. *L'Oeuvre* is just as much a variation on the theme of Jacob and the Angel as *La Curée* is on the theme of Phaedra, or *La Faute de l'abbé Mouret* on the theme of Adam and Eve.

Claude, this new Claude of Zola's, takes the place of Jacob, just as the first had done. Nature is substituted for the Angel. Like Jacob, Claude Lantier is not a weak man, but a strong man whom God is testing. Like Jacob, Claude wants too much, attempts the impossible. Both try to bend their divine opponents to their will, force them to divulge their secrets. As in *La Confession de Claude,* the Angel's laming of Jacob is echoed in the fictional hero's name itself. As in that novel, too, even the timing of the Biblical tale, so important symbolically, is reflected in the story; for just as Jacob's and the first Claude's struggles end at dawn, so does Claude Lantier's. Significantly, it is just at the crack of dawn, while the day is still striving to disengage itself from night, that he dies.

But the analogy with the Biblical story does not end there. If Claude Lantier is Jacob before his defeat, Sandoz is Jacob after his defeat. That is to say, he is the Jacob whose name has been changed by the victorious Angel to Israel, the Jacob purified and cleansed by his mystical ordeal. The old Jacob loves God, but he loves himself too and tries to bend God to his will. The new Jacob, having been vanquished by God, has become thereby God's meek instrument and thus fit to play his divinely ordained role as the progenitor of the people of Israel. Similarly, Claude Lantier's arrogance, his limitless ambition, gives way in Sandoz to humble submission to nature.

The historical context of the Biblical story, in the book of Genesis, the beginning of the world and of the chosen race, corresponds, furthermore, to Zola's visionary conception of his own historical context, the nineteenth century, that century when a new world was being born. One of the reasons he loved the Jacob story was that he too dreamt of playing a cosmogonic role, of being one of the founders of a new and better society, of helping to hasten the approach of the Kingdom of God on earth. It is significant in this respect that, among the titles that he considered giving the novel before choosing *L'Oeuvre* (rendered as *The Masterpiece* in the latest English version), were *La Lutte avec l'ange (The Struggle with the Angel)*, *Procréer (Procreate)*, *La Défaite (The Defeat)*, *Être Dieu (To Be God)*, *L'Immortalité (Immortality)*, *Créer (Create)*, *Création (Creation)*, *Notre Chair (Our Flesh)*, *Les Faiseurs d'hommes (The Men Makers)*, *Les Créateurs du monde (The World Creators)*, *Les Couches du siècle (The Century in Labor)*.

Strangely, Zola's compulsive preoccupation with this symbolic theme undermined the realism of the novel in much the same way that Claude's obsession with his symbolic woman undermined the realism of his painting. The novelist could have said of himself what he says of Claude – that he was an artist whose 'anguished concern with truth led him to exalt the unreal.'

When Goncourt first heard, back in April, that Zola was writing the book, he had been furious. He had nothing but contempt for Zola's tastes in art. (Among other things, he definitely did not share Zola's enthusiasm for Manet and the Impressionists.) 'I cannot help being amused, privately, at his attempt to rewrite my *Manette Salomon*,' he had noted in his journal. 'It is dangerous for a man who knows nothing about art to compose a whole volume on the subject.' His suspicions, overheard in conversation, had been more or less faithfully reported by a gossip columnist in *Le Figaro*. Zola, deeply wounded, had replied in a letter published in the same newspaper: '*L'Oeuvre* will not be at all what was announced. It is not at all a question of a series of tableaux on the world of painters, a collection of etchings and water colors.' Goncourt, seeing his novel referred to in those terms, had hit the ceiling.

Daudet, as full of jealousy and ill will towards Zola as the older writer, had made things worse by pretending to intervene in the name of friendship. He informed Zola that he thought the remark 'unjust' and urged him to write Goncourt directly. Zola had written him back that he could not see why it was 'unjust,' that he was beginning to be annoyed by Goncourt's mania for accusing him of plagiarism, that he could not see why he should write Goncourt, since he had done nothing to apologize for, that indeed, it was Goncourt who should have written him after the first article appeared. In the end, Goncourt had written him; he had responded and, convinced that 'the whole stupid affair,' as he put it, was ended, dismissed it from his mind.

The newspaper reviews of *L'Oeuvre* were on the whole fairly disappointing. Some praised it to the skies, but without giving any very precise reasons for the high opinions they expressed. Other expressed moral outrage at certain passages describing Christine posing in the nude for Claude or vividly recounting their making love together. Many of the more serious critiques including a long one by Jules Lemaître, discussed the accuracy of the novel or its apparent 'pessimism' (the word was now more than ever in fashion). Along with its 'frightful sadness,' Lemaître noted admiringly 'a violence of hyperbolical vision which overwhelms and hurts,' and went on to say that 'no one has seen more tragically the exterior of the human drama. M. Zola has something of Michelangelo in him. His figures remind one of *The Last Judgement.*' Several commentators compared the novel with *Manette Salomon* and Balzac's *Le Chef-d'oeuvre inconnu*. Some accused Zola of plagiarizing from this latter work. The novel sold hardly better than *La Joie de vivre*, the least popular of the *Rougon-Macquart* volumes.

Zola's old painter friends were in general surprised, hurt, and bewildered. Guillemet wrote him: 'Fortunately, reality is not so sad.' Monet remarked quite bluntly,

> You have deliberately avoided making any of your characters resemble one of us, but nevertheless I am afraid that our enemies in the press and public may drag Manet's name or at

least our names into it in order to make us out to be
failures – something which I don't want to think you intended.

There was a story that Monet, Pissarro, George Moore,
Mallarmé, and several others had met together one night over
dinner to share their displeasure.

Cézanne wrote Zola curtly from his home in the neighborhood
of Aix: 'My dear Émile, I have just received *L'Oeuvre*, which you
kindly sent me. I thank the author of *Les Rougon-Macquart* for this
token of his remembrance, and I beg to be permitted to press his
hand, musing on the bygone years. All yours inspired by times
which shall be no more.'

Upon reading the first installment of *L'Oeuvre* in *Le Gil Blas*,
Goncourt had noted that it reminded him of the beginning of a
novel by Restif de la Bretonne. Later, after having read more of
the novel, he found the style vulgar, the plot old-fashioned, the
psychology superficial, the 'revolutionary' artistic ideas ascribed
to its fictional artists a mish-mash of ill-digested tirades and
'morceaux de bravoure' from Chassagnol and other critics. He
also detected much that did indeed appear to him to be lifted
from *Manette Salomon*. 'Fundamentally,' he concluded, 'Zola is
nothing but a resoler of literature, and now that he has finished
reediting *Manette Salomon*, he is getting ready to recommence
Balzac's *Les Paysans*.'

VII

Indeed he was – in the sense that *La Terre*, his next novel, had to
do, like Balzac's work, with the peasantry. But he had long felt
that neither Balzac nor George Sand, the only other major
nineteenth-century French writer who had treated the subject,
had grasped the peasant soul in all its complexity. As for Sand,
she had deliberately idealized her rustic heroes. He had
remarked, morever, that no French novelist had as yet ventured
to recount what, in his opinion, constituted the 'true dramas' of
peasant life, mostly because of the difficulties involved in
acquiring all the necessary information. *La Terre* would thus be
the first novel about peasants to show them as they really were.

His maternal grandmother had been born in Auneau, in the

Beauce, one of the great grain-growing regions of France. His grandfather had come from Dourdan, on its border. Before their move from Dourdan to Paris, both had always been in close contact with peasants. As a boy, Zola had listened to their tales about them. He had also been struck, during his excursions around Aix, by the traits of the small local peasants – their avarice, laboriousness, attachment to the earth, brutality, sensuality, irreligion, and superstitiousness. First in Bennecourt, then Médan, where, since 1881, he had been a member of the municipal council, he had had many additional opportunities to carry on his observations. His valet and cook, Henri Cavillier and his wife, Zélie, had been an especially precious source of information about the local peasants' families. Naturally, he had also read everything he could find on the subject. Ever since the idea of writing the novel had occurred to him, in 1878, the year he had moved into Médan, he had been piling up notes.

On May 2, 1886, he had an interview with the great Marxist leader and theorist Jules Guesde. Guesde (with whose general socialist theories he had already familiarized himself while preparing *Germinal*) discussed at length with him the major agricultural problems facing the nation. The next day, Alexandrine and he set off on a research trip to the Beauce. With its immense, gently undulating, almost treeless plain largely given over to wheat, it would provide, he thought, just the sort of epic agricultural setting he wanted. They hired a two-horse landau, capacious enough to serve as a mobile study, and explored Châteaudun and the surrounding region. Romilly-sur-Aigre, a village a few miles from Cloyes, provided a near perfect model for his fictional village of Rognes. He attended a cattle fair, visited farms, watched sheep being sheared, drew maps, asked questions, and, in less than a week, had all the precise local facts he needed.

La Terre was, however, one of the most difficult tasks he had ever dared to undertake. Its scope frightened him. On May 27, he was still laboring on the plan and by no means sure as yet that he could bring the project to a successful conclusion. But as usual, he was not a man to recoil before difficulties. By June 16, he had finished the first chapter. He wrote Céard that he was afraid that it was not 'sublime' enough. Céard, in his reply, reassured him, 'The public knows very well now that you are powerful enough. That battle has been won. What is necessary now is to astonish it in another way: by the breadth of your serenity.'

That September, overcome by fatigue, he had to take a three-week vacation at Royan, on the mouth of La Gironde, with the Charpentiers, who had an estate there named 'Paradou.' Alexandrine, of course, accompanied him. By November, he had still not completed even the first half. It was hard going. The stage version of *Le Ventre de Paris,* which he had prepared in collaboration with Busnach, delayed him. So did the polemic with the critic Sarcey that followed its opening on February 19, 1887. In April, another press controversy with Sarcey, over *Renée,* his dramatized version of *La Curée,* absorbed more of his time. He increased his working hours, sometimes slaving away over sentences until two o'clock in the morning. By March, 1887, he still had one-third of the manuscript left to do. 'This novel is going to be the longest I have written,' he wrote Van Santen Kolff, 'and it's giving me a lot of trouble.' When the serialization began on May 29, in *Le Gil Blas,* he still had more than a quarter to write. 'I'm working myself to death,' he wrote Alexis. Finally, on August 18, he finished the last page, altogether more than fourteen months after he had begun the first chapter.

The Rougon-Macquart family is represented in the novel by Jean Macquart, Gervaise's brother. After having fought valiantly at Solferino, Jean has returned to France and found work on a large farm in the Beauce. Not far from there, in Rognes, there lives an old peasant, Fouan, well-known for his avarice, selfishness, and attachment to the soil. His two sons, Buteau and Hyacinthe, nicknamed 'Jésus-Christ,' have inherited the same traits. The dramatic plot mainly consists of two interconnected stories. One revolves about Jean's and Buteau's rivalry over Françoise Mouche, Buteau's sister-in-law, at first Jean's mistress, then his wife. Buteau's attempt to seduce her away from Jean is motivated not only by raw passion, but also by his ambition to own her land. Although she bears Jean's child within her, she really loves Buteau and little by little comes to sympathize with his conviction that their property should be kept out of the hands of 'outsiders.' In the end, he brutally rapes her to prevent the child from being born, thus preventing the land from passing on to the Macquarts. His wife, Lise, Françoise's sister, as greedy as he is, helps hold her down and, during the ensuing quarrel, pierces her with her scythe. Françoise dies shortly afterwards, refusing to name her murderers and leaving no will. Consequently Buteau and Lise are her legal heirs. At the end of the novel, they unceremoniously evict Jean from his house, which now belongs to them.

But the most terrible and unforgettable part of the story is the one centering on old Fouan. Like Balzac's *Le Père Goriot,* it is a variation on the theme of *King Lear.* Seventy years old, no longer able to till the fields, Fouan divides his land among his children, Buteau, Hyacinthe, and Fanny, on the condition that they will provide him with a stipend agreed upon in advance. However, they soon fail to keep their part of the bargain. In the following pages, Zola traces the old man's continuing decline and the increasingly brutal treatment he receives from them.

The second chapter of Part Five, portraying him wandering out of doors, on a cold autumn day, after having been thrown out by Buteau, with whom he has just quarreled, is as heart-rending as the comparable scenes in Shakespeare or Balzac's account of Goriot's death. In writing it, Zola demonstrated once again his genius for endowing the lowliest characters and events with tragic grandeur. The reader's pity for Fouan mingles with fear. 'When one has lost everything,' Zola remarks, 'do not expect justice – or pity.' Too proud to return to Buteau's, afraid to seek shelter with Hyacinthe, whose daughter, La Trouille, has tried to rob him, too proud, also, to knock at the door of his own daughter, Fanny, with whom he has also quarreled, Fouan has nowhere to go. His sister La Grande slams her door in his face. Night falls. He staggers about at random, lashed by the icy wind and rain. At times his legs can no longer carry him. He suffers atrociously from rage, shame, and hunger. At dawn, no longer able to bear his hunger, he goes back at last, mute and defeated, to Buteau's. His son, who had predicted he would return when he was hungry enough, greets him with a sneer: 'I knew you would not have the stomach to do it.'

Unfortunately, Fouan witnesses Buteau and Lise's murderous attacks on Françoise. In the culminating scene of the novel, Buteau and Lise kill him in his turn, first by nearly suffocating him with a pillow, then by setting fire to his bed.

There are dozens of interesting secondary characters, each

with a separate story. Some of these stories are as nightmarish – or nearly so – as Jean's and Fouan's. But the novel also contains some hilariously funny episodes – as earthy as the title itself. As in the other major *Rougon-Macquart* novels, the dramatic action is couched in a comprehensive study of a social milieu – in this case, of course, the French peasantry: its history, mores, politics, religious attitudes, historical role.

However, the better one knows the novel, the more apparent it becomes that the human dramas recounted in it and the sociological study underlying it are only parts of a larger literary entity. *La Terre,* as Zola from the outset intended it to be, is above all else an immense lyrical and epic poem of the soil, earth, Nature. The hero, or more precisely heroine, of the book is Earth, the Great Mother, herself. The vastness of the novel, its frank, earthy language, preoccupation with the physical, total lack of squeamishness and prudery, exaggerations, unhurried pace, and slow, powerful rhythms are inspired by this central theme and the necessity of presenting it in suitable poetic terms. As in 'Les Quatre Journées de Jean Gourdon,' there is a sustained analogy between individual human lives and the natural cycles of nature. The overall rhythm of the novel, the pattern of its principal divisions, is governed by the alternation of the seasons. The narrative is interspersed with descriptions of the Beauce and accounts of sowing, ploughing, hay-making, grape gathering, the mating of cattle, and all the other operations that make up farming. There is a splendid description of a violent, destructive hail storm. The many portraits of sowers remind one of Millet or Corot. Placed against their vast natural setting, Fouan, Buteau, Jean, Lise, Françoise, and all the other human characters who loom up like giants in the foreground of certain scenes diminish into insignificant specks. Once again, Zola insists on the oneness of all creation, juxtaposing, for example, graphic descriptions of the birth of Lise's daughter, Laure, with equally vivid evocations of the birth of La Coliche's calf. Primordial agricultural metaphors take on fresh vitality, as when Fouan's blond pine coffin lying on his freshly dug grave is poetically transformed into a grain of wheat.

The final pages are filled with a great hymn to Earth – the confused thoughts passing through Jean's head as he leaves Rognes for the last time – thoughts that recall, like numerous pages in *Germinal*, the 'new religion' that Zola had once tried to base on geology:

> The earth does not interfere in the quarrels that divide us, ill-tempered insects that we are. The great worker, eternally at her task, she takes no more interest in us than she does in the ants . . . . perhaps blood and tears are necessary for the world to function. What does our suffering count for, in the great mechanism of the sun and stars? God does not care a fig about us. The only way we can earn our bread is by a terrible, daily duel. Only the earth is immortal, the mother from whom we come and to whom we return, she whom we love to the point of committing crimes, who continually recreates life for her unknown goal.

The pantheistic vision inherent in this hymn – the same vision as that which informs the entire text – is a major source of the novel's power. At the same time, it redeems the novel. All the repellent ingredients that Zola felt compelled to pour into it, blood, semen, vomit, farts, excrement, are explained, justified, and purified by it.

Like *Germinal*, *La Terre* ends with the word 'earth.'

He had written another supreme masterpiece. Nevertheless there were, from the outset, many who regarded it as anything but one. On June 24, less than a month after it had started coming out in serial form, *La Gazette de France* declared that the peasants depicted in it are 'perfectly ignoble.' On August 18, the day he finished it, *Le Figaro* published a long, verbose, pompously worded statement violently attacking not only the book, but its author as well. Immediately baptized *Le Manifeste des cinq*, the article was signed by five aspiring young authors: Paul Bonnetain, J. H. Rosny, Lucien Descaves, Paul Margueritte, and Gustave Guiches. The first two had composed it. None of them was a friend of Zola's. Each had cultivated the patronage of Goncourt or Daudet. Not any of their creative works would survive. Posing as the spokesmen of the younger generation, they excoriated the novel. They rejected, among many other things, its characters, 'these ill-drawn human figures of Zolist rhetoric, these enormous silhouettes, superhuman and mis-shapen, devoid of complication, hurled brutally, in heavy masses, into milieux glimpsed by chance from the windows of an express train.' They rejected, above all, what they considered to be the moral depravity of the novel, which they characterized as nothing but a collection of scatological tales. 'The Master,' they asserted, 'has sunk into the lowest depths of filth.'

But what was even graver, they repudiated Zola as their literary leader. They accused him of betraying his own naturalistic principles, of fleeing the battlefield of Paris for the luxurious peace and quiet of Médan, of deserting the literary revolution which, they pointed out in passing, not he, but the Goncourts and others had started. They perceived in all his writings a taste for obscenity which, they theorized, was due not only to his insatiable desire for profit, but also to certain psychological and physical disorders: 'a malady of the writer's lower organs,' 'eccentricities of solitary monks,' 'his kidney trouble.' 'It is necessary,' they concluded,

> with all the force of our laborious youth, with all the loyalty of our artistic conscience, to adopt a dignified attitude towards a literature without nobility, which we protest in the name of sane, virile ambition, in the name of our cult and of deep love and supreme respect for *Art*!

Zola refused to honor the article with a reply, but he could not ignore the notes from friends or the newspaper comments expressing the suspicion or assumption that Goncourt or Daudet or perhaps both of them had instigated it. He publicly stated that he personally refused to believe this, while conceding that several passages would indeed seem to support the possibility that they had. Goncourt gave him his word of honor that he was innocent and reproached him for having been 'Machiavellian.' His remarks had, the old man asserted, been widely interpreted as, in fact, an indictment of himself and Daudet. As a result, he had, he complained, been the innocent victim of ferocious attacks in the newspapers – had even been accused of being basely jealous of Zola's financial success. Daudet, too, protested his innocence. In the end, Zola, anxious to preserve their old friendship, accepted their explanations.

Yet whoever was ultimately responsible for the *Manifeste des cinq*, it created a lasting sensation. It set the tone for most of the subsequent reviews of *La Terre*. The great majority were devastating. Anatole France called it 'the *Georgics* of crapulence' and, aiming at the man as well as the novel, went on to say, 'His work is bad, and he is one of those unfortunates of whom one can say that it would have been better if they had never been born.' Brunetière, while loftily admitting that the novel contained some pretty good passages, that Zola's inspiration had not as yet completely dried up, that, in places, the book could almost be described as powerful, discerned in it 'no conscience, no observation, no truth.' As for the naturalistic movement, he proclaimed it bankrupt.

'All that is quite comical and sad,' Zola wrote Huysmans from Médan on August 21. 'You know how I feel about insults. The older I get, the more I thirst for unpopularity and solitude.' But did he really? In his heart of hearts, was he not still the youth who had confessed to Baille his fear of solitude and limitless need to love and be loved? Moreover, were not his main objectives still, whether he was loved or not, to impose himself upon his contemporaries and create works that would last? It was comforting to know that the public at large was snapping up *La Terre* almost as avidly as it had *L'Assommoir* and *Nana* (which were still selling very well). But it was disturbing to know that so many respected commentators had condemned the novel – and him to boot – and that so few had praised it. Now that he was approaching fifty, adverse criticism was harder to take than it had been when he was younger.

Meanwhile, the mood of French intellectuals was obviously undergoing one of its frequent periodic changes. It was quite apparent that many members of the avant-garde had tired of science, positivism, and naturalism. Zola could sense as well as anyone else a growing hunger for faith. Concern with the ideal, the spiritual, the mystical, the irrational was increasing. Huysmans' *A rebours,* published in 1884, had, in Zola's own words, dealt naturalism 'a terrible blow.' Led by Brunetière and others, the reaction to naturalism was clearly gathering momentum, turning into a redoubtable movement. More recently, in *Le Roman russe,* published in 1886, Count Eugène Melchior de Vogüé had revealed to the French public Tolstoy and Dostoevsky, stressing their Christian qualities. The book had been a great success. It was not hard to see that the new generation which was then emerging would probably march to a different drummer.

[6]

Life Persisting, Recommencing

I

Now that he was approaching fifty, another storm was raging inside of Zola, a tempest of old and new doubts, hopes, fears, regrets, aspirations. He was tired, restless. The days when he had enjoyed battling on behalf of his fellow naturalists were long gone. 'I have cooled off considerably,' he wrote Van Santen Kolff on January 22, 1888. 'From now on, I shall fight just for myself.' He longed to be young again, to experience once more the joys of love. In late 1887, he decided to lose weight. He gave up wine and starchy foods and by March, 1888, had gone down from 212 to 163 lbs. Goncourt, who had not seen him since the publication of the *Manifeste des cinq,* was astonished. His paunch had melted away. He seemed taller and more taut. The delicately molded features that had for years been lost and buried in his fat, round face had reappeared, so that he once more looked like his Manet portrait, except for what struck Goncourt as 'a hint of wickedness' in his expression.

His relationship with Alexandrine being as unsatisfactory as ever, he had come to take a dour view of matrimony in general. In an interview with a British journalist, he ventured the opinion that marriage, like the Church, was an old and faulty institution that would, nevertheless, probably have to go on until something better could be found to take its place. He himself, he said, thought that living together out of wedlock might be every bit as good as marrying. 'In any case,' he peevishly concluded, 'marriage . . . is a failure and a grievance.'

For years he had had fantasies about sleeping with a young girl, a girl almost, but not yet, a woman – the Ninon of his *Contes.* In 1877, he had flirted so heavily with a charming young maid that Alexandrine had had to let her go. Planning his new novel, which he wanted to be something very pure and dreamlike, he considered for a moment making its subject 'a forty-year-old man ignorant of love, totally absorbed in science up till then, who becomes passiontately attached to a girl of sixteen.' A bit farther on, he had written between parentheses: 'Myself, my work, literature, which has devoured my life, and the inner turmoil, the crisis, the need to be loved.'

When, that May, his wife engaged a good-looking, very modest and placid twenty-year-old girl to help with the mending and sewing, he could not help eyeing her, too, longingly. A miller's daughter from a small village in Burgundy, she was a delight to look at, with her heavy crown of black hair and large, bright, gentle eyes. She resembled a girl he had once fallen in love with in a Greuze painting. Her name was Jeanne Rozerot. She had lost her mother at a very early age. Her father had remarried and had many more children by his second wife. She was pretty much on her own.

That summer, in Royan, where he and Alexandrine went for their vacation again, accompanied by Jeanne, he spent hours courting her. He gave her a little gold watch. He took some beautiful photographs of her threading a needle at her work table in the garden or strolling along a country road, her face shielded from the bright sunshine by a wide-brimmed hat and a parasol. His days were completely free. For once, he had brought no work along. His friends had rarely seen him so idle or happy. He had also become, as he continued to follow his diet, quite dashing. His beard was trimmer than it had been for years, his cravat impeccably tied. Although Jeanne did nothing at first to encourage his advances, she could not help loving him, too. His literary reputation dazzled her. His adoration, his eloquence, his gentleness, his generosity, his concern with her well-being deeply moved her. Everything about him fascinated her. From then on, he would be the center of her life. After they returned from Royan, he put her up in an apartment that he had found for her at no. 66, Rue Saint-Lazare, not far from the station. On December 11, she finally gave herself to him.

He had come to the conclusion that there were things more important than literature. In January, 1889, he confessed to Goncourt that he was experiencing a new burst of life, heightened desire for physical pleasure. Then, impulsively, he added, 'My wife isn't here . . . . Well, I can never see a girl pass by like that one over there without asking myself: "Now isn't that worth more than a book?" ' He was still deeply troubled, full of stormy thoughts. He would be depressed for weeks at a time. All he wanted to do was sleep. On March 6, he wrote Van Santen Kolff, 'I'm in the midst of a crisis – no doubt the one that comes to so many men on the brink of fifty.' The same day he confided in Huysmans: 'All my repressed laziness is coming out. It would take very little effort to make me put down my pen for ever. It's a crisis of indifference, a feeling of what's the use.'

Within a few weeks after Jeanne had agreed to be his mistress, she had become pregnant. As the expected date of her confinement drew nearer, his mood improved. 'I'm going through a very healthy period of hard work,' he wrote Charpentier. 'I am in tiptop condition. I feel just the way I did at twenty, when I wanted to devour mountains.' On September 20, 1889, Jeanne gave birth to a baby girl. They named her Denise. He let his faithful friend, Paul Alexis, in on the secret, and Marie, Paul's wife, consented to be her godmother. Céard, who had also become a close confidant, stood as godfather. Barely more than a year later, a second child was born, this time a boy, Jacques.

Alexandrine was still in the dark. The news of her husband's infidelity had leaked out, however. Alexis had been indiscreet. The guilty couple had been seen together. People were gossiping about it all over Paris. Shortly after the birth of Jacques, an anonymous 'well-wisher' apprised her of the truth. In her fury, she forced open her husband's desk, seized Jeanne's letters, and destroyed them. For a while Zola feared she was really going mad. He had to have their bedroom padded to deaden the noise of her screams. Month after month, their life was sheer hell. At one point, after an unusually violent quarrel, she started packing her bags, and he took refuge in his room, determined not to stop her. Céard, who happened to be visiting them at Médan, could no longer contain himself. He told Zola that he was a swine and a brute if he let this woman go, after she had shared the poverty of his bad years. It soon became apparent to both Zola and Alexandrine that, while they could not be happy together, they could not be happy apart either.

Consumed by guilt, resolved not to hurt her any more than he had, he continued to live with her, while still seeing his darling Jeanne (in one of his letters he told her, 'You are my prayer') and beloved children. Finally, Alexandrine, calmer but still heart-broken, reluctantly accepted the situation. In the summer of 1892, they took another long trip to the south. When they got back, he rented a house at Cheverchemont, a small village where Alexis and his wife were then living. It was in sight of Médan. After lunch, he would bicycle over there. In the morning, when the weather was clear, he would stand at the window of his study and gaze through a pair of binoculars at Denise and Jacques playing on their lawn.

II

During most of this period of inner crisis and domestic turmoil, Zola kept on with his literary activities, reluctant as he frequently was to do so. In the spring of 1888, the stage adaptation of *Germinal*, which he had written with Busnach's help, failed miserably, but his *Madeleine*, directed by Antoine at the Théâtre Libre the following year, was a great success.

Meanwhile, he had written his next novel, the one which he had wanted to be as pure and dreamlike as possible to contrast with its predecessor, *La Terre*. He liked to think that this new work could be put in the hands of anyone. Entitled, appropriately, *Le Rêve*, it recounts the love story of a beautiful, frail, very pious girl who dreams of love, realizes her dreams, and then dies.

The setting, Beaumont-l'Eglise, is a fictional cathedral town reminiscent of Coucy-le-Château in Picardy. Born out of wedlock, Angélique is abandoned by her mother, Sidonie Rougon. At the age of nine, she runs away from the cruel nurse to whom the authorities have entrusted her and, caught in a violent snowstorm, takes refuge under the portal of the Beaumont-l'Eglise cathedral. It is Christmas night. The next morning, the Huberts, a devout middle-aged couple who live in a fifteenth-century house adjacent to the cathedral and make chasubles for a living, find her shivering there. Having no children of their own, they raise her as their own daughter, sheltering her from the world and teaching her the art of ecclesiastical embroidery.

One moonlit night in May as she gazes from her balcony at the cathedral, the dominant feature of her environment, she imagines that a stained-glass image of Saint George which she has long admired and fantasized about has miraculously come to life and is walking in the cathedral close. What she really sees is a young painter, Félicien d'Hautecoeur, the son of a world-weary aristocrat who, after taking orders, has become the local bishop. Angélique and Felicien fall in love, but his father at first opposes their marriage because of the difference in their social ranks. When, however, Angélique nearly expires from grief, he relents. She seems to recover, and, in a splendid ceremony, the nuptials take place. But her joy is too much for her. As she and Félicien walk out through the great portal, passing from the dream of the cathedral to the reality of the outside world – the bright sunlight, the tumultuous, cheering crowd in the square outside – she suddenly collapses, her lips pressed against his. 'Everything is nothing but a dream,' the novel concludes. 'And, at the peak of happiness, Angélique passed away, in the faint breath of a kiss.'

Le Rêve is, of course, another variation on the Greek pastoral romance – like the idyll of Silvère and Miette, Maxime and Renée, Marjolin and Cadine, Serge and Albine, or Etienne and Catherine. It also partakes of folklore, the fairy tale, the *Golden Legend*. Yet unlike most of its predecessors in Zola's fiction, it is neither sinister nor tragic, even though the heroine dies. The ending is joyously sad and lovely – the sort of ending that a dreamy, romantically inclined reader would like to have. One is reminded, in this respect, of Zola's youthful fairy tale, 'Simplice.'

The most extraordinary feature of the novel is, however, its poetic universe. It is a universe in which romantic dreams come true. Like Cinderella, Angélique ends up by marrying her aristocratic lover. But, at the same time, it is clearly meant to be a nineteenth-century scientific universe. Angélique's naively Christian, unscientific view of reality, embellished by the *Golden Legend,* contrasts in most respects with the one adopted in the book by Zola, each bringing the other out in sharp relief.

The main differences are carefully emphasized, especially in the fourth chapter, where the 'miraculous' transformation of the stained-glass image into the true Saint George (in reality

Félicien) takes place. One of Zola's motives in writing the book was to create a naturalistic equivalent to, or substitute for, Christianity. The question as to whether miracles can really happen is a major theme. So also is the problem of salvation. To the Christian answers, Zola opposes a theory compatible with his naturalism. He replaces the Christian God with nature, divine providence with scientific determinism, original sin with heredity. For Divine Grace, he substitutes a beneficent environment. Salvation is possible, he declares, but only through the action of natural forces. If Angélique had not been taken in by the Huberts and raised in the shadow of the cathedral, she might well, he remarks, have succumbed to the demon lurking in her Macquart blood.

> Was this not grace, this milieu composed of what she had learned by heart, the faith she had imbibed, the mystical eternity in which she was immersed, this milieu of the invisible where miracles seemed completely natural, everyday events? It armed her for life's combats, just as grace armed the holy martyrs. She had created it herself, unknowingly. It was born of her imagination . . . . Everything came from and returned to her. Man created God to save man. Everything is a dream.

Le Rêve thus represents Zola's answer to the idealistic reaction that was beginning to characterize French thought as the century approached its close – the revival of Catholicism, a heightened impatience with the limitations of positivism, a disillusionment with the wild promises made by many of the supporters of science, a renewed penchant for the irrational, the mystical, the unknowable.

The book went on sale on October 15, 1888. One critic raved about the 'suppleness of Zola's talent.' Another regarded the novel as further proof of Zola's 'poetic genius.' Others praised the musical, compelling style or cited, more generally, its 'exquisite art.' Others, while admiring certain passages, had reservations. Anatole France remarked: 'If I had to choose, I would still prefer, to M. Zola with wings, M. Zola with four feet.' Lemaître found the novels a disconcerting and rather unpleasant mixture of genres – the fable, the physiological study, the romantic novel, and the epic. The subject deserved, he

thought, to be expressed in a form less massive, less materialistic. The very qualities that contributed to the beauty of Zola's
best works are, he concluded, definitely out of place in a work on
such a subject. The public at large loved *Le Rêve*. For years, the
sales figures were just as impressive as those of *Germinal*, up to
then Zola's fourth best selling novel.

III

La Bête humaine, the seventeenth volume of the *Rougon-Macquart*
series, came out during the first week of March, 1890. Begun just
after Zola had fallen in love with Jeanne and set her up in the
apartment on the Rue Saint-Lazare, it is as dark, brutal, and
grim a work as anything he had ever written. After having, in *Le
Rêve*, offered the public a pure and lovely revery, he now plunged
once again into the realm of nightmare, a heaving, thunderous
catastrophic world dominated by egoism, lust, anger, greed, and
hatred. Ever since he had written up his original plans for the
series, he had wanted to write a novel about crime. After moving
to Médan, where every day he could watch the trains passing by,
a stone's throw from his study window, he had also played with
the idea of doing something about the railroads. The two
projects fused in this new novel.

The main characters are all, like Thérèse Raquin or Buteau,
human beasts lashed on by instinct and appetite. Most of them
also harbor guilty secrets. The hero is Jacques Lantier, Etienne's
tardily invented older brother. (There is no mention of him in
any earlier Zola novel.) Jacques is a good engineer; but his bad
heredity has made him into a monster. Like Jack the Ripper, one
of his real-life models, he is devoured by the desire to kill the
objects of his sexual desire. 'It seemed like a sudden outburst of
blind rage, an ever-recurring thirst to avenge some very ancient
offences, the exact recollection of which escaped him.'

One scene of sex and violence follows another. After having
witnessed a brutal murder committed by a fellow southerner,
Roubaud, an assistant station-manager, and his wife, Séverine,
Jacques refuses to inform the authorities of what he has seen.
The Roubauds' alibi holds. To secure his silence, they befriend

him. Séverine and he fall in love and plot to kill Roubaud, but, at the last moment, his long suppressed frenzy overwhelms him, and he murders her instead. By another miscarriage of justice, Roubaud and an equally innocent companion are charged with the crime, tried, and sentenced to life imprisonment. Not much later, however, Jacques and his fireman, Pecqueux, are cut to pieces by the wheels of their locomotive after they fall from the engine during a fight over another woman. The locomotive, devoid of control, continues its mad rush on through the night, pulling its cargo of soldiers bound for the front at Sedan.

The overall effect of the novel is similar to standing too close to the tracks as an express train hurtles by. Its two main subjects, crimes of passion, the railroads, perfectly go together. The characters' world is a projection into space and time of their inner world. The scenes showing crimes being committed and those depicting railroad catastrophes – a major collision, the driverless train – complement and reinforce each other. The noises connected with railroading, the tinkling of telegraph signals, the scream of train whistles, the click of racing wheels, the thunder of passing carriages, fill the novel, providing a suitable musical accompaniment to its human dramas. As in most of Zola's other novels, there is, moreover, an attempt to portray fully a milieu, this time, a giant railroad, and, more generally, the whole world of the railroads. Zola's locomotives are endowed with as intense a life as Au Bonheur des Dames or Le Voreux. The death of Jacques' beloved La Lison, a locomotive, is as moving as any human death.

Of course, everything in this book too cries out for symbolic interpretation. Some of the symbolism would seem quite simple, but that part of it which has to do with the trains themselves is clearly many-leveled. They obviously stand for technological progress – the equivalents in this respect of today's rocket ships and computers. In this capacity, they help bring out one of the larger messages of the novel: that the moral progress of mankind has not kept up with scientific and technological progress and that terrible catastrophes will surely result from this discrepancy. They symbolize the hectic quality, the impersonality, the inhumanity, the irresistible force of mass culture and technological civilization. They symbolize the mad cult of progress, a contemporary Moloch. In the conclusion, the

196

driverless train with its cargo of soldiers symbolizes in particular the France of Napoleon III heading towards the débâcle of the war with Prussia:

> What matter the victims which this locomotive might crush on its way! Was it not hurtling on into the future all the same, mindless of the blood spilt? Driverless in the black darkness, like a blind, deaf beast unleashed among death, it plunged on through the night, on and on, loaded with this cannon flesh, these soldiers, already stupid with fatigue, singing drunken songs.

But the trains are also iron and brass extensions of the human beasts of the novel; and they also reflect Zola's own persistent phobias – his obsessive fear of death, his terror of thunder, his recurrent nightmare of being trapped in a tunnel. In one of the most memorable scenes of the novel, a crossing guard, Flore, crazed by Jacques' failure to return her love, commits suicide by walking towards a train advancing towards her through a tunnel:

> But the train had just entered the tunnel, the frightful roar approached, shaking the earth with its tempestuous breath, while the star had become an enormous eye, growing bigger and bigger, protruding as if from the orbit of the shadows. . . . The eye was changing into a blazing furnace, a fiery mouth vomiting forth flames. The monster's breath approached, already moist and warm in this roll of thunder, more and more deafening. And she kept on walking straight towards this inferno, so as not to miss the locomotive, fascinated like a nocturnal insect attracted by a flame.

Anatole France, so cruelly critical of *La Terre*, could barely contain his admiration of this new work of Zola's: 'His genius, lofty and simple, creates symbols. He has given rise to new myths. The Greeks had created the Dryad; he has created La Lison.' Lemaître proclaimed, in a long laudatory review: 'He is the poet of the shadowy depths of man . . . . Under envelopes borrowed from thirty years of humanity, one sees the action of elementary powers more antique than chaos . . . . It is a prehistoric epic in the form of a modern story.' An eminent physician praised Zola's portrayal of criminal physiology. More than one other critic tried to tear the novel apart. Lombroso, the great Italian criminologist, had reservations. Goncourt privately condemned the characters as pure figments of Zola's imagination and wrote Zola that it was now evident that they had different literary ideals. The sales, while nothing spectacular, were not bad either.

IV

The end of the series, one of the most ambitious literary projects ever conceived, was now in sight. Zola could hardly wait to finish it. Only a few weeks after finishing *La Bête humaine,* he started working doggedly, without any great pleasure, on the eighteenth volume, *L'Argent.* Its subject, money, the world of high finance, was one of the most difficult he had ever tackled. He finished the manuscript on January 30, 1891. It was published in book form on March 4. Another long novel, it continues the story of Saccard more or less where it left off at the end of *La Curée.* Ruined by a disastrous speculation, he is shown creating a new fortune, founding a bank which, thanks to advertising, almost at once becomes a great success. Carried away by his good luck, he indulges in wild speculation, using the bank's funds. In the end, the bank crashes, impoverishing thousands of depositors, and Saccard himself flees from France, taking refuge in Belgium.

The novel, based on some major financial scandals of Zola's time, contrasted with its predecessor chiefly by its optimism. 'What I want to do in this novel,' he wrote in his preliminary outline, 'is not to conclude that life is disgusting (pessimism). Life as it is, but accepted, despite everything, out of love, with all its power.' The most interesting character is not Saccard, but a thirty-six-year-old woman, Mme Caroline, first his housekeeper, then his mistress. In her, Zola has embodied the essential philosophy of the novel, the philosophy that he himself was trying to follow at the time he wrote it. The wife of a brutal millionaire brewer, whom she could no longer bear to live with, she has been through everything, and has no illusions left. 'Has been married, beaten, known all of life's horrors, and yet she is always gay, courageous, and beautiful. She is hope itself,' Zola had jotted down in his notes.

She loves life without knowing why. She is like humanity living in the midst of a thousand evils, yet cheered up by the youth of each new generation. As soon as she finds herself outdoors, in the street, in the sun, she can love again, hope again, be happy again. Even her approaching old age has no hold over her. I must pour all of myself into her.

Also, like humanity, Mme Caroline does not know where she is going. She wants to believe that life is something gay and happy. Like, for example, Pauline, whom she recalls, she is actually not so much Zola as one of Zola's ideals of himself. It is through her, too, that he voices the specific moral of the novel: that *laissez-faire* capitalism, while inhuman, may ultimately be beneficent. Money is as necessary to the world's well being as fertilizer. 'My God! Over and above all this mud that has been stirred, all these victims crushed, all this abominable suffering that each forward step of humanity costs it,' she muses at the novel's end,

> is there not some obscure, far off objective, something
> superior, good, just, definitive, towards which we are ad-
> vancing without knowing it and which swells our hearts with
> the obstinate need to go on living and hoping: . . . Why then
> blame money for all the dirty things and crimes which it has
> caused? Is love any less soiled, the creator of life?

It is with this word, 'life,' that the novel ends.

Most of the critics, having said so much about Zola, had a hard time finding anything new to say. Most discussed the book's general significance. One pointed out how Zola always translates ideas into symbols. Another compared his use of repetition to Wagner. Anatole France was impressed again. For the first time he recognized the apocalyptic, prophetic character of Zola's genius. 'One must pardon many things in prophets,' he remarked, 'especially with respect to measure and taste. It is a fact that they speak of the vices of the peoples with figures that would not be tolerated in less inspired authors.' Like *La Bête humaine*, the novel was not one of Zola's biggest successes, but it sold well enough by the standards of his day.

V

With *La Débâcle*, Zola had, however, another roaring best seller – and another masterpiece. As the next-to-the-last volume of his series, it has to do, quite logically, with the end of the Second Empire and the disasters that immediately followed. More specifically, it is an epic account of the Franco-Prussian war and the Civil War of the Commune. Told largely from the points of view of two soldiers, Jean Macquart and his friend Maurice Levasseur, the novel begins with the early defeats, marches and countermarches, vacillations and confusions, gross incompetence, and widespread demoralization that resulted in the Battle of Sedan. The second part recounts the Battle of Sedan itself, culminating in the French surrender. The third, commencing in the prison camp in the Iges loop of the Meuse River, shifts to Paris under siege and, after recounting the futile efforts of the French to break the Prussians' iron circle, concludes with the Commune.

The book not only relates these events; it seeks to account for them. How is it that France, victorious under Napoleon I, went down to ignoble defeat under Napoleon III? And how grave was this defeat? What possible use might it serve? These questions had plagued many Frenchmen, including Zola. In his opinion, the causes were largely to be found in the inexorable workings of evolution. In 1870, France was not so fit to survive as Bismarck's Prussia with its discipline, advanced science, and recently accomplished social reorganization. Since the glorious days of Austerlitz, the French nation had become exhausted. The Algerian war, with its idiotic chauvinism, had perverted its military morale. Trusting in the legend of its invincibility, the country had failed to keep up, like Prussia, with the latest advances in the technology of warfare. The Second Empire had, moreover, produced a type of Frenchmen very different in some crucial respects from the old Napoleonic heroes – high-strung, generous, enthusiastic, but unstable, vulnerable to every passing idea, quick to hope and despair. To this Darwinian explanation, the novel adds hints of a more moralistic one, reminiscent of the Biblical prophets: the France of Napoleon III had some terrible sins to expiate.

But, the novel also tells us, the French defeat, terrible as it was, was necessary, if France was to be reborn. Sedan put an end once and for all to the dangerous old cult of war – the chauvinistic poetry, the frenzied flag-waving. Henceforth, no Frenchman would want war or commit his country to foreign adventures as rashly as Napoleon III and his entourage had. The defeat of the Commune, the last expression of the unhealthy elements in the French mentality, symbolized by Maurice, resulted in their final eradication. The spirit which had always made France a great nation, symbolized by Jean, well-balanced, brave, attached to the soil, hardworking, thrifty, not eager for war, but willing to fight if necessary, would once again prevail.

In the course of explaining Sedan, the Commune, and their immediate national consequences, the novel also proposes, in opposition to the old jingoistic myths, 'the true vision' of war in general. According to this vision, all warfare is, in reality, atrocious, yet it is also an indispensable part of the struggle for survival and, indeed, the whole process whereby eternal life perpetuates, purifies, and renews itself. It must therefore be 'accepted with a solemn and resigned heart, like a law.' 'It is necessary perhaps, this blood-letting,' thinks Maruice as he lies dying. 'War is life which cannot exist without death.'

La Débâcle is one of the most realistic and conscientiously researched of all Zola's novels. It is also one of those in which his gift for story-telling, his genius for bringing out the full drama of history, and his extraordinary poetic imagination may be seen at their best. All those other ingredients that contributed to the power of his earlier epic novels are present once again: the universally interesting subject matter; the clear, impersonal, impassive, unhurried prose, carrying the reader along like a slow, but mighty river; the spectacular panoramas; the powerful rhythms and repetitions; the brilliant descriptions of vast masses of men in action; the tendency to choose a collectivity (in this case, the French army minus its incompetent leaders) as his real hero; the bigger-than-life qualities of the principal individual characters (including the Emperor himself, his face painted with rouge to hide the pallor); the idyllic subplots; the realism; the poetry; the marriage of eternal and passing historical themes and forms.

Few authors have portrayed more deliberately or powerfully

the ugly, unromantic side of war. But even as Zola debunks the glamorous old jingoistic myths, he invests his accounts of the Franco-Prussian war with images and meanings drawn from his personal fantasies, cults, and mythology. French cuirassiers crossing the Meuse are transformed by his imagination into awesome figures straight out of folklore and legend. Prompted by his conception of nature as supremely indifferent to human woes, he contrasts the terrible carnage going on during the Battle of Sedan with the serene blue of the sky. The men locked in combat are nothing more than 'human dust, a few black specks, lost in the midst of eternal, smiling nature.' He also expresses his animism. Struck by a Prussian cannon ball, an ancient oak in the Garenne Forest topples with the tragic majesty of a hero; the screams of wounded men mingle with the sobs of shattered trees. 'Everywhere felled trunks were lying, denuded, full of holes, ripped open like breasts; and this destruction, this massacre of branches weeping sap, was just as horrible and heartbreaking to see as a human battlefield.'

Especially in the second and third parts of the novel, he gives full reign, moreover, to the mixture of apocalypticism and humanitarianism that was becoming, as he approached old age, an increasingly important element of his still uncertain and confused thought. There are allusions to the Last Judgement, Babylon, Sodom and Gomorrah. The herds of riderless horses galloping madly over the dead and wounded in Part II are decidedly apocalyptic images, reminiscent of the horses of Saint John of Patmos. The Cross is summoned up as a paganized symbol of the agony of France: 'From now on the cadaver had reached the terrifying peak of its agony. The crucified nation was expiating its sins and was going to be reborn.'

The defeat and rebirth of France is metaphorically transformed, furthermore, into a cosmic process. The apocalyptic tradition dissolves, at the novel's end, into a vision inspired by one of the most primordial myths of all – eternal return, life's persistence and ever recurrent renewal. As he had composed the last chapter, Zola had been haunted by, among other personal memories of the Commune, the flames of the burning buildings and the crimson night sky that had so impressed him during its final hours. In the concluding paragraphs, he elaborates upon these motifs, transforms them into a complex symbol of death and regeneration. Paris burning becomes in his eye 'the field ploughed up once again so that from the renewed and purified soil might spring the idyll of a new golden age.' The setting sun is 'the final pyrotechnic display, the shower of sparks reserved for the grand finale of the imperial celebration.' But even as the blazing sun goes down and the city burns, it seems that a new day is already dawning. He says of Jean,

> And yet, beyond this fiery furnace still roaring about him,
> Hope, the eternal, was being reborn in the depths of the vast,
> tranquil sky. It was the certain rejuvenation of an everlasting
> Nature, of an imperishable Humanity, the renewal promised
> to him who keeps on working and does not despair . . . .

The volume came out on June 24, 1892. Goncourt was incapable of finding in it a single page of any true literary merit. The first published reviews, including those of many critics who had severely judged Zola's preceding works, tended to be favorable. One commentator compared him to the greatest poets that had ever lived. Émile Faguet, a major critic and scholar, thought it 'a very great work' and found it much more epical in the grand manner than either *Germinal* or *La Terre*. No one challenged Zola's patriotism. There were, however, numerous quibbles concerning the historical details. Many conservative readers were afraid that it would have a deleterious effect on French morale. Eugène de Vogüé praised Zola's romantic gifts, comparing him to Hugo, but criticized, among other things, the predictability and, in his opinion, insufficiently complex psychology of the novel's main characters, its failure to show precisely in what ways the Prussians were superior, and its too unflattering portrait of the France of 1870. He thought the book insufficiently comforting, still preferring in this and other respects *War and Peace*. Other reactionaries also joined in, bitterly lambasting *La Débâcle* on ideological and political grounds. According to one indignant priest, it was 'a hideous nightmare, as unhealthy as antipatriotic.' Numerous right-wing Frenchmen would never forget or forgive this attempt on Zola's part to undermine the old militarism or desacralize the personage of Napoleon III. By October 10, less than four months after the novel came out, 150,000 copies had already been printed, not counting those in the numerous foreign editions. (It was now customary for translations of Zola's novels into English, Spanish, Portuguese, Italian, Dutch, Danish, Russian, and other languages to come out simultaneously with the original French version.)

VI

Of the next and last *Rougon-Macquart* volume, he wrote Van Santen Kolff on January 25, 1893, 'I cannot wait to finish *Le Docteur Pascal*, to have the series over and done with.' As soon as he had been able to, after finishing *La Débâcle* in May, he had gotten seriously down to work on it. His main motive, now, was not to try to surpass that novel in dramatic or epic impact, but, as he had written at the head of his preliminary sketch, 'to sum up the philosophical significance of the series.' 'I believe that I have put into it,' he had gone on to remark,

> despite all the dark pessimism it contains, a great love of life,
> continuously exalting the forces of love . . . . I have not
> liked some of the pictures I have drawn, and I did not display
> them out of sheer perversion, but to show as courageously as I
> could existence as it truly is, so that I could end up by saying
> that despite everything life is great and good, because we go on
> living it with such fierce obstinacy.

A few pages later, he had pointed out another explanation for his frequently harsh realism – the sort of realism that Hugo had so passionately condemned in *L'Assommoir*: that the only way to make possible an eventual cure of the ills of society, was to have a good idea of what they are.

As he had gone on meditating on what he wanted the overall meaning of his series to be, his own ideas about God, man, nature, and history, always so confused, like those of his contemporaries, had continued to evolve. Its highest, most general theme, he fully realized now, was life continuing, always renewing itself, forever recommencing. But what was life? How was it connected to progress, science, work, and all his other major, only slightly less central themes? In his attempt to pin down once and for all the answers, he began by turning to a recently published summary by Melchior de Vogüé of Renan's credo:

> The Universe obeys inexorable laws . . . . Two elements, time and the tendency to progress, explain the universe. A kind of intrinsic spring mechanism, a nisus, impells everything towards life and a life that is more and more developed. There is a consciousness at the heart of the universe which is progressively taking shape and of which the 'becoming' has no limit. The future of humanity lies in the progress of reason through science . . . .

The fact that thirteen years earlier he had, in his positivistic zeal, savagely attacked Renan, one of the three main intellectual leaders of his generation along with Taine and Michelet, did not particularly trouble Zola. 'Essentially,' he went on to remark about Renan's faith, 'it is a faith in life.' It would serve very well as the credo of Dr Pascal, one of his two fictional alter egos in the novel. 'Life,' he wrote,

> is, for Pascal, the manifestation of the divine. Life is God. Everything through life. The great motor, the only one, the soul of the world. And it is because nothing counts for him but life, living nature, this life which is nothing but movement, that he devotes himself to the study of heredity. Heredity is a movement passed on. In a word, heredity makes life, and if one could intervene, understand it well enough to manipulate it, one could create the world.

He also wanted to evoke indirectly, through Pascal, something of his own intellectual evolution particularly with respect to the relationship between life and the science of life. In his attempt to do so, he was already struggling with questions that would, a hundred years later, with the arrival of new techniques of genetic engineering, take on the most crucial importance. Should one make use of science to improve life and hasten the advent of universal happiness, the great joyful city of the future, by eliminating sickness, old age, and death? Or would it not be wiser to pursue scientific knowledge for its own sake, leaving life to its own resources? Is not life perfectly capable of fulfilling its own needs? Is not any attempt to intervene in life's business stupid and criminal? It is not possible that everything which seems to us hurtful or offensive is in actuality a necessary occurrence? He had finally come to the conclusion that the scientists should not try to interfere.

As he meditated, he formulated in clear, didactic, almost theological terms intuitions that he had had for years, but had not as yet codified in any methodical, systemic way. He was indeed growing old! It came to him that history, too, is the movement of life, like heredity, but on a grander scale. Work, he now saw very well, is nothing but the movement of life also. The two terms, 'work,' 'movement of life,' are, indeed, synonymous. The work of individual workers is always part of this universal action, this unceasing effort, of life in pursuit of its mysterious goal of world creation. This being so, he also could go on to say (through Pascal),

> This gigantic labor of humanity, this stubborn clinging to life, is its excuse, its redemption . . . . One must live for the effort that life requires, one must live to add one stone to the far-off and mysterious edifice, and the only peace of heart one can find here on earth lies in the joy of having accomplished this task.

He could also assert (through Clotilde Rougon, Pascal's young niece, the daughter of Aristide and his first wife, Angèle Sicardot):

> Life, with the brave defiance of its eternity, was not afraid to make yet another life . . . . Even at the risk of forming monsters, it had no choice but to create, to go on creating, because, despite all the sickly and the mad that it creates, it never grows tired of creating, in the hope, no doubt, that the sound and the wise will some day appear.

The final version of the plot emerged partly out of his struggle to give dramatic expression to these ideas and all the others that were now crowding into his conscious mind, partly out of another, very different motive: he wanted to make the book into a monument to his liaison with Jeanne. The notion of writing a novel about an older man who has singlemindedly devoted most of his life to science and then falls in love with a girl still intrigued him. The story, set in Plassans, focuses not only on Pascal, but also on Clotilde. Between them, they embody Zola's favorite philosophical and religious notions at the moment that he composed the novel. They represent, too, what was then his general state of mind, still torn between faith and doubt, hope and despair.

A large portion of the story has to do with Pascal's scientific career: his attempt to write a study of heredity based on his observations of all the other Rougon-Macquart family members; his struggle against provincial prejudices and the pious intolerance of some of those closest to him; his discovery of an amazing panacea, a brief attempt to apply it, and then the decision that it would be wiser not to do so. Considerable space is also devoted to Clotilde's intellectual and spiritual questioning, confusion, and vacillation and to her gradual conversion (not without some lingering doubts) to Pascal's creed of science, work, and life. Although the story unfolds presumably between 1872 and 1874, her mentality is, at least to start out with, similar to that of many thoughtful French young people in 1892, a blend of doubt, pessimism, religiosity, fascination with the irrational, the supernatural, the unknown.

But the idyll of the old man and the girl occupies an equally important place in the novel. In its essential lines, it resembles Zola and Jeanne's own love story partly as it was, partly as Zola would have liked it to be. Pascal has no wife. Not long after Clotilde becomes Pascal's mistress (Zola compares them to Abraham and Hagar, Boaz and Ruth, and King David and Abishag), Pascal dies, leaving her two months pregnant. The child, resembling them both, is, as a recent critic has pointed out, Pascal's true masterpiece.

The novel and, with it, the whole *Rougon-Macquart* series ends with a domestic scene at once intensely poetic and profoundly realistic. Clotilde, as she suckles her baby, has thoughts that might occur to any mother. Languid and content, she feels that her milk, the pure essence of her maternal love, is binding this precious new being ever more closely to her. What will he be? A scholar? A captain? A pastor? Like all mothers, she dreams that he will be the expected Messiah. The final sentence focuses on the newborn child, and, as in *L'Argent*, the last word is 'life': 'In the tepid silence, in the solitary peace of the workroom, Clotilde smiled at the infant, still sucking away, his little arm raised in the air, very straight, like a flag summoning life.'

It is one of the oddest of all Zola's novels. Certainly, as Zola was himself aware, it is not made of the stuff of best sellers, and it is too eccentric to please most critics. Many readers have found the love idyll repellent despite Zola's attempt to ennoble it through Biblical comparisons. The lengthy philosophizing is hardly calculated to enthrall the common reader. As for the form, it involves a baroque combination of themes and genres which, one might think, should never be combined. In more than one scene, the work trembles on the brink of the outright ridiculous (the passages, for example, where the old drunk Antoine Macquart, his body diffused with alcohol, catches fire by spontaneous combusion and is quickly reduced to a mere handful of fine ashes. 'It was,' Zola wrote, 'the most beautiful case of spontaneous combustion that a doctor had ever observed'). Yet there are other pages, including the final ones, which are, without any question, sublime. Zola's narrative genius and the emotion reflected in the style make the work harder to put down than one might imagine. The general effect is somewhat like that of a nineteenth-century steam engine running at full speed.

He finished *Le Docteur Pascal* on May 15, 1893. Three days later he gave a talk at a banquet of the General Association of Parisian Students. While characterizing himself as a hardened old positivist, he nevertheless spoke sympathetically of the heightened spiritual unrest that marked the *fin de siècle*. He noted the widespread disillusionment with science. He could understand, he said, why the younger generation wanted to go back to religion or take refuge in escapist reveries. But, he claimed, science never had offered happiness, only truth. To be content with this truth someday, he said, a great deal of stoicism would probably be necessary, an absolute self-abnegation, the sort of serenity which comes from having satisfied one's intelligence and which is found only among an elite. For those of his auditors who absolutely needed a faith, he recommended faith in work. It had saved him, he said. And it was in itself a whole religion – 'the unique law of the world, the regulator that leads organized matter to its unknown end!' 'Life,' he proclaimed, 'has no other meaning, no other *raison d'être*. Each one of us is born only to produce his or her quota of work and then disappear.' As he spoke, he looked infinitely sad.

After the novel came out in volume form, that June, he sent a copy to Jeanne inscribed with the words:

To my beloved Jeanne – to my Clotilde, who has given me the royal feast of her youth and made me feel like thirty again, in presenting me with my Denise and my Jacques, the two dear children for whom I wrote this book, so that they might know, reading it some day, how much I adored their mother and with what respectful tenderness they should reward her later on for the happiness with which she has consoled me, in my times of troubles. Émile Zola, Paris, June 20, 1893.

As he had expected, the critics, without damning the book, were generally reserved. But the important thing was that he had finished the series. Begun in 1869, it stood complete at long last. It was different in many ways from what he had at first envisaged. It had grown from the originally conceived ten volumes to twenty, becoming with each new addition more imposing in its sheer mass. But what was more important, the initial, rather narrow and rigid formula had expanded and grown more supple. He was, by temperament, too much of a fighter and reformer to have been satisfied with his originally self-imposed role as a detached scientific observer. In the end, he had turned out to be just as much of a moralist as any of his predecessors, including Balzac. The positivist in him, far from being in complete command, had been in constant competition with the cosmic pessimist. Both had had to contend with the optimistic dreamer, the metaphysical speculator, the seeker after a new religion, the would-be prophet. The novels had expressed the deepest stirrings of his heart, his loves, hates, hopes, fears, doubts, leaps of faith. They had been shaped by his unconscious as well as his conscious mind.

The best of them were essentially great poems. The scientific mentality carried to its extreme had provoked, in accordance with some mysterious law of compensation, a return to pre-scientific modes of thinking. Myth had mingled with fact, primitive archetypes cast their long shadows over narrations of modern history. The act of reading had become, at least in the case of *Germinal*, a manner of participating vicariously in primitive rites of birth, death, and renewal. Through the lens of metaphor, an almost photographic realism had been transformed

209

into overwhelmingly powerful poetic visions. A revolutionary art preoccupied with contemporary life and remarkable for its freshness had, nevertheless, in pursuing its modern goals, helped keep alive the greatest of the older literary traditions – the tradition of Hesiod, Homer, and Dante, the tradition of Shakespeare, and, last but not least, the tradition of Isaiah and John of Patmos.

What had started out as an attempt to conform to a theoretical ideal of the modern novel pioneered by Balzac had ended up as a complex intermingling of the Balzacian and the Hugolian novels and much more besides. Melodrama, comedy, tragedy, the Greek romance, the epic – there was hardly any great form of the recent or distant past that had not entered into the commodious structure of the series. Looking back, one could even perceive the beginnings of an immense, shadowy mystery play complete with variations on Biblical stories and the 'mansions' of Eden, for example, or Heaven, or Hell.

All in all, his gigantic work conformed rather closely, whether he and his contemporaries were fully aware of all the ways it did so or not, to the sort of fiction that the period in which he had written it had required: a fiction that would mirror its most distinctive traits, satisfy its deepest aspirations, reflect its doubts, phobias, instabilities, ambiguities, tensions, its attempt to find a new vision of reality, its obsession with facts, its fascination with photography, its cult of science both as a refuge from metaphysics and possible source of a new philosophical or religious faith, its dynamism, individualism, love of big, strong, bold constructions, its industriousness, its quest for novelty, its love of color, its impressionism, nascent expressionism, sensualism, its nervousness, self-exaltation, fear of death, its sense of being caught up in the throes of a momentous transition, its need for a mirror to show it what and where it was and where it was going.

VII

In June, 1893, Charpentier and his recently acquired partner, Eugène Fasquelle, gave a banquet to make the conclusion of the series. It took place at the Chalet des Iles in the Bois de Boulogne. Neither Goncourt, nor Daudet, nor Huysmans, nor any representative of the French Academy attended, but two hundred artists and writers did. Although Zola's repeated efforts to gain admission to the Academy had been and always would be unsuccessful because of the enemies he had made there, he had, in 1888, become a knight of the Legion of Honor. Now, on July 14, he was promoted to the rank of officer.

Since April, 1891, he had been the president of the Société des Gens de Lettres.

In England, as recently as the spring of 1888, Zola's fiction had been denounced in the House of Commons as 'only fit for swine.' That same year, Henry Vizetelly, a distinguished, sixty-eight-year-old publisher, had been heavily fined for publishing translations of *Nana, Pot-Bouille,* and *La Terre.* The following year, he had been sentenced to three months in prison for bringing out other works by Zola and Maupassant's *Bel-Ami* and Bourget's *Crime d'amour.* Yet in September, 1893, the Institute of Journalists invited Zola to attend their annual meeting. The paper on anonymity which he read before an international audience of journalists at Lincoln Hall was well received. Afterwards he was the center of attention at a dinner for the Congress at the Crystal Palace, a reception at the Imperial Institute, and another reception, given by the Lord Mayor, at the Guildhall. On this last occasion, he could be perceived marching in a sort of state procession, preceded by the City's trumpeters.

The following year, while he was visiting Rome to do research for his next major project, *Les Trois Villes,* another banquet was given in his honor. Held in a magnificently lighted room at the Hôtel de Rome, it was a splendid affair with over a hundred guests. The table was decorated with a profusion of flowers. His hosts gave him an artistic goblet, containing the visiting cards of all those present. At dessert, he was toasted as 'the illustrious representative of intellectual and moral France.' The Pope refused to grant him an audience, but the King and Queen of Italy received him. On the way home, he stopped in Venice, the city of his paternal ancestors, was presented by the municipality with a blue and gold glass goblet to mark his visit, and feted at another banquet.

Everywhere he went, groups of reporters followed him. Admirers made pilgrimages to see him in his sumptuously furnished apartment at no. 21 *bis,* Rue de Bruxelles, where he had moved from the Rue Ballu in 1889. He was now, in his middle fifties, at the peak of fame. He was rich, honored, decorated. Yet he was still far from being completely happy or at rest.

In late December, 1893, he finished one of the saddest works he had ever written. It was a libretto for a composer friend, Alfred Bruneau, whose light operas drawn from *Le Rêve* and *L'Attaque du moulin* had recently enjoyed considerable critical acclaim. As the title, *Lazare,* suggested, it was a retelling of the story of Christ's raising of Lazarus from the dead – but with a difference. Zola's Lazarus, instead of being grateful, begs the Saviour to allow him to go back to sleep again:

> It was so good, O Jesus, this deep, black sleep, this deep, dreamless sleep . . . . Live again? Oh, no, no, no! Haven't I paid with enough suffering my frightful debt to life? I was born without knowing why, lived without knowing how; and you would have me pay it twice. You would have me start all over again my term of pain on this sorrowful earth!

Jesus, in his infinite compassion, grants Lazarus's request.

At a dinner party that he gave on March 22, 1895, the conversation turned to whether there really is such a thing as happiness. None of his guests, including Goncourt, thought so. Zola denied its existence more emphatically than anyone else. Afterwards, he fell into a deep depression, saying nothing more for the rest of the evening.

His domestic situation remained difficult. 'This sharing, this double life that I am obliged to lead, is making me desperate,' he wrote Jeanne on July 13, 1894. 'I dreamt of making everyone around me happy, but I see quite clearly that this is impossible, and I am the first to be hurt.' It is true that his home life improved somewhat as time went by. One day, Alexandrine asked him to bring Denise and Jacques to the house so that she could see them. Thereafter, she became more and more interested in them. She welcomed the latest news about their activities – for example, the progress Denise was making with her Scripture lessons. She did not object to his daily visits with them and their mother in their new, larger apartment at no. 8, Rue Taitbout or the one they moved to after that, at no. 3, Rue du Havre. To the great amusement of Goncourt, Daudet, and others, it gave her pleasure, starting out in the spring of 1893, to take the children out for walks. She showered them with presents, particularly after her annual trips to Italy (which she had fallen in love with). Yet there were still many moments when Zola was still tortured by guilt and regret.

He still frequently suffered, also, from real or imagined ill health, complaining to his friends of pains in his intestines and elsewhere. Curiously, the intestinal pains would occur whenever he started to read or write.

He no longer had all the close friends he used to have, and his relations with several of those who remained had cooled. Cézanne and he had stopped corresponding after the publication of *L'Oeuvre*. For a while, Céard had almost taken Cézanne's place in his affections, but towards the end of 1893, Céard broke with him too, tired of being involved in his domestic battles. Huysmans, going along with the times, had gradually detached himself from naturalism, ending up in 1892 as a Catholic convert. Maupassant, one of the first of his disciples to drift away, died of syphilis on July 6, 1893.

He saw Goncourt and Daudet from time to time. At rare intervals they would dine together, keeping up the pretense that they were still friends. Yet the attitudes of these two fellow writers towards him had become by now implacably venomous. They could not forgive him for being so successful. They could not stand his overwhelming personality. In page after page of his journal, Goncourt portrayed him in the worst possible light, heaping scorn on his art, accusing him over and over again of plagiarism, scornfully characterizing him as nothing more than a powerful vulgarizer of stolen ideas, a 'machine lubricated for industrial use, never pausing, never resting.' He agreed with a critic who had compared *Les Rougon-Macquart* to mass-produced rental housing put up by masons solely interested in profits. He repeated all the malicious gossip he could gather about him. He regularly imputed to him the crassest of motives. He accused him of dishonesty, slyness, hypocrisy, cowardice, egoism. He alluded disdainfully to his humble origins, Italian blood, physical ugliness, youthful privations. He snickered at his furnishings, his ignorance of painting, his and Alexandrine's manners, accents, social pretensions, clothes, and style of entertaining. Once, after a party on the Seine at Médan, he even made fun of the way Zola swam, like, he wrote, 'a big wood louse.'

Daudet was just as spiteful. Agreeing with Goncourt's picture of Zola, he termed him nothing but a giant 'dredging machine.' He called him a 'capon.' He spoke sneeringly of his penchant for little girls 'who smelled of piddle.' Daudet's wife, Julia, eagerly joined in the criticism. She never had been able to regard Alexandrine as her social equal. The Daudets' elder son, Léon, made his parents and their intimates laugh with his imitations of Zola's high, chiming, slightly lisping voice.

Zola did his best to avert a complete break with either Goncourt or Daudet. He repeatedly reaffirmed his affection and respect for both of them. On March 1, 1896, he wrote Goncourt, 'You are the master of all of us when it comes to disinterestedness and daring.' On May 30, he thanked him for a copy of the last volume of his *Journal,* noting in particular the elder writer's 'sovereign passion for literature.' 'We, of course, love it also,' he added, 'but I really believe that you love it more than we do.'

This was Zola's last letter to Goncourt. The old man died on July 16. At the funeral, Zola delivered an oration in which among other things he lauded this same trait. He also went back and reviewed their friendship from the beginning, the enthusiasm that he had always had for the Goncourt brothers' works. He noted the pioneering role that they had played in the evolution of the novel. He spoke of their longing for immortality and intimated, in his conclusion, that they had, indeed, achieved this noble aim.

VIII

Throughout this same period, from 1893 to 1897, Zola was also haunted more than ever by the thought of his advancing age. The longing for death that he expressed in *Lazare* was rooted in only one of his conflicting moods. His old dread of death returned, too. He was terrified not only by the certainty that his own extinction was approaching – the extinction of the graying flesh-and-blood Zola whose always anxious, doleful reflection he could regard every day in his valet's mirror. He also agonized about the future of his works. The possibility that they might not survive, that he might even outlive them, was more than he could bear. He compared himself to a worker who has just finished the house destined to shelter his old age and who worries about what the weather will be like from then on. Would the rain damage the walls? Would a north wind blow away the roof? Was the building solid enough to resist the worst storms that might come along?

He was thoroughly aware now of the new aspirations and tastes that had been radically transforming the French cultural climate since 1885. The world that he had conquered was almost gone. Its intellectual leaders were disappearing one by one. Renan had died in 1892. Taine passed away the following year. New, very different leaders had arisen – Bourget, Brunetière, Anatole France, Paul Desjardins, Edouard Drumont, Vogüé, Maurice Barrès, Léon Bloy, and all the others. The younger generation, now reaching the age of manhood, had sharply broken with its elders. The spiritual revival was in full swing. People were talking about a Catholic renaissance. After reading Bourget's *Le Disciple*, Taine had remarked: 'I can only conclude that taste has changed and that my generation is finished.' The new literary avant-garde, with the exception of Verlaine and Mallarmé and one or two other writers, detested Zola and all he stood for. In 1893, Brunetière's opposition to naturalism won him a seat in the French Academy – the very one that Zola himself had foolishly coveted. In the *Revue des deux mondes* of January 1, 1895, the same critic, recently converted with much public fanfare to Catholicism, jubilantly proclaimed 'the bankruptcy of science.'

With each passing year, the danger that Zola would become only a glorious has-been grew more acute. 'March at the head of the ideas of your century,' Napoleon III had declared, 'and they will follow you and support you. March behind them, and they will drag you after them. March against them, and they will overthrow you.' Zola had always conducted his literary career in accordance with these same principles. For fifteen years, he had brilliantly succeeded. But now he found it harder and harder to do so. It was obvious that time and his own failing creative powers were against him. When he wrote, it was more than ever difficult not to imitate what he had already done. Most of his ideas were set. So were his style and literary techniques. After finishing a long work, he was more exhausted than he had almost ever been before.

He kept on coping with the phantoms of old age, cultural change, and approaching death in the only ways he knew how. He had never been one to accept unpleasant things passively. The old warrior had once again become thoroughly aroused. From 1881 to 1896, he had stayed away from the newspapers, except to grant an interview now and then or defend his novels or literary principles. In 1896, he returned to journalism. It was, after all, an arm that had served him well in the past. He waged a new press campaign consisting of seventeen articles in *Le Figaro*. Many were on technical matters of concern to him as president of the Société des Gens de Lettres – the legal rights of novelists, for example. But in nearly every one of them, no matter what his main topic might be, he battled for himself. This was equally true of the speeches, prefaces, and opera scenarios he composed during the same period.

Above all, he was struggling to capture the younger generation, on which he depended to keep his name and works alive. He stalked his prey patiently, studying it for hours. Sometimes, he adopted an arrogant, blustering tone. He exulted in his triumphs, as when he asked rhetorically, after evoking the more than a thousand characters he had created, 'Have I not proved enough my virility as a creator of men?' While vaunting himself, he spoke contemptuously of his detractors. He would have it known how little their insults hurt him, how, indeed, they had stimulated some of his best pages. At other times, he took a humbler, more conciliatory approach, admitting, for example, that he was not really a scientist, just a novelist. He did his best to justify himself. He gave vent to his fear that he would be forgotten, that his works would not be understood. He tried to dispel current myths about himself, to explain himself, open his heart, reveal the workings of his mind. He reasserted his values and principles, defending science, for example, against its Catholic enemies. He flattered his young readers, vaunting the beauties of youth. He also chided them for their lack of ardor and vigor. He challenged them to debate with him the issues that divided himself and them. He insisted on his own rightness and on the futility of the ideas that they had embraced. He held himself up as the best model for them to follow: 'A sound, strong, happy man, proclaiming by his own example, like Goethe, like Hugo, the eternal power of life.'

Furthermore, he was trying hard to adjust to the tastes and preoccupations of the new generation. In an interview granted the journalist Jules Huret in March, 1891, he had briefly defined his revised literary ideal. What he foresaw, he said, was a kind of 'classicism of naturalism' – an expanded, more complex, tender, and logical naturalism, with a broader approach to humanity. At the annual banquet of the Association Générale des Etudiants on May 18, 1893, he admitted that he had perhaps been too much of a sectarian. He had undoubtedly erred, he said, in trying to confine art to proven truths. The younger novelists had done well, he said, to widen the horizon of fiction by reconquering the realm of the mysterious and the unknown. He had himself, he said, come to the opinion that that marginal, indeterminate area of doubt and exploration which lies between acquired truths and those as yet undiscovered belongs to literature as well as science.

In fact, he had moved in several of these directions long before completing *Les Rougon-Macquart*. Since when, for example, had he really restricted his fiction to proven truths? Questions of faith, dissatisfaction with the limits of scientific knowledge, the lure of the beyond, had all very definitely found a place in his series, in *La Joie de vivre*, for example, not to mention *Le Docteur Pascal*. Not all his novels had been brutal, and some had even been quite 'tender.' But now, in his newest literary project, *Les Trois Villes*, he made religion and the contemporary quest for faith the major theme. He adopted a broader, gentler, more compassionate, more obviously religious view of humanity than he had in most of his earlier fiction. While clinging to his old ideal of a scientific realism, he also became more overtly evangelical.

The hero and main viewpoint character of each of the thick volumes of this vast trilogy is an intelligent, intellectual, spiritually troubled young priest, Pierre Froment. He is the son of an illustrious chemist, killed in a laboratory accident, and of a pious, mystically minded mother. Convinced that her husband's death was a divine punishment for his incredulity, she had insisted on Pierre's entering holy orders as an act of atonement, and he had done so only because he loved her and wanted to comply with her dearest wish. But from the outset it had never been easy for him to accept blindly the Church's teachings.

Although each of the three novels has its own separate actions, they are linked together, above all by the story of Pierre's conversion from Catholicism to a new 'Religion of Science.' The central drama is a spiritual one, pitting science, democracy, and social justice against religion, aristocracy, *laissez-faire* capitalism, and charity.

In the first volume, *Lourdes*, published in 1894, the reader accompanies Pierre on a pilgrimage from Paris to the shrine of Lourdes. One of the hundreds of other passengers on the specially chartered train is a young woman, Marie de Guersaint, Pierre's former sweetheart. She has been paralyzed by a mysterious illness. He has told her that if her prayers for a miraculous cure are granted, his faith will be restored. Yet even though the miracle does take place, he still remains, despite his sincere desire to believe, as skeptical as before.

In *Rome*, the second volume, published in 1896, Pierre travels to Rome. He has written a book promoting a system of Christian socialism which, he has learned, is about to be put on the Index. He hopes to submit his case to Leo XIII himself, a pope known for his liberalism. After surmounting many obstacles, he does indeed manage to obtain an interview with him. But again he is disappointed.

In the concluding volume, *Paris*, concluded in 1897 and published in 1898, Pierre has returned to Paris, the great modern city where the society of the future is taking shape. Although what is left of his Catholicism now crumbles, he does not immediately discard his cassock and persists in devoting himself to acts of charity. But it soon becomes apparent that what has passed for Christian charity – permanently rich people giving alms to permanently poor people – is incapable of curing the ills of modern society. He concludes that the Christian experiment has failed. But more and more, he falls under the influence of his older brother, Guillaume, a brilliant chemist like their father. He becomes a member of Guillaume's circle of scientists and revolutionary social thinkers and activists. Gradually, as he takes part in their lively discussions, the Religion of Science, the religion of the future, takes shape in his mind: the idea of duality, monism, human solidarity, the unique law of life evolving from the first atom to condense out of the ether into a whole world – the religion announced by Darwin, Fourier, and all the other great nineteenth-century scientists or socialist prophets. In the conclusion of the novel, Pierre accepts this religion and settles down to live in conformance with it, together with his new wife. Together, they help prepare the equitable and happy society of the future by working in his brother's laboratory.

Quite as much as *Germinal* or any of Zola's other novels, *Les Trois Villes* is the work of a social reformer and prophet. In it, Zola was also fighting the same very personal battle that he was in his nonfictional writings of the time – promoting everything he held sacred, attacking everything he hated, trying to capture the new avant-garde public, especially the younger generation. As usual in his fiction, he was also living, as he had put it in *Mes Haines,* 'out loud.' As his ever-faithful disciple, Alexis, pointed out in a review of *Lourdes,* its priestly hero is none other than Zola himself – 'a Zola troubled by doubt, but also tormented by the desire to believe and forever humiliating his reason in order to attain this objective, but always in vain, thanks to the predominance of his reason . . . .'

Les Trois Villes takes up pretty much where *Le Docteur Pascal* leaves off, treating the same philosophical and religious questions, but changing the scene. After having portrayed the Second Empire and the first few years of the Third Republic, Zola had now turned to what was then the present. On the artistic level, he was still, despite his growing fatigue and tendency to repeat himself, a very great artist. Each of the three volumes contains powerful passages, although some, particularly in *Paris,* suffer from Zola's having treated their subjects even more powerfully in earlier writings. He had lost none of his genius for portraying human masses. This is particularly evident in *Lourdes,* with its numerous crowd scenes – the train full of passengers traveling to Lourdes, the crowds pouring into the town, the collective excitement, the screams and moans filling the nights, the flame-lit processions, the multitudes swarming about the shrine, singing hymns, invoking the Virgin, surging forwards to be healed.

From beginning to end, the trilogy is permeated by the mood of world destruction and renewal which was so widespread in Europe in Zola's lifetime and which he himself had often shared – the same mood that colored much of *Les Rougon-*

Macquart too; but in none of the individual novels of that series, except *Germinal*, had he expressed it with such overwhelming force.

Critics have rightly singled out *Lourdes* as a great novel, on the same level as *La Débâcle*, for example. It has always been, moreover, one of Zola's most widely read works. Seventy thousand copies were sold the first year alone. 'Drenched in tears like a prayer' (to quote Alexis), it expresses even more movingly than *Rome* and *Paris* Zola's ambivalent attitude towards the faith of his childhood. The work of a disbeliever, it is, nevertheless, a religious book not only in its subject matter, but also in the way it recounts its story. It is, furthermore, the best example of the 'tenderness' that Zola wanted to cultivate in his new works. Its sales were not hurt, of course, by the huge scandal it provoked upon its publication or by its having been placed on the Index shortly afterwards.

IX

It was during these same years that the Dreyfus Affair, a major event in modern French history, went through its initial stages.

In 1893, Captain Alfred Dreyfus, the son of a rich Jewish textile manufacturer, was sent as a staff learner to the Ministry of War. Three years earlier, he had married Lucie Hadamard, daughter of a Parisian diamond merchant. The couple had two young children. He had been up to then in every way a model officer.

On September 26, 1894, an unsigned letter reached the Statistical Section of the ministry. Known henceforth as the *bordereau*, it contained evidence of the betrayal of military information to Germany. On October 15, Dreyfus was provisionally arrested by the Army authorities and charged with high treason. Later that same month, a virulently anti-Semitic Parisian newspaper, *La Libre Parole*, founded by Edouard Drumont, announced the arrest, and Dreyfus's trial by press, fed by false rumors and reports, began. Since 1882, when the failure of a large Catholic-royalist bank had been blamed on a syndicate headed by the Rothschilds and other wealthy Jews, anti-Semitism had become increasingly rife in France. It was generally assumed that Dreyfus was guilty. Actually, the hardest evidence against him was that three of the five experts consulted had said that his handwriting and that of the *bordereau* were the same.

General Mercier, the Minister of War, was aware of the meagerness of the case against Dreyfus, but he was afraid to buck public opinion. If he were to release the 'traitor,' people would say that he had succumbed to Jewish blackmail. He would also have a hard time explaining why an officer could have been arrested on so grave a charge without adequate proof. Mercier, therefore, not only permitted Dreyfus to be brought to trial, but did everything necessary to obtain a verdict of guilty. He even went so far as to have assembled a 'secret dossier' which contained no additional facts of any real value but could be used to impress the members of the court-martial. Dreyfus and his defenders were not permitted to see it. The proceedings took place behind closed doors, and the record was not made public. Found guilty, he was condemned to degradation and to deportation for life. His family supported his plea of innocence. However, the French public and the French press as a whole, led by *La Libre Parole* and other anti-Semitic newspapers, exulted over the verdict and the harsh sentence.

On January 5, 1895, Dreyfus's degradation took place in the presence of the whole corps of his comrades drawn up in lines in the courtyard of the École Militaire. He protested his innocence again, and cried, 'Long live France!' On February 21, he was packed off to Devil's Island, a leper colony hastily cleared to receive him, off the coast of Guiana.

Mercier ordered his fellow officers not to discuss the case. However, certain lingering doubts about the validity of the verdict were impossible to repress. Dreyfus's family, who knew that he could not have committed such a crime, kept on tirelessly agitating for reconsideration. General Boisdeffre, the Chief of the General Staff, aware of Dreyfus's irreproachable character, decided that further investigation into his motives was needed. Lieutenant Colonel Georges Picquart, the new head of the Statistical Section, acting on Boisdeffre's orders, pursued the matter. At the beginning of March, 1896, the section, charged with anti-espionage matters, intercepted an express letter originating in the German Embassy and addressed to a Major Esterhazy. Picquart started investigating Esterhazy, a dissolute man who frequently speculated on the stock market, was always short of money, and had been living with a registered prostitute. He was soon convinced that Esterhazy was the real author of the *bordereau*.

But when he informed his superiors of his findings, they reacted coldly. They were adamantly opposed to reopening the Dreyfus Case. General Gonse, Picquart's immediate superior, remarked, 'What difference does it make to you if that Jew remains on Devil's Island?' 'But what if he is innocent, sir?' 'That is something that can no longer be discussed. Mercier, Boisdeffre, Saussier himself would be compromised.' (General Saussier, the Military Commandant of Paris, was the one who had actually summoned Dreyfus's court-martial.) Since these high officers embodied, as it were, the honor of their country, the honor of France itself was at stake. When Picquart persisted in pursuing his inquiries, his superiors, on November 15, 1896, had him removed from his post and sent on a protracted mission abroad. That December he was dispatched to Tunisia. His career lay in shambles.

Meanwhile, Picquart's assistant, Major Henry, had forged and given to General Gonse a letter supposedly from the Italian military attaché, Panizzardi, to his German counterpart, Schwartzkoppen, which seemed to confirm Dreyfus's guilt. Henry, one of the most vehement prosecution witnesses during Dreyfus's trial, had every reason not to want the case reopened. In order to forestall this eventuality, he had already forged or altered other documents and would do so again, but this particular one was especially damning.

Dreyfus's family, friends, and sympathizers had also continued their campaign on his behalf. On November 6, 1896, a pamphlet by an idealistic young Zionist writer, Bernard Lazare, *La Vérité sur l'Affaire Dreyfus* was printed and distributed to leading government officials and influential citizens. It had little impact, however.

Four days later, *Le Matin* published a facsimile of the *bordereau* bought from one of the graphologists who had testified that Dreyfus had written it. Although Schwartzkoppen and at least two other men recognized Esterhazy's hand, no one came forward to name him.

In June, 1897, Picquart, in strict confidence, apprised his

lawyer, Louis Leblois, of his situation (without mentioning, however, the intercepted express letter). He also entrusted to him fourteen letters from General Gonse in which Gonse admitted the possibility of a judicial error in the Dreyfus trial. Without Picquart's permission, Leblois confidentially informed Auguste Scheurer-Kestner, vice-president of the Senate, of what he had learned from Picquart and showed him the Gonse letters. This was enough to convince Scheurer-Kestner of Dreyfus's innocence. In his turn, he contacted Georges Clemenceau, who, after his defeat in 1893, had joined *L'Aurore,* a pro-Dreyfus left-wing newspaper. Scheurer-Kestner persuaded Clemenceau to denounce the irregularity of the trial. The Dreyfus Affair had now grown into an important political issue.

The Army, the nationalists, and many French Catholics were united in their opposition to the campaign to have the court-martial reviewed. It had become an article of faith with them that the Jew was guilty. Dreyfus was no longer a man. He had turned into a myth, a symbol, an abstraction. Among other things, he had become a scapegoat for Sedan. His name evoked the image of the defeated fatherland, butchered, treacherously delivered into the hands of the Germans. In the popular mind, France could never have been invaded and captured by a foreign enemy without the help of some traitor from within. Dreyfus stood for that traitor. He was that traitor. Whoever denied his guilt was a heretic and a bad citizen. For having spoken up in Dreyfus's behalf, Scheurer-Kestner, a wealthy former munitions manufacturer and till then a much respected patriot, one of the founders of the Third Republic, was savagely vilified by the whole nationalist press.

On November 9, 1897, one of Dreyfus's brothers, Mathieu, had a facsimile of the *bordereau* broadcast everywhere throughout Paris. A banker named de Castro recognized Esterhazy's handwriting and told a friend, who passed the discovery on to Mathieu. Encouraged by Scheurer-Kestner, Mathieu reported it to the Minister of War. It now had become impossible to avoid an investigation. Esterhazy himself was obliged to attend first an army inquiry, then a full-dress court-martial. The military authorities conducting it did everything they could, however, to subvert justice. In collusion with Esterhazy, a small group of officers in charge of the court-martial investigation or directly

223

affected by it, including Major Henry, tirelessly forged misleading evidence and spread false rumors calculated to discredit Picquart and his testimony. Day by day, the Dreyfus Case became murkier, more complicated.

On January 5, 1895, the day of Dreyfus's degradation, Zola had dined at the Daudets'. Léon had been present at the ceremony and had described it in detail – the hostile crowds, Dreyfus's protestations of innocence and cry, 'Long live France!', the breaking of his sword, the whole drama. Although Léon's account had been passionately hostile to Dreyfus (the Daudets were friends of Drumont's and thoroughly sympathized with his anti-Semitism), Zola had nevertheless not been able to help feeling sorry for the poor fellow. However, like most other people, he had assumed that Dreyfus was guilty. It had occurred to him that the incident was something that he could use some day in a novel. But he had given it little more thought. He had been too caught up in his own personal affairs – his domestic life with Alexandrine, Jeanne, and the children, *Les Trois Villes*, his struggle to cope with old age, preserve his reputation, ensure the survival of his works, adjust to changing tastes, and regain his position as one of the leaders of the avant-garde.

In 1897, just as the Dreyfus Case was beginning to loom up as a major political issue, Bernard Lazare sent him his pamphlets. Shortly afterwards, he called on him to find out what he thought of them. Although the same young writer had treated him rather unfavorably in a series of essays entitled *Les Figures contemporaines*, Zola received him courteously and congratulated him on his courage. Yet he had hardly glanced at the pamphlets. He still assumed that Dreyfus was guilty.

Then, that October, Leblois, Picquart's lawyer, approached him, cautiously acquainted him with certain confidential facts of the Case, and persuaded him to meet with Scheurer-Kestner for lunch. Even the old senator could not entirely convince him. He discussed the Affair with others. Only gradually, as he thought about it, analyzing the facts with his own novelist's mind, trying to extract from them answers to the questions troubling him, did the truth dawn on him.

At first, primarily the novelist was stirred. The three leading characters of Dreyfus's story as he originally envisaged it formed in his imagination a fascinating triptych: 'a trilogy of types," as he put it:

the innocent victim over there with a tempest inside his skull; the real criminal running around scot-free here at home and all that must be going on inside him while someone else pays for his crime; and his unmasker, Scheurer-Kestner, quietly working hour after hour to bring the truth to light.

The whole spectacle had something frightfully beautiful about it. It was gripping, thrilling, horrible. It was also grand. 'I do not know what I shall do about it, but no human drama has ever filled me with a more poignant emotion,' he wrote Scheurer-Kestner on November 20. 'It is the battle for truth, and that is the only good one, the only great one.'

Zola's first article on the Affair, published in *Le Figaro* of November 15, 1897, reflects this attitude. He was still a spectator, a passionately interested one, but nothing more. Entitled 'M. Scheurer-Kestner,' it was a tribute to the old man's sense of duty and honor. It closed with the words, destined to become famous: 'Truth is on the march, and nothing will stop it.'

But when Zola wrote his second article on the subject, 'Le Syndicat,' published in the same newspaper on December 1, he was already fully committed to the campaign for revision. Exploding the myth that a vast, shadowy organization of wealthy Jews had been formed to buy Dreyfus's release even if it meant putting an innocent Christian in his place, he named Dreyfus's actual supporters. He proudly included himself among them. In doing so, he was risking his peace of mind, his chances of getting into the Academy, some of his closest friendships, his popularity, but it did not matter. The old fighter was aroused once again. Once again he was a soldier reveling in battle and hungering for glory. Once again he was also the Zola who had declared at twenty-one, 'The poet's role is sacred. It is to be a regenerator, to devote himself to the progress of humanity.'

His third article, published in *Le Figaro* of December 5, expressed his conviction that Esterhazy's court-martial, to take place in January, would set matters straight by revealing the true criminal. After that, he predicted, a chastened France would return to the path of humanitarianism and justice. Worried by the possible reactions of its conservative readers, *Le Figaro* now closed its columns to him.

He was already beginning to pay the price of his boldness. On December 7, at a dinner party attended by both himself and Daudet, he and his old 'friend' publicly clashed over the Affair. Immediately afterwards, the atmosphere became icy. The dinner dragged on in futile and extremely sad conversation.

Daudet, long ill with an agonizing disease of the spinal cord, died suddenly on December 16. At the funeral, on December 20, the crowd jeered Zola as he paced along dejectedly holding one of the strings of Daudet's pall. 'Down with Zola! Down with the traitor! Bandit! Sellout!' A band of young men followed him step by step, resolved not to leave him until he had safely returned to the Rue de Bruxelles.

Meanwhile, he had fired off a pamphlet, *Lettre à la jeunesse.* He followed this with another, *Lettre à la France,* published on January 6, 1898.

On January 10, Esterhazy's court-martial began. On the 11th, to the stupefaction of Dreyfus's supporters, he was unanimously acquitted. The court broke into applause. There were shouts of 'Long live France!' and 'Down with the Syndicate!'

Zola was already hard at work on an open letter to Félix Faure, the President of the Republic. There was a grave danger that the whole matter of Dreyfus's guilt or innocence would disappear from the headlines and be forgotten once again. The jingoist newspapers were already declaring the Affair over. No broad movement in favor of Dreyfus as yet existed, because the evidence of Dreyfus's innocence was unknown except to a handful of supporters. From the government's point of view, the Dreyfus Case was of only minor importance. Something had to be done to force the government to order a review of Dreyfus's court-martial and ensure that it would result in Dreyfus's exoneration. Fully aware of what he was doing (he had checked the libel laws), Zola composed the letter in such a way as to make it certain that he would be arrested. His trial and the uproar and civil suits that would inevitably result would help achieve his objectives.

At the same time, he kept on, as he had in his earlier writings on the case, trying to wake up France – that is to say, his France, the France of Voltaire, the Rights of Man, the republic – to what was really happening.

He worked on feverishly hour after hour. A day passed. Another day. He kept on writing, sustained not only by his passion for truth and hatred of injustice but also by his thirst for glory and very human fear that someone else might be doing the same thing and finish first. Informed of what he was doing, Clemenceau had almost insisted on writing the letter himself. As Zola's pen scratched away, a mob shouted outside, 'Down with Zola! Long live Esterhazy!' A stone crashed through a window. Policemen standing by in the street merely shrugged. A package of excrement arrived in the mail.

Towards noon of the third day Zola was finished. Late that afternoon, he took the manuscript to *L'Aurore* and read it to the editors and a few visitors who happened to be there. They saw the drama in all its horror for the first time and burst into applause. The next day, January 13, the letter appeared on the front page with the banner headline '*J'accuse . . . !*' – chosen at the last moment by Clemenceau.

It was everything that Zola had meant it to be: a premeditated provocation, a cry of anger, a brilliant exposé of the facts of the Affair, an appeal to the humanitarian idealism which for millions of Frenchmen like himself still had the force of a religion.

Although even more passionate in style than anything that he had written before on the Affair, it had a remarkable terseness and clarity. It flashed and stabbed like a deftly wielded sword. It named names. It recounted in damning detail what had really happened. It ridiculed the charge against Dreyfus. It denied the competence of the three graphologists who had testified that the *bordereau* was in his handwriting. It dared to accuse General Mercier and General Billot, the two War Ministers involved in the Case, with either hiding the truth, deliberately lying, or yielding weakly to others. It accused the War Office of conducting a despicable newspaper campaign to lead public opinion astray and hide its mistakes. It claimed that Esterhazy had been acquitted by order. Adopting an outright religious terminology, it characterized Dreyfus's persecutors as 'sacrilegious' and compared them to 'inquisitors.' It appealed to the great republican and humanitarian values – justice, liberty, brotherhood, science, humanity, and progress. The words *truth* and *justice* in particular resounded again and again.

It was a crime, it said, 'to exploit patriotism in works of hatred,' a crime to make the saber 'a modern god, when all human science was striving to construct the great future edifice of truth and justice.' It asserted once again Zola's faith in the power of truth: 'I have said this elsewhere, and I repeat it here; when you try to bury truth underground, it grows there, it acquires such explosive force that, the day it erupts, it blows up everything with it.'

The whole edition of *L'Aurore*, all 200,000 copies, was sold out by evening. The complete text or excerpts of *J'accuse . . . !* appeared in hundreds of other publications in France and abroad. Millions of people throughout the world were stirred. Zola received 14,000 letters and telegrams of support and congratulation, some from as far away as San Francisco. The great socialist statesman Jaurès called *J'accuse . . . !* 'the greatest revolutionary act of the century.'

Marcel Proust and some other young writers from *La Revue blanche* circulated a petition among French savants, writers, philosophers, painters, teachers, and students. It called for a revison of Dreyfus's court-martial. Soon they had gathered one hundred and four signatures. Clemenceau had it published in *L'Aurore* under the title 'The Manifesto of the Intellectuals.' It was the first time the word *intellectual* was used in its contemporary sense. Zola's name came first, then that of Anatole France. Durkheim gave his support. So did Lanson, Maeterlinck, Gide, Mallarmé, Péguy, Signac, Ensor.

Monet, who had been deeply hurt by *L'Oeuvre*, wrote Zola, 'Once again I say bravo, with all my heart, for your valor and courage.'

The vast majority of foreigners were pro-Zola. Mark Twain wrote in *The New York Herald:* 'Such cowards, hypocrites, and flatterers as the members of military and ecclesiastical courts the world could produce by the millions every year. But it takes five centuries to produce a Zola.' In Rome, however, Leo XIII remained silent. The official Jesuit review, *Civilià Cattolica* asserted: 'The Jews have invented the allegation of a judicial error. The plot was worked out at the Zionist Congress in Basel, invoked ostensibly to discuss the deliverance of Jerusalem. The Protestants made common cause with the Jews for the creation of a syndicate.'

But in France the growing number of revisionists was still far outweighed by those who opposed revision or wanted nothing to do with the case. Furious mobs paraded through the streets. Zola was burnt in effigy. Drumont and other yellow journalists called for the sacking of his house, incarceration, assassination. Anti-Semites staged a series of riots in Bordeaux, Montpellier, Marseilles, Le Havre and other French cities. In Algiers, a mob sacked the Jewish quarter.

The government had no choice but to grant Zola's bold request that it prosecute him. The charge was cautiously restricted to solely those passages in *J'accuse . . . !* stating that Major Esterhazy had been acquitted by order. Thus not only would the trial be limited to matters on which the defense could produce no evidence; there would be no need to mention the Dreyfus Case at all.

The trial lasted sixteen tumultuous days. While a vast, ugly crowd milled about the Place Dauphine outside the Palace of Justice, only a few steps from Notre-Dame, the spectators jamming the courtroom excitedly watched the drama unfold. Many of them were officers in mufti under order to cheer or disrupt the trial on command. There were numerous society women. Delegorgue, the portly, complacent, red-faced president of the three-man tribunal, suppressed any attempts of the defense to introduce new testimony. The jury consisted almost entirely of tradesmen. Their names and addresses had been published in the nationalist press. Zola appeared nervous but elated. Much of the time he was bored. Dressed in a black coat and white vest, he would get up now and then, stroll here and there, exchange a few words with his sympathizers, converse with journalists, read telegrams expressing support from all over the world. His Counsel, Fernand Labori, had a stentorian voice and was a dogged debater. But whenever he asked a leading question, the president stopped him with the dry formula: 'The question will not be put!'

At one point on the second day, Zola leapt to his feet, furiously demanding the freedom 'granted to murderers and thieves; they can defend themselves, they can call witnesses.' Delegorgue interrupted him: 'You are aware of Article 52 of the law of 1881.' Beside himself, Zola cried, 'I don't know the law and I don't want to know it!' All over the courtroom, angry voices shouted in

229

chorus, 'Down with Zola!' 'We shall know how to make you respect the law!' said the Court. 'I did not mean to place myself above the law,' Zola quickly said, trying to make himself heard above the din. 'I meant that to use only fifteen lines of what I said, in order to inculpate me is beneath justice.'

That evening he risked his life passing through the surging, jeering, spitting, cane-waving mob outside the Palace. If, just in the nick of time, he had not been able to jump aboard a special police van, he would surely have been torn to pieces. On other evenings, toughs chased his carriage as he rode away.

On the thirteenth day, he read a short address to the jury. He spoke of the contribution that he had made to French literature and then went on to say, his voice shaking, 'May all that crumble, may my works perish, if Dreyfus is not innocent.' In conclusion, he stated that France would some day thank him for having helped to save its honor.

It took the jury only forty minutes to arrive at a verdict. They found Zola guilty, seven to five. He was condemned to imprisonment for twelve months and fined 3,000 francs. He was also to be suspended from the Legion of Honor. Outside the Palace, the news of the verdict brought yells of triumph. There were cries of 'Death to the Jews! Death to the dirty Jews!' Two thousand police struggled to maintain order.

An American newspaper published by blacks, the *Bee* of the District of Columbia, editorialized: 'French justice seems to have fled to brutish beasts, for the verdict is simply an expression of the prejudice and race hate of a uniformed and inferior mob.'

Zola had by now become one of the most loved and detested men in history. The attitude of Chekhov, then at Nice, was typical of that of thousands of intellectuals around the world. 'I would not exchange one of his fingernails,' he wrote a friend back in Russia, 'for all of those who are sitting on his case at the court, all those generals and high-born witnesses.' Mallarmé (who died only a few weeks later) wrote Zola: 'The spectacle has just been given for all time of limpid intuition opposed to the competitive spirit of the mighty. I venerate this courage and am filled with admiration at the thought that, from a glorious labor of creation that would have worn out anyone else, a man could still emerge, new, whole, so heroic!' On February 26, Monet, who had been too ill to attend the trial, wrote him: 'I am among those who believe that you have just done a noble service to France . . . . She will be proud some day that she gave birth to you.'

Immediately after the trial, there was formed the League for the Defense of the Rights of Man and of the Citizen. More than two hundred Roman Catholic supporters of Dreyfus banded together in a Committee for the Defense of Right and Justice. Numerous prominent citizens courageously spoke up for Dreyfus at meetings that often turned tempestuous. There was a strong revival of religious humanitarianism. As one French intellectual recalled twelve years later, 'It was through the Dreyfus Case that the men of our generation communed for the first time in Humanity. For us, it was, and it remains, a religion. All our lives, we will bear gloriously on our brows this baptism of outrages and of tears. By this sign we shall know each other.' During this same period, a former priest, Victor Charbonnel, even went so far as to invent a new Humanitarian Church with its own ritual and Hugo, Michelet, Anatole France, and, of course, Zola as its patriarchs.

But far more Frenchmen rejoiced at the court's verdict than condemned it. The journalistic abuse to which Zola was now submitted knew no bounds. Because of his partly Italian ancestry, the gutter press branded him a half-breed. One widely circulated penny newspaper, *Le Petit journal,* ran the headline: 'Emile Zola's Father a Thief!' Pious French families, including that of the young François Mauriac, called their chamber pots 'Zolas.' A chauvinist sent Denise, now eight, a photograph of her father with the eyes poked out.

By now the larger issues of the Affair by far overshadowed the question of Dreyfus's guilt or innocence. Anticlericalism had become involved. So also had the rivalry between republican civil authority and a military body claiming to be autonomous within the state and the question of individual civil rights versus public authority. In opposing revision, rightists continued to believe that they were championing the cause of national security against international socialism and Jewry and of France against Germany.

Zola's unpopularity with the general public resulted in a disastrous collapse in the sales of his novels. Since he had put almost no money away he was threatened with financial collapse. Yet he had never been more serene. Although he had

231

lost his position at the head of the literary avant-garde, he had won something even better. He was marching once again at the head of the great ideas of his century. Like Hugo before him, he embodied the best of republican France. He was helping more effectively than ever before create the world of the future.

After his trial, he had appealed on technical grounds to the Cour de Cassation. There was every reason to fight for time. Not only was pro-Dreyfus sentiment growing and the question of Dreyfus's guilt under debate everywhere. Ministries were falling. Forgers and spies connected with the case were committing suicide. There was a rash of law suits related to the Affair. As a result, new facts, some of which might be useful to him, were being bared every day.

His second trial began on May 23, 1898, at the Cour d'Assises in Versailles. Labori immediately appealed, again on technical grounds, but this time with no success. The desired new evidence had failed to turn up. On July 18, Zola was again condemned to the maximum penalties. As Labori explained to him, there was only one way now of keeping his case operative and thereby making sure that the Dreyfus Affair would remain alive; he would have to avoid punishment by going into exile. He hated the idea, yet had to agree with Labori's reasoning.

That very evening, with only a nightshirt and a toilet bag wrapped in a newspaper, he left for Dover. After staying a couple of days at the Grosvenor Hotel, next to Victoria Station, he moved to the Oatlands Park Hotel in Weybridge, then rented a detached villa at Oatlands Chase, Walton-on Thames. About four weeks later, he shifted to another furnished house in the village of Addlestone, not far away. In October, he took up residence in The Queen's Hotel, in Church Road, Norwood. All of this had to be done in great secrecy, under assumed names, M. Pascal, for example, or M. Beauchamp; for he was in constant danger of being served with a French summons. Luckily, it was rumored in France that he had fled to Norway or Switzerland.

While in England, he suffered dreadfully from homesickness. He could hardly bear being separated from his loved ones. He spoke no English. He found it impossible to adjust to English food. The news from Paris was sometimes quite depressing. On July 26, he was suspended from his rank in the Legion of Honor.

The following month, he was shocked to learn that a damage suit brought against him by the three graphologists whom he had criticized as incompetent in *J'accuse . . .!* had succeeded.

He was as passionately attached as ever to his dogs and other animals. In particular, he missed his toy Pomeranian, Pinpin. He would gladly have brought it with him, but foreign dogs were not admitted into England. Fierce, intensely loyal, jealous, barking at anyone who approached its master, it had accompanied him everywhere it could – when he was out bicycling, or napping in his chalet on the island, or writing in his study. After his departure, it had pined away and early that autumn had died. He mourned for it as he would have one of his own children.

He seethed with resentment at the way his beloved France had treated him. He hated having to stand by idly while other men carried on the fight for truth and justice. Although he was confident that their cause would triumph in the end, it seemed to him that the victory that they were all so impatiently waiting for was very slow coming. 'Oh yes, the truth advances,' he wrote an artist friend, Fernand Desmoulin, on August 10, 'but at a snail's pace!'

Yet he had been through worse times. Ernest Vizetelly, the journalist son of his English publisher, and other Englishmen were extraordinarily kind and helpful. Jeanne, Denise, and Jacques joined him for a few weeks before school recommenced in the fall. Alexandrine came to see him on October 30 and, although the climate made her ill, stayed until December 5. Jeanne and the children returned briefly during the Easter holidays. As usual, he found solace in his work. 'I have never believed in anything but work,' he wrote Desmoulin on August 13, 1898. 'It is always what has saved me,' he remarked in a letter to Labori a few days later. Moreover, his optimism about the Affair was justified. Although the chances of Dreyfus's being proven innocent were not improving as rapidly as he would have liked, progress was indeed being made.

On August 31, Henry committed suicide, after admitting to having forged the Panizzardi letters. On June 3, 1899, the Cour de Cassation quashed the judgement of Dreyfus's court-martial and demanded a re-hearing of the case.

The next day, Sunday, June 4, at nine o'clock in the evening,

Zola boarded a train in Victoria Station and, the following morning, arrived back in Paris. His exile had lasted almost eleven months.

The national duel went on. The verdict brought by Dreyfus's second court-martial on September 9, 1899, was absurd: guilty with extenuating circumstances. Ten days later, President Loubet pardoned the man. This too was absurd, since he had committed no crime. He would not be completely exonerated until 1906. But after Zola's return to France, his own part in the Affair was largely over. He had already made his main contribution. It was not until March, 1901, however, that he had completely extricated himself from all the criminal and civil legal proceedings that he had been involved in as a result of his intervention. In a public statement, he renounced all further action against Ernest Judet, the journalist who had alleged that his father was a thief. He also decided at the same time not to press his suit to have set aside the judgement awarding the three handwriting experts damages for his having accused them of incompetency. 'Let them keep the money, let them go off with their pockets full,' he wrote. 'The irony of it all will be the greater, and there will be yet a little more baseness in the Affair.' He did not want his noble battle to end in sordid bickering over sums of money.

X

Once he had arrived back in France, his private life had returned pretty much to normal. His income would never rise again to quite what it had been before *J'accuse . . . !* But as the months went by, it gradually improved, and by 1900 he was making about 400,000 francs a year. He spent many happy hours with Jeanne and the children, strolling or bicycling with them, photographing them, discussing botany with Jacques, or helping Denise with the homework assigned in her catechism class. He particularly enjoyed going over her essays on Biblical history with her, whipping them into shape, recounting with gusto all the most sanguine crimes, massacres, and wars of the Old and New Testaments. Not surprisingly, many of these essays received from their priestly reader very high marks. On their walks, Denise would insist on resting on her father's arm, in order to be with him and bask in the atmosphere of fame that surrounded him.

One of the high points of 1900, along with Denise's First Communion, was the Paris Exposition, on the theme of electricity. Accompanied by Alexandrine, Zola took numerous photographs of the Palais de l'Électricité and other attractions. In October, after he had dined with Jeanne and the children at the Eiffel Tower, they watched the light display and admired the illuminated fountains in front of the Château d'Eau.

Alexis, his close friend and the only member of his original group of disciples who had not deserted him, died suddenly in July, 1901. In his grief, it seemed to him that one of the most precious parts of his own past had vanished with the dear man. At the funeral, he praised Alexis's sure taste and noble character, and ended, 'Farewell, friend, with all my heart.'

Since his flight to England, he had also become absorbed once again in his creative writing. As before, he stuck to a regular schedule, and his pen scratched on as productively as ever. He was still capable at times of composing passages reminiscent of his best earlier novels – for example, a powerful realistic description, in *Travail*, of L'Abîme, a vast, sinister steel works, with its flames, thunderous rhythms, and forest of steam- and soot-belching chimneys, in the reddish light of dusk. Like Le Voreux, in *Germinal*, the whole mass assumes a monstrous life, breathes, devours its daily quotient of human flesh. But more than one of those traits which had endowed his naturalistic masterpieces with their peculiar power was largely missing from what he was doing now. Among other things, he had grown tired of exploring the real world, trying to emulate as he did so the ruthless, unflinching objectivity of science. 'I have been dissecting for forty years,' he wrote Octave Mirbeau in November, 1899. 'I must be allowed in my old age to dream a little.' As a result of this attitude, the fertile tension between the imaginative and realistic elements of his genius had been broken. The poetic element in his writings dating from this period no longer has that splendidly dynamic, explosive quality that it has in *L'Assommoir*, for example, or *Germinal* – all the more powerful for being contained by his realism like a gas under pressure. The symbols, instead of darting about in the ocean of Zola's naturalistic prose

235

challenging the reader to catch them, lie in full view, like fish displayed on a counter.

In his dreams the reveries now far outweighed the nightmares. It was more pleasant, no doubt, for him, but it made for less intriguing literature. Readers have always been more interested in descents into hell than they have in ascents into heaven. Moreover, his literary manner also had changed, again. It had grown more didactic. More than ever, he was devoured by a need to codify, theologize, and preach. Hypotheses, theories, intuitions, reveries that, before, he had almost always expressed tentatively, indirectly, subversively, in his creative writings – rarely committing himself to them entirely or overtly – he now proclaimed from the roof tops as certain truths. Discarding the laboratory jacket of a scientist, he had donned the white robe of the seer. It was not that he had really found the one, harmonious, all-embracing Truth which he had been looking for most of his life. In his more sober moments, he remained an anguished skeptic. But just because even now he still had no real religion, he more than ever found, like many of his spiritually troubled, questing contemporaries, a fleeting solace in fictional faiths.

While in exile, he had written his last short story, 'Angéline ou la maison hantée.' First published, in English translation, in *The Star,* on January 11, 1899, it is about a 'haunted' house in which the 'ghost' of a beautiful, long-dead young girl turns out to be another beautiful young girl distantly related to her and bearing the same name. 'Ah! the dear ghost! Death had been vanquished,' the narrator proclaims upon making the discovery. 'My old friend, the poet V*** was absolutely right, nothing is ever lost, everything recommences, beauty as well as love.' The story ends with the sentence: 'It was with the child's awakening that this house was haunted, this house that has become young and happy again today, in the finally regained happiness of eternal life.'

After *Lazare,* he had composed another light-opera for Bruneau, *Messidor.* First performed at the Académie Nationale de Musique on February 19, 1897, it had been a huge success, outlasting even Wagner's *Lohengrin.* Historically, it marked the triumph of prose over verse in the opera. But whereas *Lazare,* which would never be produced during Zola's lifetime, expresses

236

Zola's pessimism, this new work, with its partly fantastic setting and fanciful ballet and pantomine recounting 'the legend of gold,' is a glowing utopian dream. In it Zola imagines that a village of gold panners finds true wealth and happiness after the source of their greedy wealth is destroyed by an avalanche and that they all become wheat farmers. It is essentially a 'poem' glorifying productive labor, preaching, as he put it, 'the necessity and the beauty of effort, faith in life and the fecundity of the earth, and hope in the just harvest of tomorrow.'

He had followed *Messidor* with a musical fairy-tale inspired by essentially the same themes, *Violaine la chevelue,* replete with fairies, shepherds, shepherdesses, nymphs, and fauns. Now he confectioned still other librettos, always for the same distinguished composer. *L'Ouragan,* produced with considerable success at the Opéra-Comique in 1901, *L'Enfant roi,* and *Sylvanire ou Paris en amour.* They lyrically evoke the storms unleashed by the human passions, chant life's eternal renewal, glorify the child, fecundity, progress, work, Paris – the Paris which kills and brings forth new life. In the most lifelike scenes, realism survives as a mere manner. Elsewhere, it is lacking altogether. Dream, myth, fantasy reign supreme.

As Zola sat behind one of his elaborate, elegant antique desks, in the peace of his study at Médan or on the Rue de Bruxelles, his head was full of ambitious projects. He toyed with the idea of doing for the Third Republic what he had for the Second Empire – only in a different genre: a vast series of plays, to be called *La France en marche,* recounting the natural and social history of an epoch, pitting the forces of the past against those of the future, and culminating in the battle initiated by the Dreyfus Affair. But his bias, this time, would be strongly optimistic. The underlying assumption would be that, as he had always wanted to think, it was France's destiny to lead the battle of progress, the battle to establish 'the just city of tomorrow.' Meditating on Renan's life of Jesus, he was also tempted to write a work about an imaginary modern counterpart of Jesus, complete with characters corresponding to the Apostles, the women around Jesus, the priests, the Romans, the whole cast. In this work, he would create another new religion. His modern Jesus, he wrote down in his notes, would be another Tolstoy – but 'more practical.' He wanted, too, to write a novel about Zionism, on

237

the theme of Jerusalem rebuilt by the descendants of an ancient, scattered race, but he found the prospect of the long research trip abroad that this would require a bit disconcerting.

Meanwhile, he kept on working on *Les Quarte Évangiles*, the colossal tetralogy that he had begun in England. He conceived of it as a sequel to *Les Trois Villes*. In planning it, he had decided that each of its four novels would have as its hero one of the four sons of Pierre and Marie Froment. They were to be named Mathieu, Marc, Luc, and Jean, after the four gospels of the New Testament. Each volume would amount, in effect, to a new, modern gospel, a social gospel centered on one of Zola's own most sacred values: fecundity, work, truth, and justice. At the same time, he would be realizing, in a sense, his old dream, going back to *La Genèse*, of embracing the whole of time, of becoming the prophet of the future after having recounted the past and present. The actions he would relate would mostly unfold in a mythical twentieth century and beyond. Each would end in a Utopia. He was well aware that none of this would be easy, that he ran the risk of boring the public, that nothing is more glacial than fantasies and symbols dragged out too long, that the dream of universal brotherhood made people smile. Yet, as he had observed in his notes, he had always been attracted by danger; and so he had gone ahead with this difficult, yet, to him, infinitely appealing project.

It was all, he insisted, to be based on science – the dream that science authorizes. But actually the visions that he wanted to communicate to his readers had little to do with scientific truth. Over the years, he had gradually managed, like many of his contemporaries, to convince himself that his favorite fantasies had a scientific foundation, whereas all those philosophical and religious institutions and ideas that he disagreed with – Catholicism, above all – were 'unscientific.' Moreover, when he actually started writing, he would forget that he was dealing in dreams, that he and his fictional surrogates were only fictional messiahs. He imagined that he was really saving the world, in and through them. What had started out as a fictional gospel, became, in his mind, a real one.

In composing the first one, *Fécondité*, he was motivated partly by his lifelong quasi-religious veneration for the productive power of life, partly by his concern about France's declining birth rate. He showed the family of Mathieu and Marianne growing generation by generation until, at their diamond wedding anniversary, three hundred people, all relatives by blood or marriage, assemble in their honor. Along with the number of their progeny, their property, the domain of Chantebled, redeemed from what was once useless land outside of Paris, has grown into an immense, very rich estate.

> And in their heroic grandeur, there was also all the desire with which they had burned, the divine desire, creator and regulator of the world, which had visited them in bursts of flame each time they had engendered a new being. They were like the holy temple that the god had constantly inhabited; they had loved each other with the inextinguishable fire with which the universe burns, for its endless creation.

Their descendants found and populate a new colony in Africa and spread elsewhere throughout the world – 'humanity on the march, eternally advancing.' On the other hand, all those characters in the story who practice birth control end up sadly. The main message is spelled out in the final pages: fecundity, the ever-expansive force of life, is the driving force of progress. 'There has never been in history a single forward step without humanity's having been pushed onwards by population growth.'

Fécondité is a novel only in the loosest sense of the term. As more than one of its original reviewers saw, it is really a long prose poem. Some readers have found it exciting, many others tedious, except for certain pages. Published by Fasquelle (who had bought out Charpentier) in early October, 1899, it stirred up considerable discussion, above all with respect to its thesis, especially among socialists. Some enthusiastically agreed. Others, like Péguy, thought it too nationalistic. In the first two years alone, 94,000 copies were sold.

Travail, the second volume, came out in May, 1901. After having composed the gospel of Venus, queen of seeds and immortal hope, Zola now preached, once again, but in vastly expanded form, what he had already called, in his talk to the student association, 'the religion of work.' Work, he now proclaimed, is the world's salvation, 'health, joy, sovereign peace, the sole truth,' the 'only master and only god, of a sovereign nobility, having redeemed humanity, which was dying from lies and injustice, healing it, giving it back the joy of life, restoring it to love and beauty.' The plot centers on the foundation of an ideal socialist community, La Crêcherie, with its own laws and religion, and the gradual spread of the new and better civilization it inaugurates around the world.

In the hero, Luc, a reform-minded engineer, Zola realized his ambition of creating a modern counterpart of Christ – or, more exactly, a Messianic figure reminiscent of Christ in many ways but succeeding where Christ had failed. 'A kind of archangel,' as one critic has put it, descending into the dark, crushing modern world to redeem it, his career parallels in some respects Christ's, including the crucifixion and resurrection. Some of the men and women around him recall those around Christ. Mary Magdalene, for example, has her opposite number in Josine, an oppressed working-class girl tottering on the brink of the gutter, whom Luc saves with his pure, unselfish love. As the founder of La Crêcherie, he presides over a mass festival that recalls the Eucharist, except that it is held out of doors and the birds take part, consuming the crumbs scattered on the tables. Like Christ, Luc radiates charity. He adheres to a variety of the golden rule. But his religion is essentially this-worldly and rooted not in the Hebrew scriptures so much as in Fourier, the anarchists Kropotkin and Grave, and Zola's own personal vision of God, man, nature and history. Luc, the savior of mankind, reigning over his grateful, happy followers like Christ among his disciples, embodies Zola's most glorious dream of what he himself wanted to be. Luc's death, moreover, represents the kind of death that Zola wanted most of all for himself:

> Below, under the window, the joyful band of children went on playing, and one could hear the cries of the tiniest ones, the laughs of the bigger ones, that joy of a future marching towards more and more happiness . . . . Then Luc, in one last look, embraced the city, the horizon, the entire earth, where the evolution begun by him was propagating itself and ending. His work was finished. The city had been founded. And Luc expired, entered the torrent of universal love, of universal life.

Despite its predominantly subjective, utopian character, *Tra-*

vail contains numerous pages capable of fascinating, if not the average amateur of fiction, at least certain types of readers, the religiously minded, for example, or those interested in the history of social ideas. Like *Les Rougon-Macquart* and *Les Trois Villes*, and *Fécondité*, but more compellingly than this last novel, it involves the reader in the central spiritual drama of modern times, the clash of old and new religious ideas, the search for a new religious and political faith, the quest for a new Messiah. It expresses even more strongly than any of Zola's earlier novels, even *Germinal*, *La Débâcle*, and *Paris*, the mood of world destruction and renewal that, as has already been noted, had set its mark upon his time. Nowhere else in his fiction does one have so intense an impression of participating in what the Greeks would have called a new metamorphosis of the gods – that is, of the fundamental principles and symbols. It is also the most luridly apocalyptic of all of Zola's novels, ending with still terrifying descriptions of the great final war between capitalism and socialism – a mechanized Armageddon anticipating World Wars I and II:

> They did not even take the time to carry away the dead; the heaps of corpses made walls behind which new regiments, ever pouring in, came to die. Night did not put an end to the combat . . . . From the sky itself, balloons hurled bombs, burning down towns wherever they passed. Science had invented explosives, engines capable of carrying death prodigious distances, of suddenly engulfing an entire population, like an earthquake . . . .

Since the Dreyfus Affair, more and more working-class readers had begun to read Zola. Péguy, Guesde, Georges Sorel, and other socialist thinkers and leaders growled, held up their hands in dismay, or shrugged (a later exception would be Lenin, who highly esteemed *Travail*); but the masses loved the novel. They recognized Zola's enormous sympathy for them and saw that he shared many of their own aspirations. All over France, this second gospel was read and commented on in working-class night schools like a Bible. In 1903, the 77,000th copy was sold.

He finished his third gospel, *Vérité*, another immense work, on August 7, 1902. In several ways it differed from both of its predecessors, which are also quite different from each other. He had tried in his original planning of the series to give the ideas to be set forth in it some systematic unity. He had noted that his four main subjects penetrate each other: 'fecundity can get nowhere without work, which can get nowhere without science, which brings about justice.' But the world view that had begun to emerge from *Les Quatre Evangiles* was almost as confused as that which had issued from *Les Rougon-Macquart*. It was as though John of Patmos, instead of writing one Revelation, had written several, each with a different Messiah, a different religion, a different supreme deity, a different vision of the shape of things to come. While writing *Vérité*, Zola had been inspired by his memories of the Dreyfus Affair, still not over. He had also wanted to play a part in the intense political and ideological battle, then rocking the whole of France, between anticlericals and clericals, the schoolmaster and the priest, those for absolute separation of church and state, and those opposing it. The hero, Marc, is a schoolmaster passionately devoted, like Zola, to truth and justice. The villains are priests and monks. The story has to do mainly with Marc's heroic and ultimately successful struggle on behalf of Simon, a Jewish friend and colleague, wrongfully accused of having sexually abused and murdered his eleven-year-old nephew. The real culprit is a monk, Gorgias, one of the boy's teachers at a school run by Gorgias's monastic order. The book attacks not only Catholicism, but the whole of Christianity, for exalting servility and poverty of spirit. In the place of the traditional Catholic catechism, Marc proposes 'the catechism of science.' All revealed truth, he informs his pupils, is a lie. Only experimental truth is true, one and entire, and eternal. The only way social progress can be achieved is through the truths that science discovers for the benefit of humanity.

Before finishing *Vérité* (which would not be published until 1903), Zola had already begun thinking seriously about his fourth gospel, *Justice*. He wanted it to include the whole of humanity, a humanity brought together by justice. It would portray a world without frontiers, a disarmed world, a peaceful and happy socialistic world of brothers working together, holding the means of production in common. It would stress the pacifying, liberating role of France. 'France the Messiah,' he wrote in his preparatory notes. 'Redeemer, Savior, Queen.'

He was never to write the novel. On Sunday, September 28,

1902, Alexandrine and he left Médan to take up their autumn and winter quarters at no. 21 *bis* Rue de Bruxelles. The building was chilly, because the basement furnace had not been used during the summer; so a fire was lighted in their bedroom. Noting that the chimney did not draw well, Alexandrine expressed her intention of having it examined by some workmen who were then making some repairs in the rooms. They sat down to dinner about eight o'clock and, after a hearty meal, decided to go to bed. The move back to Paris had exhausted them. She noted that the bedroom fire was burning poorly and asked Zola if he wanted to have it extinguished. He decided that there was no need to do so. It would seen burn itself out, he thought. Not long afterwards, they fell asleep. The room slowly filled with coal gas. (In 1927, a fitter of heating appliances, a zealous nationalist, would confess, shortly before his death, that he and some fellow workmen repairing the roof of a neighboring house had deliberately stopped the Zolas' chimney up. They had then unblocked it very early the following morning, without being seen. But whether this was what had really happened, would never be proved.) About nine o'clock that same morning, after repeatedly knocking on their door, one of the servants, a man named Monnier, became alarmed and, together with his wife, broke it down. Alexandrine was lying unconscious on Zola's and her bed. He was lying in his nightshirt on the floor, his feet just touching a bedside rug. He was dead.

For hours, his two most recent pet dogs, both Pomeranians like his beloved Pinpin, went about the apartment looking for him everywhere and whining plaintively because they could not find him. Meanwhile, the news of his death had spread throughout Paris, France, and much of the rest of the world. Newspapers announced it in special editions. Drumont's *Libre Parole* ran on its front page, in large letters, the headline: 'A Naturalistic Miscellaneous News Item: Émile Zola Asphyxiated.' *Le Peuple Français* declared that God had punished Zola. It was rumored that the agent of His divine wrath had been none other than the Archangel Michael. In Aix, Cézanne, informed of the sad event by his gardener, retired to his studio and did not come out for the rest of the day, overcome with grief. Pope Leo XIII reportedly commented, 'He was an adversary of the Church, but a frank, honest adversary. May his soul find rest in Heaven.'

Telegrams and letters of condolence flooded in from all over France and nearly every foreign country. Hundreds of distinguished figures crowded into the vestibule of the house on the Rue de Bruxelles to inscribe their names in the registers. The air of the apartment was heavy with the fragrance of a host of wreaths and coronals. In his will, Zola had left all his property to his wife. He had also specified that the interment should be in Paris and include no religious rites. A gigantic public funeral, devoid of such rites, took place on Sunday, October 5. Police and municipal guards lined the streets between his home and the place of burial, the Montmartre Cemetery. Out of sight, two cavalry squadrons stood on the ready, in case rioting should break out. As the coffin was brought out of the house, escorted by Charpentier, Fasquelle, Bruneau, and other pallbearers, drums beat and soldiers presented arms. Two chariots laden with flowers preceded the hearse, draped in the antique arms of the Venetian Zollas. Alexandrine, too distraught to attend the ceremony, was confined to her bed, but among the friends and relatives who followed after, were Ernest Vizetelly and another man between whom, his hands in theirs, walked little Jacques. Jeanne, in full mourning, heavily veiled, and Denise were there too. She also, pacing along sadly in perfect order, their heads uncovered, their voices stilled, were Alfred Dreyfus, the chiefs of all the main government departments, a crowd of well-known writers, artists, and other celebrities. Then came innumerable deputations, including a troop of miners from Denain rhythmically shouting: 'Germinal! Germinal!' Altogether, the *cortège* consisted, according to one report, of 50,000 persons. A vast multitude watched the spectacle. Only a few shouted insults. The common people in general had by now accepted Zola as their own.

At the cemetery, the last and principal oration was delivered by Anatole France. He spoke of the immensity of Zola's work, his kindliness, candor, and simplicity, the idealism that complemented his realism, his hatred of injustice, his reforming zeal, his love for mankind. Zola, in his youth, had posed for his painter friend Chaillan as Amphion, the mythical singer who, with his brother Zethus, had built Thebes, huge blocks of stone forming themselves into walls at the sound of his lyre. Knowing nothing of this, Anatole France compared Zola to the same mythological figure, contrasting him at the same time with Tolstoy: 'At the two extremities of European thought the lyre has raised two vast ideal cities. Both are generous and pacific; but whereas Tolstoy's is the city of resignation, Zola's is the city of work.' He spoke on, reviewing Zola's role in the Dreyfus Affair. After doing so, he said, 'Gentlemen, there is only one country in the world where such great things could have been accomplished. How beautiful is the genius of our fatherland!' He concluded: 'Let us envy him: he honored his country and the world by an immense literary work and by a great deed. Envy him! His destiny and his heart made his lot that of the greatest: *he was a moment of the conscience of man!*'

On the night of June 4, 1908, his coffin was removed from its tomb in the cemetery and transferred to the Panthéon, where it was laid under the dome. The six marble columns surrounding it were draped in gold and flowers. Outside, thousands of *cuirassiers* with shining brass helmets and breast-armor stood at attention. After a second funeral ceremony, in which music from *Messidor* was played, his remains were placed, not far from Voltaire's and Rousseau's sarcophagi, in the crypt below. They are still there today, sharing a small vault with Victor Hugo's.

Selected Bibliography

The principal contemporary editions of Zola's works are *Les Rougon-Macquart*, ed. Henri Mitterand, 5 vols, Gallimard, Bibliothèque de la Pléiade, Paris, 1960-7; *Les Oeuvres complètes*, ed. Henri Mitterand, 15 vols, Cercle du Livre Précieux, Paris, 1962-9; and *Contes et Nouvelles*, ed. Roger Ripoll, Gallimard, Bibliothèque de la Pléiade, Paris, 1976. A major new critical edition of Zola's letters, containing thousands of previously unpublished ones (*Correspondance*), is being issued currently by the University of Montréal Press. Edited by a large international team of scholars under the direction of B. H. Bakker, the set, when completed, is projected to run to ten volumes. For those interested in Zola's art criticism, mention should also be made here of F. W. J. Hemmings' and R. J. Niess's scholarly edition of his *Salons*, Droz, Geneva, 1959 and of the excellent critical anthology of Zola's writings on art edited under the title *Le Bon Combat de Courbet aux Impressionistes* by Jean-Paul Bouillon with a preface by Gaëtan Picon, Hermann, Collection Savoir, Paris, 1974. A list of fifty-nine films based on Zola's novels or short stories compiled by Leo Braudy may be found in *Yale French Studies*, no. 42 (1969), pp. 85-7.

The locations of Zola's manuscripts in so far as they are known and bibliographical information about the publication of his writings are given in the first three works cited above. A list of the serial publication dates of his novels is provided by F. W. J. Hemmings in *Emile Zola*, 2nd edn, Clarendon Press, Oxford, 1966 (republished as an Oxford Paperback in 1970). A complete chronological and descriptive bibliography of Zola's articles, short stories, and poems published between 1859 and 1881 has been prepared by Henri Mitterand and Halina Suwala, *Emile Zola Journaliste: Bibliographie chronologique et analytique – I. (1859-1881)*, Les Belles Lettres, Annales Littéraires de l'Université de Besançon, vol. 87, Paris, 1968. See also the sections entitled 'Bibliographie des articles de Zola recueillis en volume' and 'La Publication des contes de Zola dans les journaux et les revues' included in the 'Annexes' of Henri Mitterand's *Zola Journaliste de l'affaire Manet à l'affaire Dreyfus*, Armand Colin, Paris, 1962. No edition of Zola's complete works has as yet appeared in English. A list of the principal translations of his individual writings up to 1967 is included in Philip Walker's *Emile Zola*, Routledge & Kegan Paul, Profiles in Literature, London, 1968 [1969]. Since 1967, several new translations of Zola's novels have been brought out, most notably, *L'Assommoir*, tr. and intro. by L. W. Tancock, Penguin, Harmondsworth, Middlesex, 1970; *The Beast in Man (La Bête humaine)*, Tr. R. G. Goodyear and P. J. R. Wright, the New English Library, Signet Classics, London, 1968; *La Bête humaine*, tr. L. W. Tancock, Penguin, Harmondsworth, Middlesex, 1977; *The Debacle*, tr. and intro. by L. W. Tancock, Penguin, Harmondsworth, Middlesex, 1972; *The Earth (La Terre)*, tr. Douglas Parmée, Penguin, Harmondsworth, 1980; *Germinal*, tr. Stanley and Eleanor Hochman, with an afterword by Irving Howe, The New English Library, Signet Classics, London, 1970; *Nana*, tr. George Holden, Penguin, Harmondsworth, 1972; *Nana*, tr. Charles Duff, Folio Press, London, 1973; *The Sin of Father Mouret (La Faute de l'abbé Mouret)*, tr. S. Petrey, Prentice-Hall, Englewood Cliffs, N J, 1969.

By far the most exhaustive listing of writings about Zola (books, articles, unpublished dissertations, etc.) is provided by David Baguley's *Bibliographie de la critique sur Émile Zola*, University of Toronto Press, 1976-82, in two volumes. The first volume covers the period from 1864 through 1970 and contains 7,974 entries. The second, covering the following decade, lists 986 titles. It also includes a lengthy supplement to volume I. Both volumes are furnished with helpful subject and author indexes. The most helpful selected bibliography for students and specialists alike is Brian Nelson's *Émile Zola: A Selective Analytical Bibliography*, Research Bibliographies and Checklists no. 36, Grant & Cutler, London, 1982, 150 pp. Mention should also be made here of the selected bibliography published by F. W. J. Hemmings in his *Emile Zola*, mentioned above. This includes the principal documentary sources of our knowledge of Zola's life, together with a selection of the more useful books and articles written about his work up through 1964. See also the excellent bibliographies provided by Henri Mitterand in the Pléiade edition of *Les Rougon-Macquart*, also mentioned above, and by Joanna Richardson in her *Zola*, Weidenfeld & Nicolson, London, 1978. The aforementioned still incomplete Montréal University Press edition of Zola's *Correspondance* contains much precious bibliographical data (as well as many fresh biographical facts, basic information about the journals in which Zola published, and numerous biographical résumés of Zola's main correspondents and the people mentioned in his letters).

The following list of studies of Zola's life and work include some but by no means all of those available. The intention is merely to provide a small selection of those which seem, at least to the author of this volume, the most indispensable.

Alexis, P., *Emile Zola, notes d'un ami*, Charpentier, Paris, 1882.
Baguley, David, *Fécondité d'Emile Zola: Roman à thèse, évangile, mythe*, University of Toronto Press, 1973.
Barbusse, H., *Zola*, Gallimard, Paris, 1932.
Bonnefis, Philippe, 'Le Descripteur mélancolique,' in *La Description. Nodier, Sue, Flaubert, Hugo, Verne, Zola, Alexis, Fénélon*, Editions Universitaires, Paris, 1974, pp. 103-51.
Borie, J., *Zola et les mythes, ou de la nausée au salut*, Seuil, Paris, 1971.

Brady, P., *'L'Oeuvre' d'Émile Zola. Roman sur les arts. Manifeste, autobiographie, roman à clef,* Droz, Geneva, 1976.
Brisson, A., *L'Envers de la gloire. Enquêtes et documents inédits,* Flammarion, Paris, 1904 ('Émile Zola: l'aube de la gloire,' pp. 70-89; 'Le Caractère d'Émile Zola,' pp. 90-105.)
Brown, C. S., *Repetition in Zola's Novels,* University of Georgia Press, Athens, Georgia, 1952.
Burns, C. A., 'Documentation et imagination chez Émile Zola,' *Cahiers Naturalistes,* nos 14-25 (1963), pp. 69-78.
Carter, L. A., *Zola and the Theater,* Yale University Press, New Haven, Conn., 1963.
Chapman, G., *The Dreyfus Case: a Reassessment,* Rupert Hart-Davis, London, 1963 (ch. 7, 'The Intervention of Zola,' pp. 178-97).
Charpentier, Georges, *Trente années d'amitié. Lettres de l'éditeur Georges Charpentier à Émile Zola: 1872-1902,* ed. Colette Becker, Presses Universitaires de France, Paris, c. 1980.
Cogny, P., 'Émile Zola devant le problème de Jésus-Christ d'après des documents inédits,' *Studi Francesi,* viii (1964), 106-11.
De Amicis, E., *Ricordi di Parigi,* Treves, Milan, 1879 ('Emilio Zola,' pp. 213-90).
De Amicis, E., *Ritratti letterari,* Treves, Milan, 1881 ('Emilio Zola polemista,' pp. 51-106).
Dezalay, A., *L'Opéra des 'Rougon-Macquart': Essai de rythmologie romanesque,* Klincksieck, Paris, 1983.
Doucet, F., *L'Esthétique d'Émile Zola et son application à la critique,* De Nederlandsche Boek-en Steendrukkerij, 1923.
Dubois, J., *'L'Assommoir' de Zola: société, discours, idéologie,* Larousse, Paris, 1973.
Faria, Neide de, *Structures et unité dans 'Les Rougon-Macquart' (La poétique du cycle),* pref. by H. Mitterand, Nizet, Paris, 1977.
Girard, M., 'L'Univers de *Germinal*,' Revue des sciences humaines fasc. 69 (1953), pp. 59-76.
Goncourt, E. and J. de, *Journal. Mémoires de la vie littéraire,* ed. R. Ricatte, Editions de l'Imprimerie Nationale, Monaco, 1956.
Grant, E. M., *Émile Zola,* Twayne, New York, 1966.
Guieu, Jean-Max, *Le Théâtre lyrique d'Emile Zola,* Fischbacher, Paris, 1983.
Guillemin, H., *Présentation des Rougon-Macquart,*' Gallimard, Paris, 1964.
Hamon, P., 'A propos de l'impressionnisme de Zola,' *Cahiers Naturalistes,* xiii, no. 34 (1967), pp. 139-47.
Hamon, P., 'Un discours contraint', *Poétique,* iv, no. 16 (1973), pp. 411-45. ·
Hemmings, F. W. J., *Émile Zola* (see above).
Hemmings, F. W. J., *The Life and Times of Émile Zola,* Elek, London, 1977.
Hemmings, F. W. J., introduction, *Salons,* by Émile Zola (see above).
Jennings, C., *L'Eros et la femme chez Zola,* Klincksieck, Paris, 1977.
Josephson, M., *Zola and his Time,* Macaulay, New York, 1928.
Kamm, Lewis, *The Object in Zola's Rougon-Macquart*', José Porrúa Turanzas,

Madrid, 1978.

Kanes, M., 'Zola and Busnach: The Temptation of the Stage,' *PMLA*, lxxvii (March 1962), pp. 109-15.

Kanes, M., 'Zola, Pelletan and *La Tribune*,' *PMLA*, lxxix (September 1964), pp. 473-83.

Knapp, B. L., *Émile Zola*, Frederick Ungar, New York, 1980.

Laborde, A., *Trente-huit années près de Zola: Vie d'Alexandrine Émile Zola*, Les Editeurs Français Réunis,Paris, 1963.

Lanoux, A., *Bonjour, Monsieur Zola*, Amiot-Dumont, Paris, 1954.

Lapp, J. C., *Zola before the 'Rougon-Macquart'*, University of Toronto Press, 1964.

Lattre, A. de, *Le Réalisme selon Zola. Archéologie d'une intelligence*, Presses Universitaires de France, Paris, 1975.

Le Blond-Zola, D., *Émile Zola reconté par sa fille*, Fasquelle, Paris, 1931.

Le Blond-Zola, D., 'Émile Zola et l'amour des bêtes,' *Cahiers Naturaliste,* ii, no. 6 (1956), pp. 284-308.

Lepelletier, E., *Émile Zola, sa vie, son oeuvre*, Mercure de France, Paris, 1908.

Levin, H., 'Zola,' in *The Gates of Horn: A Study of Five French Realists*, Oxford University Press, New York, 1963, pp. 305-71.

Lewis, D. L., *Prisoners of Honor: The Dreyfus Affair*, William Morrow, New York, 1973.

Matthews, J. H., *Les Deux Zola*, Droz, Geneva, 1957.

Matthews, J. H., 'Things in the Naturalist Novel,' *French Studies*, xiv (1960), pp. 212-23.

Max, S., *Les Métamorphoses de la grande ville dans 'Les Rougon-Macquart,'* Nizet, Paris, 1966.

Mitterand, H., *Zola journaliste: De l'affaire Manet à l'affaire Dreyfus*, Armand Colin, Paris, 1962.

Mitterand, H., études, notes et variantes, *Les Rougon-Macquart*, by É. Zola, ed. H. Mitterand, 5 vols, Gallimard, Bibliothèque de la Pléiade, Paris, 1960-7.

Mitterand, H., *Le Discours du roman*, Presses Universitaires de France, Paris, 1980.

Nelson, Brian, *Zola and the Bourgeoisie: A Study of Themes and Techniques in 'Les Rougon-Macquart'*, Barnes & Noble, Totowa, New Jersey, 1983.

Newton, Joy, 'Émile Zola impressionniste,' *Cahiers Naturalistes*, xiii, nos 33-4 (1967), pp. 39-52, 124-38.

Niess, R. J., *Zola, Cézanne, and Manet: A Study of 'L'Oeuvre,'* University of Michigan Press, Ann Arbor, 1968.

Pasco, Allan, 'Love *à la* Michelet in Zola's *La Faute de l'abbé Mouret*,' *Nineteenth-Century French Studies*, VII, nos 3, 4 (1979), pp. 232-44.

Patterson, J. G., *A Zola Dictionary: with a Biographical and Critical Introduction, Synopses of the Plots of the 'Rougon-Macquart' Novels, and a Bibliographical Note*, Routledge, London, 1912.

Proulx, A., *Aspects épiques des 'Rougon-Macquart' de Zola*, Mouton, The Hague, 1966.

Présence de Zola, Fasquelle, Paris, 1953 (essays by various hands).

Selected Bibliography

Rewald, J., *Paul Cézanne: A Biography*, Simon & Schuster, New York, 1948.

Richardson, J., *Zola*, Weidenfeld & Nicolson, London, 1978.

Ripoll, Roger, *Réalité et mythe chez Zola, thèse présentée devant l'Université de Paris IV le 18 juin 1977*, 2 vols, Honoré Champion, Paris, 1981.

Robert, G., *Émile Zola. Principes et caractères généraux de son oeuvre*, Les Belles Lettres, Paris, 1952.

Robert, G., *'La Terre' d'Émile Zola, étude historique et critique*, Les Belles Lettres, Paris, 1952.

Robert, G., 'Zola et le classicisme,' *Revue des Sciences humaines*, fasc. 49 (1948), pp. 181-207.

Sadoul, Georges, 'Zola et le cinéma français (1900-1920),' *Europe*, 83-4 (1952), pp. 158-70.

Schor, N., *Zola's Crowds*, John Hopkins University Press, Baltimore, 1978.

Serres, M., *Feux et signaux de brume: Zola*, Bernard Grasset, Paris, 1975.

Snyder, L. L., *The Dreyfus Case: A Documentary History*, Rutgers University Press, New Brunswick, New Jersey, 1973.

Suwala, H., *Naissance d'une doctrine: Formation des idées littéraires et esthétiques de Zola (1859-65)*, Wydawnictwa Uniwersytetu Warszawskiego, Warsaw, 1976.

Ternois, R., *Zola et son temps. Lourdes – Rome – Paris*, Les Belles Lettres, Paris, 1961.

Ternois, R., *Zola et ses amis italiens: documents inédits*, Les Belles Lettres, Paris, 1967.

Toulouse, E., *Enquête médico-psychologique sur les rapports de la supériorité intellectuelle avec la néuropathie. Emile Zola*, Société d'Editions Scientifiques, Paris, 1896.

Tuchman, B. W., *The Proud Tower: A Portrait of the World Before the War, 1890-1914*, Macmillan, New York, 1966.

Vizetelly, E. A., *Émile Zola, Novelist and Reformer: an Account of his Life and Work*, Bodley Head, London, 1904.

Walker, P., 'Prophetic Myths in Zola,' *PMLA*, LXXIV (1959), pp. 444-52.

Walker, P., *Émile Zola*, Routledge & Kegan Paul, London, 1968 [1969].

Walker, P., *'Germinal' and Zola's Philosophical and Religious Thought*, John Benjamins, Purdue University Monographs in Romance Languages, Amsterdam/Philadelphia, 1983.

Wilson, A., *Emile Zola. An Introductory Study of His Novels*, revised edn, Secker & Warburg, London, 1965.

Xau, Fernand, *Emile Zola*, Marpon & Flammarion, Paris, 1880.

Index

About, Edmond, 138
Alexis, Marie, 191
Alexis, Paul, 76, 91, 92, 94, 96, 98, 99, 108, 115, 116-17, 125, 136, 191, 219, 220, 235
Antigny, Blanche d', 77-8, 142, 145
Antoine, André, 192
Aristotle, 137
Arnaud, Léopold, 73, 94
Assi, Adolphe, 123
Aubanel, Théodore, 15
Aubert, Louis Auguse, 1, 4, 5, 17, 24, 48, 182
Aubert, Mme Louis Auguste, 1, 4, 5, 9, 14, 16, 181-2

Baille, Jean Baptistin, 11-12, 15-16, 17, 18, 19, 21, 22, 26, 28, 49, 56, 66, 75, 76, 98, 116, 177
Balzac, Honoré de, 57, 71, 76, 80, 81, 82, 86, 89, 90, 102, 109, 111, 124, 133, 138, 169, 180, 181, 184, 209, 210
Banville, Théodore de, 75
Barbey d'Aurevilly, Jules, 63, 120
Barbier, Auguse, 18
Barlatier, A., 96
Barrès, Maurice, 215
Basly, Émile, 164
Baudelaire, Charles, 52, 57, 76
Bazille, Frédéric, 49, 66-7, 76, 94, 98
Beauharnais, Eugène de, 1
Belot, Adolphe, 80
Bernard, Claude, 138-9
Bernardin de Saint-Pierre, 24
Berthe, 38-9, 43, 52, 61, 62, 144
Berthelot, Marcelin, 138
Berthet, Élie, 14
Bertrand, 94

Billot, Jean Baptiste, 227
Bismarck, Otto von, 200
Bloy, Léon, 215
Boisdeffre, Raoul Le Mouton de, 221, 222
Bonnetain, Paul, 186-7
Boudet, 46
Bourdin, Gustave, 64, 65
Bourget, Paul, 211, 215
Bruneau, Alfred, 212, 236
Brunetière, Ferdinand, 111, 139, 173, 188, 215
Busnach, William, 140, 192

Cambronne, comte Pierre, 63
Caro, Elme Marie, 47, 79
Castiglione, Virginia di, 121
Castro, 223
Cavillier, Henri, 182
Cavillier, Mme Henri, 182
Céard, Henry, 136, 139, 144, 154, 158, 182-3, 191, 213
Cézanne, Louis Auguste, 11, 100
Cézanne, Paul, 11-12, 15-16, 17, 18, 19, 21, 25, 26, 29, 30, 32, 49-50, 51, 56, 58, 66, 67, 75, 76, 77, 78, 85, 92, 109, 116, 117, 136, 141, 167, 174, 176, 177, 181, 213, 243
Chaillan, Jean Baptiste, 24, 68, 244
Champfleury, 57, 138
Charbonnel, Victor, 231
Charlemagne, 21
Charpentier, Georges, 106-7, 116, 183, 210, 239, 244
Charpentier, Marguerite, 116, 134, 136, 183
Chassagnol, 181

Chateaubriand, François René, 141, 160
Chekhov, Anton Pavlovich, 230
Chénier, André, 26, 31
Cherbuliez, Victor, 138
Chevreul, Eugène, 176
Claretie, Jules, 53
Clemenceau, Georges, 223, 227, 228
Coppée, François, 75
Coquelin cadet, 145
Corneille, Pierre, 31, 33
Corot, Jean Baptiste, 67, 76, 78, 185
Coste, Numa, 49
Courbet, Gustave, 58, 66, 68, 76, 98, 124
Cousin, Victor, 79
Cuvier, Georges, 44, 59

Dante Alighieri, 26, 97, 129, 169, 173, 210
Darwin, Charles, 57, 177, 219
Daubigny, Charles, 67
Daudet, Alphonse, 115-16, 117, 136, 138, 141, 158, 180, 186-7, 210, 213, 214, 224, 226
Daudet, Ernest, 80
Daudet, Léon, 214, 224
Daudet, Mme Alphonse, 116, 214, 224
Daumier, Honoré, 124
David d'Angers, Pierre Jean, 75
De Amicis, Edmondo, 152
Degas, Edgar, 66-7, 76, 94, 124
Delegorgue, Jules, 229-30
Desjardins, Paul, 215
Delacroix, Ferdinand Victor, 66, 173
Delavigne, Casimir, 26
Descaves, Lucien, 186-7
Deschanel, Émile, 42-3, 47, 51, 53, 57-8, 84
Dickens, Charles, 57, 83
Doret, Gustave, 60
Dostoevsky, F. M., 188
Dreyfus, Alfred, 220-34, 242, 244, 245
Dreyfus, Mathieu, 223
Dreyfus, Mme Alfred, 220
Drumont, Édouard, 162, 215, 220, 224, 229, 243
Dumas, Aleandre (père), 14
Dumas, Alexandre (fils), 14, 18
Duranty, Louis, 57, 66-7, 99, 138, 151
Duret, Théodore, 74
Durkheim, Émile, 228

Edward VII, 145

Émile-Zola, Jacques, 191, 192, 209, 212-13, 224, 233, 234-5, 244
Ensor, James, 228
Erckmann-Chatrian, 138
Esterhazy, Ferdinand (Walsin-), 221-2, 223, 225, 226, 227, 229
Étienne, 19
Eugénie (Empress), 20, 77
Euripides, 124, 170

Faguet, Émile, 203
Fantin-Latour, Théodore, 49, 66-7
Fasquelle, Eugène, 210, 239, 244
Faure, Félix, 226
Feuillet, Octave, 138
Féval, Paul, 14
Fischer, Mme, 2
Flaubert, Gustave, 57, 80, 103, 111, 115-16, 129, 135, 136, 137, 138, 141-2, 144, 145, 147, 148, 151, 160
Flourens, Marie Jean Pierre, 44
Fourier, Charles, 219, 240
Fourtoul, Hippolyte, 8
France, Anatole, 111, 187-8, 194, 197, 199, 215, 228, 231, 244-5

Galliffet, Gaston Auguste, marquis de, 4
Gautier, Théophile, 18, 57, 84, 103, 106
Geffroy, Gustave, 173
Gérôme, Jean Léon, 68
Giard, Alfred, 164
Gide, André, 228
Gill, André, 147
Girardin, Émile de, 64
Glais-Bizoin, Alexandre Olivier, 95-6, 121
Gleyre, Charles, 51
Gobineau, Joseph Arthur, comte de, 47
Goethe, 160, 217
Goncort, Edmond de, 57, 63, 75, 80, 81, 84, 86, 92, 115-16, 124, 136, 138, 141, 148, 152, 158, 173, 174, 179-80, 181, 186-7, 189, 198, 203, 210, 212, 213-14
Goncourt, Jules de, 57, 63, 75, 80, 81, 84, 86, 92, 124, 187, 214
Gonse, Charles, 222, 223
Gonzalès, Emmanuel, 14
Goujon, Jean, 30
Grave, Jean, 240
Greuze, Jean Baptiste, 30
Guesde, Jules, 182, 241
Guiches, Gustave, 186-7
Guillaumin, Armand, 49

Guillemet, Antoine, 49, 51, 66-7, 94, 136, 180
Guizot, François, 47
Guyot, Yves, 163

Hachette, Louis, 46-8, 50, 64
Halévy, Ludovic, 144
Harmant (Gustave Dardoize), 61
Hartmann, Eduard von, 173
Haussmann, Georges, 47, 77, 104, 123
Hawthorne, Nathaniel, 57, 83
Hegel, Georg Wilhelm Friedrich, 71
Heine, Heinrich, 55
Hennique, Léon, 136
Henry, Hubert Joseph, 222, 224, 233
Hesiod, 210
Hetzel, Pierre, 53-4, 61
Holtzapfel, Jules, 67
Homer, 30, 71, 102, 124, 170, 173, 210
Horace, 15, 27
Houchard, Aurélien, 24
Houssaye, Arsène, 75, 80, 81
Hugo, Charles, 75
Hugo, Georges, 174
Hugo, Victor, 9, 15, 16, 18, 26, 28, 32, 33, 34, 38, 54, 75, 76, 78, 86, 92, 93, 108-9, 110, 123, 133, 137, 138, 141, 145, 173, 174, 203, 204, 210, 217, 231, 232, 245
Humbert, I., 211
Huret, Jules, 217
Huysmans, Joris Karl, 136, 139, 148, 154, 158, 173, 188, 210, 213

Isaiah, 210
Isoard, 6, 7

Jack the Ripper, 195
Jacob, 62, 178-9
Jaures, Jean, 228
Jesus Christ, 35-6, 212, 237, 240
Joan of Arc, 52
John (of Patmos), 202, 210, 242
Jongkind, Johann Barthold, 76, 78, 108
Jonson, Ben, 112
Jourdain, Frantz, 157
Jourdan, Louis, 34-5
Judet, Ernest, 234
Judic, Anna, 144
Juvenal, 86

Kant, Immanuel, 59
Kropotkin, Petr Alekseevich, 240

Labori, Fernand, 229, 232
Labot, Alexandre, 4, 5, 17, 22, 23
La Bruyère, Jean de, 33
Lacroix, Albert, 53-4, 61, 81, 85, 86, 91, 106, 107
La Fontaine, Jean de, 26
Lamarck, Jean Baptiste de, 87
Lamartine, Alphonse de, 15, 16, 18, 26, 27, 28, 138
Lanson, Gustave, 228
La Païva, 142
Laporte, Edmond, 144
Laprade, Victor de, 26, 41
Laurent, Marie, 112
Lautréamont, 171
Lavergne, Alexandre de, 72
Lazare, Bernard, 222, 224
Lazarus, 212
Leblois, Louis, 223, 224
Leblond-Zola, Denise, 191, 192, 209, 212-13, 224, 231, 233, 234-5, 244
Lemaître, Jules, 173, 180, 194-5, 197
Lemoine-Montigny, *see* Montigny
Lenin, 241
Leo XIII, 211, 218, 228, 243
Letourneau, Charles, 90
Levasseur, Calvaire, 69, 113
Levasseur, Pierre Émile, 18
Littré, Émile, 47, 50, 60, 71, 79
Lombroso, Cesare, 197-8
Longus, 102
Loubet, Émile, 234
Louis Philippe, 2
Lucas, Prosper, 85, 87-8, 90
Lucretius, 44, 52

MacMahon, Edmé Patrice de, 97
Maeterlinck, Maurice, 228
Mallarmé, Stéphane, 115, 141, 171, 181, 215, 229, 230
Malon, Benoit, 123
Malot, Hector, 138
Manet, Édouard, 51-2, 67, 68, 69, 72, 75, 76, 94, 115, 116, 159, 174, 176, 179, 189
Margherita Teresa Giovanna, 211
Margueritte, Paul, 186-7
Marguery, Louis, 11, 48
Marion, Fortuné, 88
Marx, Karl, 172
Mary Magdalene, 240
Mary (Virgin Mary, The), 35, 219

Index

Maupassant, Guy de, 115, 120, 136, 144, 154, 173, 211, 213
Mauriac, François, 231
Meissonier, Ernest, 68
Meley, Edmond Jacques, 56, 151
Mendès, Catulle, 133
Mercier, Gen. Auguste, 221, 222, 223, 227
Meurice, Paul, 75, 76
Michelangelo, 35, 113, 180
Michelet, Jules, 18, 28, 32, 34, 36, 37, 47, 50, 71, 75, 78, 79, 85, 86, 88, 93, 119, 146, 205, 231
Migeon, Jules, 5, 28
Millaud, Moïse, 64
Millet, Jean François, 185
Millière, Jean Baptiste, 123
Mirbeau, Octave, 136
Mirès, Jules, 64
Mistral, Frédéric, 15, 78
Molière, 27, 52, 54, 110, 111
Monet, Claude, 66, 68, 76, 108, 180-1, 228, 230
Monnier, 243
Montaigne, 26, 40, 44, 59, 60, 153
Montigny (Adolphe Lemoine), 61
Moore, George, 181
Moreau, Hégésippe, 18
Murger, Henri, 56
Musset, Alfred de, 15-16, 18, 34, 35, 41, 54, 55, 62
Mustapha, 7

Napoleon I, 210
Napoleon III, 20, 54, 93, 100, 101, 104, 107, 121, 131, 132, 145, 200, 203, 215

Offenbach, Jacques, 77, 142, 144
Oller, Francisco, 49
Otway, Thomas, 146

Pagès (du Tarn), A., 24, 31, 105
Pajot, Georges, 20, 24-5, 49, 63
Panizzardi, Alessandro, 222
Pascal, Blaise, 60
Pasteur, Louis, 88, 138
Pearl, Cora, 142
Péguy, Charles, 228, 239, 241
Perrault, Charles, 54
Petrarch, 27
Petronius, 102
Picquart, Georges, 221-4
Pinpin, 233, 243

Pissarro, Camille, 49, 51, 56, 66-7, 68, 76, 78, 108, 181
Plato, 137
Poe, Edgar Allen, 57, 83
Pontmartin, Armand, 133
Poulot, Denis, 125
Prévost, Antoine Françoise, 145
Proudhon, Pierre Joseph, 58
Proust, Marcel, 169, 228

Rabelais, François, 33
Racine, Jean, 31, 124, 137
Remondet-Aubin, 77
Renan, Ernest, 59, 71, 138, 205, 215, 237
Renoir, Auguse, 76
Restif de la Bretonne, Nicholas Edmé, 144, 181
Rhunka, 75
Rimbaud, Arthur, 171
Rochefort, Henri, 123
Rosny, J. H., 186-7
Rouher, Eugène, 121
Roumanille, Joseph, 15
Rousseau, Jean Jacques, 245
Roux, Marius, 7, 49, 55, 66, 73, 92, 94, 99, 117, 136
Rozerot, Jeanne, 190-2, 195, 206, 207, 209, 212, 224, 233, 234-5, 244
Rubens, Peter Paul, 66

Sade, marquis de, 147
Sainte-Beuve, Charles Augustin, 26, 47, 50, 82, 84
Sand, George, 15, 26, 30, 36, 123, 181
Sandeau, Jules, 138
Sarcey, Francisque, 183
Saussier, Gen., 222
Scheffer, Ary, 30
Scherer, Edmond, 133
Scheurer-Kestner, Auguse, 223, 224, 225
Schneider, Hortense, 77-8, 142, 145
Schopenhauer, Artur, 154, 159, 160, 173
Schwartzkoppen, Maximilian von, 222
Shakespeare, 26, 31, 34, 82, 170, 173, 184, 210
Signac, Paul, 228
Simon, Gustave, 97
Solari, Louise, 13
Solari, Philippe, 7, 13, 49, 56, 66, 77, 92, 116-17, 136, 174
Sorel, Georges, 241
Spinoza, Benedictus de, 70-1
Stendhal, 57

254

Index

Sue, Eugène, 14, 73, 123

Taine, Hippolyte, 47, 50, 57, 59, 60, 65, 70, 71, 79, 80, 81, 82, 84, 88, 89, 90, 115, 120, 138, 205, 215
Thiers, Adolphe, 3, 5, 96
Tintoretto, Jacopo, 66
Tolstoy, L. N., 188, 245
Turgenev, I.S., 115-16, 134, 149, 158
Twain, Mark, 228

Ulbach, Louis, 81, 138, 147

Vacquerie, Auguse, 75
Valabregue, Antony, 50, 55, 58, 67, 69, 74, 76, 80, 91, 145
Vallès, Jules, 51
Valtesse de la Bigne, 145
Van Santen Kolff, Jacques, 175
Varlin, Eugène, 123
Verlaine, Paul, 75, 215
Vermorel, Auguste, 43
Verne, Jules, 138
Vernet, Horace, 68
Veuillot, Louis, 78
Villemain, Abel François, 71
Villemessant, Hippolyte de, 64-5, 67, 68, 69
Villon, François, 109
Virgil, 15
Vizetelly, Ernest Alfred, 233, 244
Vizetelly, Henry, 211
Vogüé, Eugène Melchior de, 188, 203, 205, 215
Voltaire, 33, 36, 52, 54-5, 60, 226, 245

Wadoux, Caroline Louise, 56
Wagner, Richard, 77, 168, 199, 236
Weiss, Jean-Jacques, 51, 52
Whistler, James Abbott McNeill, 66-7

Zimmermann, Charles, 44
Zola, Alexandrine, 56, 66, 69, 73, 74-5, 92, 94, 95, 96, 97, 134-5, 149-50, 151, 158, 182, 183, 189-92, 212-13, 214, 224
Zola, Émile Édouard Charles Antoine, advice to younger writers, 50-1; aesthetic theories, 29-33, 41-3, 49, 52-3, 56-9, 71, 78-9, 81, 114, 137-9, 217; affair with a prostitute, 38-9, 61; artistic development, *see esp.* 14-16, 18-19, 21, 25-34, 38-45, 49, 52-3, 56-9, 70-1, 74, 86, 217, 235, 209-10, 216-
17, 235; battle to launch his career, 20, 26, 47-8, 50-1, 52, 53-4, 56, 60-4, 66, 71, 74, 86; birth, 1; campaign against Second Empire, 93; campaign for Manet and impressionists, 67-8, 76-7; campaign for naturalism, 81, 99, 136-9; campaign on behalf of father's reputation, 20, 77; Catholic upbringing, 7-8, 11, 13; character, 5-6, 10, 32, 33, 51, 74, 97, 219, 238; children, *see also* Émile Zola *and* Leblond-Zola; choice of a career, 20, 23, 27-9; Commune, impact of, 96-8; conception of his age, 32, 72; death, 242-3; and the Dreyfus Affair, 224-34, 242; dwellings, 1, 4, 5, 7, 17, 20, 22, 24, 48-9, 66, 69, 74-5, 94, 95, 96, 97, 134-6, 212-13; education, 6-13, 16, 17-22; encounters with death, 4, 16, 19, 38, 48, 97-8, 151, 158-9, 174, 214, 226, 235; entombment in the Panthéon, 245; financial situation, 4-5, 17, 21-2, 23, 38, 46, 48-9, 64, 65, 72-3, 91, 92, 94-5, 106-7, 134-6, 150, 158, 231, 234; Franco-Prussian War, impact of, 93-6; friends and disciples, 7, 10-12, 19, 24-5, 49, 50, 56, 66-7, 69, 75-6, 92, 98-9, 115-17, 133, 134, 136, 141, 148, 173-4, 179-81, 186-7, 191, 198, 203, 210-11, 213-14, 226, 228, 230, 233, 243; funerals, 244-5; at Hachette's, 46-8, 50-2, 64; identification with the Biblical Jacob, 62; ill health, 6, 19, 23, 38, 73, 149, 152, 153, 213; journalism, 50, 60-1, 64-6, 67-71, 72-4, 76-8, 89, 92-3, 94, 96, 114-15, 134, 216-17; liaison with Gabrielle Alexandrine Meley, 56; liaison with Jeanne Rozerot, 190-2, 207, 209, 212-13, 234-5; literary achievement, 209-10; love of animals, 6, 38, 75, 135-6, 233; and *Le Manifeste des cinq*, 186-7; marriage, 92, 149, 189-92, 212-13; motives, 7, 24, 27-9, 50, 78, 86, 88, 89, 113, 136, 150-1, 159, 173-4, 188, 204, 216, 238; mystical experience, 79; and the myth of Amphion, 24, 244; naturalism, use of term, 78, 81, 137; necrophobia, 152-3, 214-15; opera librettos, 212, 236-7; patriarch of Humanitarian Church, 231; physical appearance, 6, 10, 13, 23, 66, 76, 96, 98, 134, 149, 152, 189,

214; political views, 20, 32, 77, 89, 92-3, 94, 96, 97, 98, 163-4, 204, 240; prophetic vocation, 28-9, 78, 164, 166, 199, 209, 219, 238; relationship with the art world, 11, 24-5, 49, 51-2, 66-9, 174, 176-7, 180-1, 228; relationship with nature, 11-12, 13-14, 22, 49, 71; religious and philosophical thought, 7-8, 12, 25, 34-7, 39-40, 44, 59-60, 70-1, 78-9, 86, 90-1, 138-9, 150, 151, 153-4, 159, 172, 194, 204-6, 208, 209, 212, 217, 219, 220, 227, 233, 237-42; sexual development, 7, 13-14, 37, 38-9; speech defect, 6, 10, 23; struggle against old age and changing tastes, 215-17, 219; symbolization of reality, 113-14, 171; and the theatre, 14, 16, 20, 26, 51, 53, 61, 73, 85, 112, 140, 183, 192; values, 12, 50, 58, 59, 70, 86, 114, 137, 164, 216, 238; works at Docks, 22-3; world view, *see* conception of his own age *and* religious and philosophical thought
WORKS:
address, banquet of the Association Générale des Étudiants, 208, 217; 'L'Aérienne', 43; 'À l'impératrice Eugénie, régente de France', 20; 'Angéline ou la maison hantée', 236; *L'Argent*, 198-9; *L'Assommoir*, 122-34, 136, 137, 140, 142, 153, 155, 156, 169, 170, 188, 204, 235; 'L'Attaque du moulin', 140, 212; *Au Bonheur des Dames*, 156-8; 'Aventures du grand Sidoine et du petit Médéric', 54-5; *La Bête humaine*, 195-8, 199; *Le Bouton de rose*, 140; 'Le Canal Zola', 20; 'Celle qui m'aime', 54; 'La Chaîne des êtres', *or* 'La Genèse', 16, 26, 27, 30, 44, 52, 59, 69, 78, 177; *La Comédie amoureuse*, 43-4, 47-8; *La Confession de Claude*, 43, 52, 61-4, 145, 178; *La Conquête de Plassans*, 110-12, 117; *Contes à Ninon*, 53-6, 62, 63, 64, 177; 'Un Coup de vent', 37-8; *La Curée*, 95, 103-6, 142, 183, 198; *La Débâcle*, 200-4, 220, 241; 'Deux Définitions du roman', 71; *Le Docteur Pascal*, 204-9, 217, 219; 'Doute', 44; 'Édouard Manet', 69; *L'Enfant roi*, 237; *Enfoncé le pion!*, 19; *La Faute de l'abbé Mouret*, 110, 117-20, 134, 162, 171; *Fécondité*, 238-9, 241; 'La Fée amoureuse', 26, 28, 54; 'Le Forgeron', 113-14; *La Fortune des Rougon*, 91, 93-4, 95, 96, 99-103, 105; *La France en marche*, 237; 'La Genèse', *see* 'La Chaîne des êtres'; *Germinal*, 163-74, 182, 186, 209, 235, 241; 'Les Grisettes de Provence', 26; *Les Héritiers Rabourdin*, 112; *Les Héroïsmes*, 65-6, 69; *Il faut hurler avec les loups*, 20; *J'accuse . . .!*, 226-9, 233, 234; *La Joie de vivre*, 154-5, 158-63, 171, 172, 180, 217; *Justice*, 242; *La Laide*, 61; *Lazare*, 212, 214; *Lettre à la France*, 226; *Lettre à la jeunesse*, 226; *Livres d'aujourd'hui et de demain*, 65; *Lourdes*, 218, 219-20; *Madeleine*, 61, 85-6, 192; *Madeleine Férat*, 85, 86, 87; *Mes Haines*, 68-9; *Messidor*, 236-7, 245; 'La Mort d'Olivier Bécaille', 150; 'M. Scheurer-Kestner', 225; *Les Mystères de Marseille*, 73, 80, 94; *Nana*, 142-8, 156, 161, 188, 211; *Nouveaux contes à Ninon*, 112-14; *L'Oeuvre*, 174-81, 213; *L'Oeuvre d'art devant la critique*, 69; *L'Ouragan*, 237; *Une Page d'amour*, 140-2; 'Paolo', 26, 35, 36, 37, 38; *Paris*, 218-20, 241; *Perrette*, 26, 53; *Le Poète*, 42; *Pot-Bouille*, 155-6, 158, 211; 'Proudhon et Courbet', 58; *Les Quatre Évangiles*, 238-42; 'Les Quatre Journées de Jean Gourdon', 70, 113, 185; *Renée*, 183; *Le Rêve*, 192-5, 212; 'Rodolpho', 21, 36; *Rollon l'archer*, 20; 'Le Roman expérimental', 139; 'Les Romanciers contemporains', 138; *Rome*, 218, 219-20; *Les Rougon-Macquart*, 86-91, 99, 106-7, 132, 142, 149, 158, 161, 180, 185, 207, 209-10, 213, 217, 219-20, 241, 242; 'Salon' (1866), 67-8; 'Simplice', 54; 'Soeur des pauvres', 48, 54; *Son Excellence Eugène Rougon*, 120-2; 'Souvenirs', 113; *Sylvanire ou Paris en amour*, 237; 'Le Syndicat', 225; *La Terre*, 181-8, 192, 211; *Thérèse Raquin*, 80-4, 85; *Travail*, 235, 239-41; *Les Trois Villes*, 211, 217-20, 241; *Le Ventre de Paris*, 107-10, 112, 117, 125; *Vérité*, 241-2; *Violaine la chevelue*, 237; 'Vive la France!', 93; *Le Voeu d'une morte*, 69-70;
Zola, Francesco, 1-6, 12, 20, 46, 77, 231
Zola, Mme François, 1, 2-10, 17, 18, 24,

38, 48-9, 74-5, 92, 94, 95, 96, 97, 134-5, 149-51, 155, 233, 235, 243, 244
Zolla, Antonio, 1

Zolla, Carlo, 1
Zolla, Marco, 2